T0214086

Lecture Notes in Computer Science 12222

More information about this series at http://www.springer.com/series/7407

Aleksander Byrski · John Hughes (Eds.)

Trends in Functional Programming

21st International Symposium, TFP 2020
Krakow, Poland, February 13–14, 2020
Revised Selected Papers

 Springer

Editors
Aleksander Byrski (ID)
AGH University of Science
and Technology
Krakow, Poland

John Hughes (ID)
Chalmers University of Technology
Gothenburg, Sweden

ISSN 0302-9743   ISSN 1611-3349   (electronic)
Lecture Notes in Computer Science
ISBN 978-3-030-57760-5   ISBN 978-3-030-57761-2   (eBook)
https://doi.org/10.1007/978-3-030-57761-2

LNCS Sublibrary: SL1 – Theoretical Computer Science and General Issues

This Springer imprint is published by the registered company Springer Nature Switzerland AG
The registered company address is: Gewerbestrasse 11, 6330 Cham, Switzerland

Preface

This volume contains a selection of papers presented at the 21st International Symposium on Trends in Functional Programming (TFP 2020), held during February 13–14, 2020, in Kraków, Poland.

TFP is an international forum for researchers with interests in all aspects of functional programming, taking a broad view of current and future trends in this area. It aspires to be a lively environment for presenting the latest research results and other contributions, with an unconventional reviewing process that allows for full single-blind peer review either before or after the symposium (or both, if the pre-symposium reviews ask for changes that need a second review before inclusion in the proceedings). Each paper receives at least three reviews in each round it participates in. This year 22 papers were submitted in total (12 reviewed before the symposium, and 10 afterwards), and 18 of them were presented in Kraków, together with a keynote by Carl Seger (Chalmers University of Technology, Sweden) on "Functional Programming for Hardware Design: The Good, The Bad, The Ugly." After the final reviewing round, revised versions of 11 papers were selected for inclusion in these proceedings. The final selection spans across domain-specific languages, testing and debugging, reasoning and effects, and parallelism.

This year TFP moved from early summer to winter dates, to provide a research-oriented functional programming event separated by around six months from the ACM SIGPLAN ICFP. We co-located with Lambda Days, an established developer conference in the area, organized by Erlang Solutions, with a strong research element. Joint registration enabled TFP to attract part of the Lambda Days audience to some of the sessions, with a peak of around 120 people in the room at times, giving TFP papers significantly more exposure than usual; co-location was a great success.

All of this was only possible thanks to the hard work of the Program Committee members, and the help and support of the Lambda Days team. We are deeply grateful to both.

July 2020

Aleksander Byrski
John Hughes

Organization

Steering Committee

Peter Achten	Radboud University, The Netherlands
William J. Bowman	The University of British Columbia, Canada
Ron Garcia	The University of British Columbia, Canada
Jurriaan Hage	Utrecht University, The Netherlands
Kevin Hammond	University of St Andrews, UK
David van Horn	University of Maryland, USA
Zoltán Horváth	Eötvös Loránd University of Sciences, Hungary
John Hughes	Chalmers University of Technology, Sweden
Pieter Koopman	Radboud University, The Netherlands
Hans-Wolfgang Loidl	Heriot-Watt University, UK
Jay McCarthy	Brigham Young University, USA
Meng Wang	University of Bristol, UK
Greg Michaelson	Heriot-Watt University, UK
Marco T. Morazán	Seton Hall University, USA
Magnus Myreen	Chalmers University of Technology, Sweden
Henrik Nilsson	University of Nottingham, UK
Scott Owens	University of Kent, UK
Rex Page	University of Oklahoma, USA
Ricardo Peña	Universidad Complutense de Madrid, Spain
Manuel Serrano	Inria Sophia-Antipolis, France
Phil Trinder	Glasgow University, UK
David A. Turner	University of Kent and Middlesex University, UK
Marko van Eekelen	Open University of the Netherlands and Radboud University, The Netherlands
Viktória Zsók	Eötvös Loránd University of Sciences, Hungary

Program Committee Chairs

Aleksandr Byrski	AGH University of Science and Technology, Poland
John Hughes	Chalmers University of Technology, Sweden

Program Committee

Edwin Brady	University of St Andrews, UK
Natalia Chechina	Bournemouth University, UK
Robby Findler	Northwestern University, USA
Jennifer Hackett	University of Nottingham, UK
Gabriele Keller	Utrecht University, The Netherlands
Pieter Koopman	Radboud University, The Netherlands

Hans-Wolfgang Loidl	Heriot-Watt University, UK
Erik Meijer	Facebook, USA
Magnus Myreen	Chalmers University, Sweden
Zoe Paraskevopoulou	Princeton University, USA
Francois Pottier	Inria Paris, France
Fernando Rubio Diez	Complutense University of Madrid, Spain
Kostis Sagonas	Uppsala University, Sweden
Eijiro Sumii	Tohoku University, Japan
Wojciech Turek	AGH University, Poland
Meng Wang	University of Bristol, UK
Niki Vazou	IMDEA Software Institute, Spain
Stephanie Wierich	University of Pennsylvania, USA
Viktória Zsók	Eötvös Loránd University, Hungary

Coorganized by

Contents

Parallelism

Domain-Specific Languages

PaSe: An Extensible and Inspectable DSL for Micro-Animations

Ruben P. Pieters$^{(\boxtimes)}$ and Tom Schrijvers

KU Leuven, 3001 Leuven, Belgium
{ruben.pieters,tom.schrijvers}@cs.kuleuven.be

Abstract. This paper presents PaSe, an extensible and inspectable DSL embedded in Haskell for expressing micro-animations. PaSe builds animations in compositional fashion, using parallel and sequential animations as basic building blocks. This differs from typical animation libraries which mostly focus on sequential composition and utilize callbacks and implicit effects for their expressivity. To provide similar flexibility to other animation libraries, PaSe features extensibility of operations and inspectability of animations. We present the features of PaSe with a to-do list application, discuss the PaSe implementation, and argue that the callback style of extensibility is detrimental for correctly integrating inspectability. To illustrate this, we contrast with the GreenSock Animation Platform, a professional-grade and widely used JavaScript animation library.

1 Introduction

Because of their ability to structure effectful code in a pure functional codebase, monads quickly became ubiquitous in functional programming [20]. They have since seen wide use in Haskell Domain Specific Languages (DSLs). However, the choice for a monadic DSL implies certain trade-offs. The obvious advantage of monadic DSLs is their expressivity, but there are also drawbacks. The main loss is that of *inspectability*, as monadic computations can only be inspected up to the next action. Techniques such as applicative functors [16], arrows [9], or selective applicative functors [18] choose the other side of the trade-off: they increase the inspection capabilities by reducing the expressivity compared to monads.

This paper develops a DSL embedded in Haskell for defining micro-animations, called PaSe[1]. PaSe employs a technique which alleviates some aspects of the trade-off between expressivity and inspectability. The expressivity of control flow is restricted by means of type classes, inspired by the MTL style originally introduced by Liang *et al.* [14]. The MTL style is an open encoding which allows extensions to the syntax of the DSL. Instantiating the abstract animation definitions with, for example, the `Const` functor provides inspectability. Expressivity can be increased, while preserving inspectability, by adding new

---

[1] Pronounced *pace* (peɪs), the name is derived from *Parallel* and *Sequential*.

© Springer Nature Switzerland AG 2020
A. Byrski and J. Hughes (Eds.): TFP 2020, LNCS 12222, pp. 3–24, 2020.
https://doi.org/10.1007/978-3-030-57761-2_1

control flow constructs to the DSL and providing a corresponding instance for inspection.

Micro-animations are short animations displayed when users interact with an application, for example an animated transition between two screens. When used appropriately, they aid the user in understanding evolving states of the application [1,7,8]. Examples can be found in almost every software application: window managers animate window minimization, menus in mobile applications pop in gradually, browsers highlight newly selected tabs with an animation, etc.

PaSe provides the features expected of animation libraries by building them with recent ideas from functional programming. Our contributions are as follows:

– We develop PaSe, which supports arbitrary composition of animations and inspectability. Animation libraries, such as the GreenSock Animation Platform (GSAP)[2], typically use callbacks as a means of extensibility/expressivity; this is detrimental to inspectability. We show an example resulting in unexpected behaviour and how PaSe correctly handles it.
– PaSe is an *extensible* DSL: the syntax can be extended with new operations. The animations use case is novel for approaches to extensibility.
– PaSe supports *inspectability*: extracting information from computations before running it. Inspectability is present in specific computation classes, such as free applicatives [2]. But, it is novel to combine it with extensibility.
– PaSe supports arbitrary nesting of parallel and sequential animations which correctly interacts with inspectability. Such parallel components exist already, see for example Ren'Py[3], React Native Animations[4] or Qt Animations[5]. Yet, general-purpose animation libraries lack them. Also, we correctly support the interaction with inspectability.
– We implemented various examples[6]: a to-do list application, a communication story example, a game-like demo application and a Pac-Man game. We combined PaSe with both `gloss`[7] and the Haskell SDL bindings[8] as graphics backend. This paper uses the to-do list as motivating application and compares the development of the Pac-Man application, developed in both Haskell with PaSe and in TypeScript with GSAP.

2   Motivation

We present a to-do list application to showcase the functionality of PaSe.

---

[2] https://greensock.com.
[3] https://www.renpy.org/doc/html/atl.html#parallel-statement.
[4] https://facebook.github.io/react-native/docs/animated#parallel.
[5] https://doc.qt.io/qt-5/animation.html.
[6] https://github.com/rubenpieters/PaSe-hs/tree/master/PaSe-examples.
[7] https://hackage.haskell.org/package/gloss.
[8] https://hackage.haskell.org/package/sdl2.

2.1 Running Example

Our application has two screens: a main screen and a menu screen. The main screen contains a navigation bar and three items. An overview of the application is given in Fig. 1. These screenshots are captured from the application built by combining PaSe with `gloss` as graphics backend.

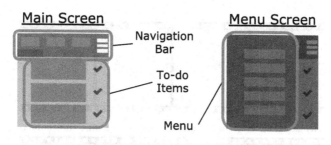

Fig. 1. Overview of the to-do list application.

In this application, various user actions are accompanied with an animation. We list these actions below. Some animations are shown in Fig. 2.

- The user marks items as *(not) done* by clicking them. The checkmark icon changes shape and color to display its status change.
- The user filters items by their status with the navigation bar buttons. The leftmost shows all items, the middle shows all completed items, and the rightmost shows all unfinished items. The navigation bar underline and to-do items itself change shape to indicate the new selection.
- The menu screen shows/hides itself after clicking the menu icon (≡). The menu expands inwards from the left, to indicate the application state changes.

2.2 Composing Animations

Animations are built in a compositional fashion. When creating an animation, we decompose it into smaller elements. For example, the `menuIntro` animation both introduces the menu screen and fades out the background. Thus, it is composed of two basic animations `menuSlideIn` and `appFadeOut` in parallel. The next sections explain how to construct such basic and composed animations.

Basic Animations. Basic animations change the property of an element over a period of time. The `linearTo` function has three inputs: a lens targeting the property, the duration, and the target value for this property. This results in a linear change from the current value to its target, hence the name. The duration is specified with `For` while the target value is specified with `To`.

To animate the navigation bar underline, we reduce the width of the leftmost underline for 0.25 s and increase the width of the middle underline for 0.25 s. These animations are expressed in respectively `line1Out` and `line2In` below, and visualized in Fig. 3.

```
line1Out = linearTo (navbar . underline1 . width) (For 0.25) (To 0)
line2In = linearTo (navbar . underline2 . width) (For 0.25) (To 28)
```

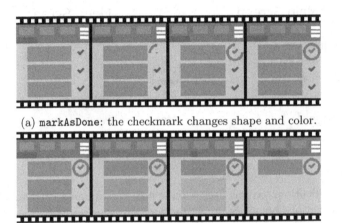

(a) `markAsDone`: the checkmark changes shape and color.

(b) `onlyDone`: the to-do items fade out and the navbar underline changes.

(c) `menuIntro`: the menu appears while the background fades out.

Fig. 2. Micro-Animations in the to-do list application.

Note on Lenses. We use lens notation `x . y . z` to target `z` inside a nested structure `{ x: { y: { z: T } } }`. This type of lenses was conceived by van Laarhoven [13], and later packaged into various Haskell libraries, such as `lens`[9].

The `menuSlideIn` and `appFadeOut` animations are other examples. For the former, we increase the width of the menu over a duration of 0.5 s, and for the latter we increase the opacity of the obscuring box, determined by `alpha`, over a duration of 0.5 s. These animations are visualized in Fig. 3.

```
menuSlideIn = linearTo (menu . width) (For 0.5) (To 75)
appFadeOut = linearTo (obscuringBox . alpha) (For 0.5) (To 0.65)
```

---

[9] https://hackage.haskell.org/package/lens.

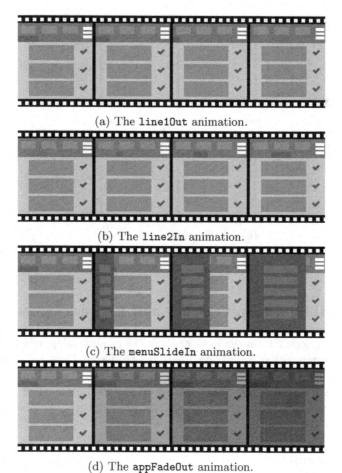

(a) The `line1Out` animation.

(b) The `line2In` animation.

(c) The `menuSlideIn` animation.

(d) The `appFadeOut` animation.

Fig. 3. Basic `linearTo` animations.

Composed Animations. A composed animation combines several other animations into a new one. We can do this either in *sequence* or in *parallel*.

We create `selectBtn2` by combining `line1Out` and `line2In` with `sequential`. This constructs a new animation which first plays `line1Out`, and once it is finished plays `line2In`.

```
selectBtn2Anim = line1Out `sequential` line2In
```

To obtain `menuIntro`, we combine both `menuSlideIn` and `appFadeOut` with `parallel`. This constructs a new animation which plays both `menuSlideIn` and `appFadeOut` at the same time.

```
menuIntro = menuSlideIn `parallel` appFadeOut
```

Both of these animations are visualized in Fig. 4.

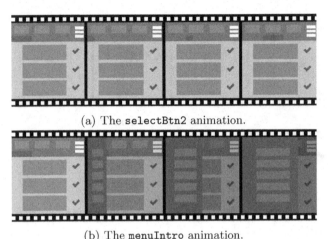

(a) The `selectBtn2` animation.

(b) The `menuIntro` animation.

Fig. 4. All of the defined composed animations.

3   Extensibility, Inspectability and Expressiveness

The features in Sect. 2 form the basis of PaSe. To provide support for additional features present in other animation libraries, we design PaSe to be extensible and inspectable. This means that PaSe can be extended with new operations and information can be derived from inspecting specified animations. To support arbitrary expressiveness in combination with those features, we also emphasize the possibility to extend PaSe with new combinators.

3.1   Extensibility

The `linearTo` operation and the `sequential` and `parallel` combinators form the basis for expressing a variety of animations. However, there are situations which require other primitives to express desired animations. For example, GSAP provides a primitive to morph one shape into another.

An example in the to-do list app is `checkIcon`, part of `markAsDone`, where we want to set the color of the checkmark to a new value. We define a custom `set` operation and embed it inside a PaSe animation. In this animation we use Haskell's do-notation to specify sequential animations.

```
checkIcon = do ...; set (checkmark . color) green; ...
```

3.2   Inspectability

PaSe is inspectable, meaning that we can derive properties of expressed computations by *inspecting them rather than running them*. For example, we want to know the duration of `menuIntro` without actually running it and keeping track of the time. The `duration` function calculates the duration by inspecting the animation. Passing it `menuIntro` gives a duration of 0.5 s, which is indeed the duration of two 0.5 s animations in parallel.

```
menuIntroDuration = duration menuIntro  -- = 0.5
```

Of course, it is not possible to inspect every animation. In the following situation we have a custom operation `get`, the dual of `set` in the previous section, returning a `Float`. If the result of this value is used as the duration parameter, then we cannot know upfront how long this animation will last. Requesting to calculate the duration then results in a type error.

```
complicatedAnim = do v <- get; linearTo lens (For v) (To 10)
complicatedAnimDuration = duration complicatedAnim  -- type error
```

Calculating a duration is a stepping stone towards other interesting features. One such example is sequentially composing animations with a relative offset. For example, to compose a first animation `anim1` with a second animation `anim2` which starts 0.5 s *before* the end of `anim1`.

```
relSeqAnim = relSequential anim1 anim2 (-0.5)
```

3.3   Expressiveness

In monadic DSLs the `>>=` and `return` combinators provide the needed expressivity. When creating inspectable animations, `>>=` is a liability since it has limited inspectability. PaSe supports extension with custom control flow combinators.

The `onlyDone` animation shows all *done* items while hiding all to-do items. This could be implemented by first showing all items with the `showAll` animation, since an item might have been hidden by a previous action, and then hiding all to-do items with the `hideToDo` animation. The definition is given below, while the definitions of `showAll` and `hideToDo` are omitted for brevity.

```
onlyDoneNaive = do showAll; hideToDo
```

However, we only intend to show completed items if needed. So instead we first check how many done items there are, if there are more than zero we play the previous version of `onlyDone`, otherwise we only hide the unfinished items.

```
onlyDone = do
  cond <- doneItemsGt0     -- check if more than 0 `done' items
  if cond then onlyDoneNaive else hideToDo
```

However, this formulation uses monadic features and is thus not inspectable. To make it inspectable, we utilize a custom combinator `ifThenElse`. We revisit this example in more detail in Sect. 5.

```
onlyDone = ifThenElse doneItemsGt0 onlyDoneNaive hideToDo
```

For this new combinator, we can define custom ways to inspect it. Since each branch might have a different duration, we do not choose to extract the duration but rather the *maximum* duration of the animation.

```
onlyDoneMaxDuration = maxDuration onlyDone  -- = 1
```

Sections 2 and 3 gave a look and feel of the features of PaSe. In the following sections, we delve deeper into the internals of the implementation.

4   Implementation of PaSe

This section implements the previously introduced operations and redefines the animations to show the resulting type signature. We develop PaSe in the style of the `mtl` library[10] which implements monadic effects using type classes [10]. This style is also called the finally tagless approach [3]. However, because the PaSe classes are not subclasses of `Monad`, they leave room for inspectability.

4.1   Specifying Basic Animations

The `mtl` library uses type classes to declare the basic operations of an effect. Similarly, we specify the `linearTo` operation using the `LinearTo` type class.

```
class LinearTo obj f where
  linearTo :: Traversal' s Float -> Duration -> Target -> f ()
```

The traditional mtl style would add a `Monad f` superclass constraint. As it hinders inspectability, we defer the addition of this constraint to the user. This allows the definition of animations which are, for example `Applicative`, if inspectability is needed or `Monad` if it is not.

The `linearTo` function is used to specify basic animations like `line1Out`, `line2In`, `menuSlideIn`, and `appFadeOut` from Sect. 2. As an example, we redefine `line1Out` with its type signature; the others are similar.

```
line1Out :: (LinearTo Application f) => f ()
line1Out = linearTo (navbar . underline1 . width) (For 0.25) (To 0)
```

4.2   Specifying Composed Animations

Section 2 used the combinators `sequential` and `parallel` for composing animations. In this section, we describe these combinators in more detail.

---

[10] http://hackage.haskell.org/package/mtl.

Sequential Composition. We reuse the `Functor-Applicative-Monad` hierarchy for sequencing animations.

The `liftA2` function from the `Applicative` class, which has type `Applicative f => (a -> b -> c) -> f a -> f b -> f c`, takes two animations `f a` and `f b` and returns a new animation which plays them in order. The final result of the animation is of type `c`, which is obtained by using the function `a -> b -> c` and applying the results of the two played animations to it.

The `>>=` function from the `Monad` class, which has type `Monad f => f a -> (a -> f b)`, takes an animation `f a` and then feeds the result of this animation into the function `a -> f b` to play the animation `f b`.

The `sequential` function is a specialization of the `liftA2` function. It only applies to animations with a `()` return value, and trivially combines the results.

```
sequential :: (Applicative f) => f () -> f () -> f ()
sequential f1 f2 = liftA2 (\_ _ -> ()) f1 f2
```

Hence, the type signature for `selectBtn2Anim` contains an `(Applicative f)` constraint in addition to the `(LinearTo Application f)` constraint.

```
selectBtn2Anim :: (LinearTo Application f, Applicative f) => f ()
selectBtn2Anim = line1Out `sequential` line2In
```

Parallel Composition. We create our own `Parallel` type class for the `parallel` function[11]. Its `liftP2` function has the same signature as `liftA2`, but the intended semantics of the `liftA2` implementation is parallel rather than sequential composition. Technically they are interchangeable, but the relation of `Applicative` to `Monad` makes it more sensible for sequential composition semantics. The `parallel` function is a specialization of `liftP2`.

```
class Parallel f where
  liftP2 :: (a -> b -> c) -> f a -> f b -> f c
```

```
parallel :: (Parallel f) => f () -> f () -> f ()
parallel f1 f2 = liftP2 (\_ _ -> ()) f1 f2
```

With that in place we can give a type signature for `menuIntro`.

```
menuIntro :: (LinearTo Application f, Parallel f) => f ()
menuIntro = menuSlideIn `parallel` appFadeOut
```

---

[11] The `Alternative` class (https://en.wikibooks.org/wiki/Haskell/Alternative_and_MonadPlus) is not suitable as the laws are not the same.

4.3 Running Animations

Now we create a new `Animation` data type that instantiates the above type classes to interpret PaSe programs as actual animations. We briefly summarize this implementation here and refer for more details to our codebase.[12]

The `Animation` data type, defined below, models an animation. It takes the current state s and the time elapsed since the previous frame. It produces a new state for the next frame, the remaining unused time and either the remainder of the animation or, if there is no remainder, the result of the animation. Note that the output is wrapped in a type constructor m to embed custom effects. We need the unused time when there is more time between frames than the animation uses. Then, the remaining time can be used to run the rest of the animation.

```
newtype Animation s m a = Animation { runAnimation ::
    s ->                                  -- previous state
    Float ->                              -- time delta
    m ( s                                 -- next state
      , Either (Animation s m a) a        -- remainder / result
      , Maybe Float )}                    -- remaining delta time
```

LinearTo Instance. The `linearTo` implementation of `Animation` constructs the new state, calculates the remainder of the animation and the remaining delta time. The difference between the `linearTo` duration and the frame time determines whether there is a remaining `linearTo` animation or remaining time.

Examples. We illustrate the behaviour on a tuple state `(Float, Float)`, of an x and y value. The `right` animation transforms the x value to 50 over 1 s.

```
right :: (LinearTo (Float, Float) f) => f ()
right = linearTo x (For 1) (To 50)
```

We run it for 0.5 s by applying it to the `runAnimation` function, together with the initial state (`s0 = (0,0)`) and the duration 0.5. We instantiate the m type constructor inside `Animation` with `Identity` as no additional effects are needed; this means that the result can be unwrapped with `runIdentity`.

```
(s1, remAn1, remDel1) = runIdentity (runAnimation right s0 0.5)
-- s1 = (25.0, 0.0) | remAn1 = Left anim2 | remDel1 = Nothing
```

Running `right` for 0.5 s uses all available time and yields the new state (25, 0). The remainder of the animation is the `right` animation with its duration reduced by 0.5, or essentially `linearTo x (For 0.5) (To 50)`. Let us run this remainder for 1 s.

```
(s2, remAn2, remDel2) = runIdentity (runAnimation anim2 s1 1)
-- s2 = (50.0, 0.0) | remAn2 = Right () | remDel2 = Just 0.5
```

Now the final state is (50, 0) with result () and remaining time 0.5.

---

[12] https://github.com/rubenpieters/anim_eff_dsl/tree/master/code

Monad Instance. For sequential animations we provide a `Monad` instance. Its `return` embeds the result a inside the `Animation` data type. The essence of the `f >>= k` case is straightforward: first, run the animation `f`, then pass its result to the continuation `k` and run that animation. We return the result of the animation, or, if there is an animation remainder, because the remaining time was used up, we return that remainder.

Examples. Let us define an additional animation `up` which transforms the y value to 50 over a duration of 1 s. Additionally, we define an animation `rightThenUp` which composes the `right` and `up` animations in sequence.

```
up :: (LinearTo (Float, Float) f) => f ()
up = linearTo y (For 1) (To 50)

rightThenUp :: (LinearTo (Float, Float) f, Applicative f) => f ()
rightThenUp = right `sequential' up
```

Running the `rightThenUp` animation for 0.5 s gives a similar result to running `right` for 0.5 s. We obtain the new state (25, 0), an animation remainder `anim2` and there is no remaining time. Now the animation remainder is the rest of `rightThenUp`, which is half of `right` and `up`. So, when we run this animation remainder for 1 s, it will run the second half of `right` and the first half of `up`. This results in the state (50, 25), the animation remainder `anim3` and no remaining delta time. This animation remainder is of course the second half of the `up` animation. If we continue to run that remainder, for example for 1 s, then we get the final state (50, 50) and the animation result ().

Parallel Instance. The `liftP2` implementation runs the animations `f1` and `f2` on the starting state. We match on the cases where `f1` and `f2` finish with a result or an animation remainder and remaining time. We check which of the animations have finished and repackage them either into a result or a new remainder, using the result combination function where appropriate. When the longest of the two parallel animations is finished while not fully using the remaining delta time, we continue running the remainder of the animation.

Examples. Let us run the animations `right` and `up` in parallel, which means that both the x and y value will increase simultaneously.

```
rightAndUp :: (LinearTo (Float, Float) f, Parallel f) => f ()
rightAndUp = right `parallel' up
```

The result of running this animation for 0.5 s gives the state (25, 25) and no remaining time. If we continue the animation remainder we get the state (50, 50) and 0.5 s of remaining time.

4.4 Inspecting Animations

To inspect animations we instantiate them with `Const`. It wraps an `a` value and has a `b` phantom type parameter to trivially make it a functor.

```
newtype Const a b = Const { getConst :: a }
```

We might wonder why this extra work is necessary. After all, it is possible to obtain the duration of an animation by running the animation and keeping track of how long it takes. First, this is not an ideal approach for obtaining the duration. We might obtain erroneous results when doing this on conditional animations. Since only one branch of the conditional will be taken, while the other branch with a different duration might be taken in reality. Also, this approach is infeasible when there are effects embedded within the animation. Second, duration is one possible inspection target. Another example is tracking the used textures within an animation so they can be loaded automatically. For this to be possible we must run the inspection *before* the animation runs for the first time, since the textures must be loaded first.

Inspecting LinearTo. To obtain the duration of a `linearTo` animation, we embed the duration in the `Const` wrapper.

```
instance LinearTo obj (Const Duration) where
  linearTo _ duration _ = Const duration
```

Inspecting Applicative. It is not possible to inspect animations with a `Monad` constraint, but it is possible for animations with an `Applicative` constraint. The `Const` data type is not the culprit here, but rather the `>>=` method of the `Monad` class, which contains the limiting factor: a continuation function `a -> m b`.

Inspecting Parallel. The duration of two parallel animations is the maximum of their durations. The `Par (Const Duration)` instance implements this.

```
instance Par (Const Duration) where
  liftP2 _ (Const x1) (Const x2) = Const (max x1 x2)
```

Examples. The duration function is a specialization of the unwrapper function of the `Const` data type, namely `getConst`. We can feed our previously defined animations `selectBtn2Anim` and `menuIntro` from Sect. 2 to this function and obtain their durations as a result.

```
duration :: Const Duration a -> Duration
duration = getConst

selectBtn2AnimDuration :: Duration
selectBtn2AnimDuration = duration selectBtn2Anim -- = For 1.0

menuIntroDuration :: Duration
menuIntroDuration = duration menuIntro -- = For 0.5
```

When we try to retrieve the duration of a monadic animation, there is an error from the compiler: there is no `Monad` instance for `Const Duration`.

```
complicatedAnimDuration :: Duration
complicatedAnimDuration = duration complicatedAnim
-- No instance for (Monad (Const Duration))
```

4.5 Adding a Custom Operation

Custom operation are added by defining a corresponding class. For example, if we want to add a `set` operation, then we create the corresponding `Set` class.

```
class Set obj f where set :: Lens' obj a -> a -> f ()
```

Now, an animation using the `set` operation will incur a `Set` constraint.

```
checkIcon :: (Set CompleteIcon f, ...) => f ()
checkIcon = do ...; set (checkmark . color) green; ...
```

To inspect or run such an animation, we also need to provide instances for the `Animation` and `Const` data types. In the `Animation` instance, we alter the previous state by setting the value targeted by the `lens` to `a`. The duration of a `set` animation is 0, which is what is returned in the `Duration` instance.

```
instance (Applicative m) => Set obj (Animation obj m) where
  set lens a = Animation $ \obj t -> let
    newObj = Lens.set lens a obj
    in pure (newObj, Right (), Just t)

instance Set obj (Const Duration) where
  set _ _ = Const (For 0)
```

5 Interaction Between Inspectability and Expressivity

Haskell DSLs are typically monadic because the `>>=` combinator provides great expressive power. Yet, this power also hinders inspectability. This section shows how to balance expressiveness and inspectability with a custom combinator. This feature is *opt-in* in the sense that it is only required when inspectability is required. If that is no concern, then it is no problem to work with the `Monad` constraint.

Let us revisit the `onlyDone` animation from Sect. 3.3. The following definition imposes a `Monad` constraint on `f`, making the animation non-inspectable.

```
onlyDone :: (LinearTo Application f, Get Application f,
  Set Application f, Monad f, Parallel f) => f ()
onlyDone = do
  cond <- doneItemsGt0
  if cond then onlyDoneNaive else hideNotDone
```

However, there is duration-related information we can extract. For example, the *maximum duration* is the largest duration of the two branches.

To express this idea in PaSe we introduce an explicit combinator to replace this particular use of `>>=`, namely an `if-then-else` construction.

```
class IfThenElse f where
  ifThenElse :: f Bool -> f a -> f a -> f a
```

This is similar to the `handle` combinator from the `DynamicIdiom` class [21] and the `ifS` combinator from the `Selective` class [18].

Now we can reformulate `onlyDone` in terms of this `ifThenElse` combinator[13].

```
onlyDone :: (LinearTo Application f, Get Application f,
  Set Application f, Applicative f, Parallel f, IfThenElse f)
  => f ()
onlyDone = ifThenElse doneItemsGt0 onlyDoneNaive hideNotDone
```

We implement an appropriate `Animation` instance for `IfThenElse`.

```
instance (Monad f) => IfThenElse (Animation obj f) where
  ifThenElse fBool thenBranch elseBranch = do
    bool <- fBool
    if bool then thenBranch else elseBranch
```

Now, we can retrieve the maximum duration, using the `newtype` `MaxDuration` to signify this. The instance for `IfThenElse` retrieves the durations of the `then` and `else` branches and adds the greater value to the duration of the preceding animation inside the condition.

```
instance IfThenElse (Const MaxDuration) where
  ifThenElse (Const (MaxDur durCond)) (Const (MaxDur durThen))
          (Const (MaxDur durElse)) =
    Const (MaxDur (durCond + max durThen durElse))
```

---

[13] Using GHC's `RebindableSyntax` extension, it is possible to use the builtin `if ... then ... else ...` syntax.

This allows us to retrieve the maximum duration of the `onlyDone` animation.

```
onlyDoneMaxDuration :: MaxDuration
onlyDoneMaxDuration = maxDuration onlyDone  -- = MaxDur 1.0
```

6   Interaction Between Callbacks and Inspectability

Many JavaScript animation libraries[14] exist, most of which allow the user to add custom behavior (which the library has not foreseen) through callbacks. A good example is the GreenSock Animation Platform (GSAP), a widely recommended and mature JavaScript animation library with a variety of features.

6.1   Working with GSAP

`TweenMax` objects are the GSAP counterpart of the `linearTo` operation. Their arguments are similar: the object to change, the duration, and the target value for the property. For example, animation `right` moves box1 to the right:

```
const right = new TweenMax("#box1", 1, { x: 50 });
```

We can add animations to a `TimeLineMax` to create a sequential animation. Below, we create `rightThenDown` which moves box1 to the right and then down.

```
const rightThenDown = new TimelineMax({ paused: true })
  .add(new TweenMax("#box1", 1, { x: 50 }))
  .add(new TweenMax("#box1", 1, { y: 50 }));
```

The `add` method takes the position on the timeline as an optional paramter. If we position both animations at point 0 on the timeline, they run in parallel. For example, the `both` animation below moves both box1 and box2 in parallel.

```
const both = new TimelineMax({ paused: true })
  .add(new TweenMax("#box1", 1, { x: 50 }), 0)
  .add(new TweenMax("#box2", 1, { x: 50 }), 0);
```

Timelines can also be embedded within other timelines.

```
const embedded = new TimelineMax({ paused: true })
  .add(both.play())
  .add(new TweenMax("#box1", 1, { y: 50 }), 0);
```

---

[14] Examples: https://greensock.com, https://animejs.com, and https://popmotion.io.

6.2 Callbacks and Inspectability

GSAP provides features related to inspectability. For example, we can use the `totalDuration` method to return the total duration of an animation. Ordinary animations correctly give their total duration when queried. For example, querying the duration of `embedded` correctly returns 2.

```
const embeddedDuration = embedded.totalDuration(); // = 2
```

However, if we want to provide animations similar to `onlyDone`, which contains an `if-then-else`, then the duration returned is not what we expect. The `add` method is overloaded and can also take a callback as parameter. Using the callback parameter we can embed arbitrary effects and control flow. For example, we can create a conditional animation `condAnim`, for which a duration of 1 is returned. This is because any callbacks that are added to the timeline are considered to have duration 0, even if an animation is played in that callback.

The resulting duration of 1 is different from the expected total duration of the animation, which is 2. Of course, in general the duration of the animations in both branches could differ, which is what makes it difficult to provide a procedure for calculating the duration of an animation in this form.

```
const condAnim = new TimelineMax({ paused: true })
  .add(both.play())
  .add(() => { if (cond) { new TweenMax("#box1", 1, { x: 50 }) }
              else { new TweenMax("#box2", 1, { x: 50 }) } });
const condAnimDuration = condAnim.totalDuration() // = 1
```

6.3 Relevance of Duration in Other Features

A wrongly calculated duration becomes more problematic when another feature relies on this calculation. The *relative sequencing* feature needs the duration of the first animation, so the second animation can be added with the correct offset. For example, we can specify the position parameter `-=0.5` to specify that it should start 0.5 s before the end of the previous animation.

```
const bothDelayed = new TimelineMax({ paused: true })
  .add(new TweenMax("#box1", 1, { x: 50 }), 0)
  .add(new TweenMax("#box2", 1, { x: 50 }), "-=0.5");
```

This feature differs from ordinary sequencing such as with `sequential`. When we state that animation B must play 0.5 s before the end of animation A, then it is not possible to wait until animation A has finished to start running animation B. This is because animation B *should have started playing for 0.5 s already*. When we have the duration of animation A available, animation B can be appropriately scheduled.

This feature behaves somewhat unexpectedly when combined with a conditional animation. In the `relativeCond` animation below we add a basic animation followed by a conditional animation. Then we add an animation with a relative position. The result is that the relative position is calculated with respect to the duration of the animations before it, which was a duration of 1.

```
const relativeCond = new TimelineMax({ paused: true })
  .add(new TweenMax("#box1", 1, { x: 50 }), 0)
  .add(() => { if (cond) { new TweenMax("#box1", 1, { x: 100 });
              } else { new TweenMax("#box1", 1, { x: 0 }); } })
  .add(new TweenMax("#box2", 1, { x: 50 }), "-=0.5");
```

Predicting the resulting behavior becomes much more complicated when conditional animations are embedded deep inside complex timelines and cause erroneous duration calculations. Clearly, being more explicit about control flow structures and their impact on inspectability like in PaSe helps providing a more predictable interaction between these features.

6.4   Relative Sequencing in PaSe

While not yet ideal from a usability perspective,[15] PaSe does enable correctly specifying relative sequential compositions by means of `relSequential`.

```
relSequential :: forall c g.
  (c (Const Duration), c g, Applicative g, Delay g) =>
  (forall f. c f => f ()) -> g () -> Float -> g ()
relSequential anim1 anim2 offset = let
  dur = getDuration (duration anim1)
  in anim1 `sequential` (delay (dur + offset) *> anim2)
```

Because this definition requires instances instantiated with `Const Duration`, it only works for animations whose duration can be analyzed. Now, we can correctly compose conditional animations sequentially using relative positioning. We use the `relMaxSequential` function to sequence animations with a maximum duration.

```
-- create synonym for multiple constraints
class (LinearTo Float f, IfThenElse f) => Combined f where
instance (LinearTo Float f, IfThenElse f) => Combined f where

relCond :: (LinearTo Float f, IfThenElse f, Applicative f) => f ()
relCond = relMaxSequential @Combined anim1 anim2 (-0.5)
```

---

[15] It requires `AllowAmbiguousTypes` (among other extensions) and explicitly instantiating the constraint c at the call-site.

7   Use Case

This section compares an implementation of a simplified Pac-Man game (Fig. 5) in Haskell with PaSe[16] and TypeScript with GSAP[17] both quantitatively and qualitatively. The quantitative evaluation compares development time and lines of code. The qualitative one compares different aspects of the libraries.

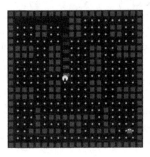

Fig. 5. Screenshot of the Pac-Man application.

7.1   Quantitative Evaluation

This section compares the PaSe and GSAP implementations on quantitative criteria. We consider the development time and lines of code for each module.

- **Development Time.** The Haskell application was developed in ~ 1.5 working days, while the TypeScript application took ~ 1 working day. We consider this approximately the same development time as the Haskell application was developed first, and thus contains design work shared by both applications. The developer is proficient in both languages.
- **Lines of Code (LOC).** Table 1 contains the LOC data (including whitespace) for both applications. Their total LOCs are roughly the same. However, the Haskell code implements its own functionality for sprites and textures while we used the existing `Sprite` class of the `PixiJS` library in TypeScript.
- **Relative LOC.** Table 1 also contains the relative LOCs. The GSAP animation definitions (AnimDefs) are slightly bigger because we had to embed effects in the animations due to differences in the used graphics library, and because of TypeScript's relative verbosity. Using the timeline feature of GSAP, the code for simple animations is comparable to PaSe. However for more complex animations and those requiring embedded effects, there are some differences which we discuss in more detail in the qualitative evaluation.

---

[16] https://github.com/rubenpieters/PaSe-hs/tree/master/PaSe-examples/Pacman.
[17] https://github.com/rubenpieters/pacman-ts.

Table 1. Lines of code comparison (including whitespace)

Module	Haskell/PaSe (LOC)	%	TypeScript/GSAP (LOC)	%
AnimDefs	127	21%	197	32%
Anims	43	7%	39	6%
Field	48	8%	77	12%
Game	130	21%	113	18%
Main	36	6%	23	4%
Sprite	45	7%	/	/
Textures	34	6%	13	2%
Types	10	2%	3	0%
View	139	23%	158	25%
Total	*612*	*100%*	*623*	*100%*

7.2   Qualitative Evaluation

This section compares PaSe and GSAP on five qualitative criteria.

- **Eco-system.** Animations are not created in isolation; they need to be coupled to a graphical backend to display them on the screen. GSAP's maturity makes it a clear winner here. It is well integrated with the browser and supports a rich set of features such as a variety of plugins, compatibility across browsers and support for animating a large range of DOM elements. Yet, for Pac-Man we only needed lenses for our own user-defined state.
- **Workflow.** It is important that animations can be specified easily and concisely. Creating pure animations, without any embedded effects, are equally convenient in GSAP and in PaSe. However, more complex interactions with effects and control flow are simpler in PaSe. We saw this in the Pac-Man use case when implementing particle animations. A particle animation is an animation that creates an object, animates it and then destroys it again. We implemented a general wrapper for such animations which takes as input a function `Int -> Animation`, where the `Int` is the unique particle identifier, and a creation and deletion function for the particle. In the GSAP library we have to add the function to the timeline as a callback, which means its duration is considered to be 0. This is problematic because the deletion of the particle should occur after its animation. This means that we are forced to manually calculate and provide the duration for the particle animation.
- **Performance.** Both libraries perform equally acceptable on Pac-Man: no visible glitches or lag at 60 frames per second (FPS) on an Intel core i7-6600U at 2.60 GHz with 8 GB memory. We have also implemented a benchmark similar to GSAP's speed test[18], which tests a large parallel animations. GSAP is slightly more optimized currently as it handles 500 parallel animations at

---

[18] https://greensock.com/js/speed.html.

60 FPS instead of PaSe's 400. This could be remedied by further performance improvements of PaSe, like fusing multiple parallel animations or improving the `Animation` data structure, which are future work.

- **Extensibility & Inspectability.** Extensibility and inspectability are key features of PaSe. Both were useful for Pac-Man. Inspectability allowed extracting all used textures in the animations to automate their loading. Extensibility enabled the definition of the particle effect mentioned earlier. We created a new `WithParticle` type class and implemented both an `Animation` instance and a `Const` instance for the texture inspection. GSAP does not support inspectability, and thus we did not implement the automatic loading of textures. The particle animation function was implemented with callbacks and implicit side-effects, which TypeScript allows anywhere.

8   Future Work

Some general improvements can be made regarding supporting new backends, more features and improving performance.

We chose the MTL style for this paper, as we believe it is simpler presentation-wise. However, an initial encoding, which is more typical for algebraic effects and handlers, can provide benefits in areas such as the implementation of the relative sequencing. This comparison is another avenue for future work.

An aspect not touched in this paper is *conflict management*. A conflict appears when the same property is targeted by different animations in parallel. For example, if we want to change a value both to 0 and 100 in parallel, what should this animation look like? PaSe does no conflict management, and the animation might look stuttery. GSAP, for example, resolves this by only enabling the most recently added animation. However this strategy is not straightforwardly mapped to the context of PaSe. Inspectability could provide a solution for this problem by providing the possibility to detect conflicts.

9   Related Work

Functional Reactive Programming. The origins of functional reactive programming (FRP) lie in the creation of animations [4], and many later developments use FRP as the basis for purely functional GUIs.

PaSe focuses on easily describing *micro-animations*, which differ from general *animations* as considered by FRP. The latter can typically be described by a time-paramterized picture function `Time -> Picture`. While a subset of all possible animations, micro-animations are not easily described by such a function because many small micro-animations can be active at the same time and their timing depends on user interaction.

We have supplied an implementation of PaSe on top of a traditional event-based framework, but it is interesting future work to investigate an implementation of the `linearTo`, `sequential` and `parallel` operations in terms of FRP behaviours and events.

Animation Frameworks. Typical micro-animation libraries for web applications (with CSS or JavaScript) and animation constructions in game engines provide a variety of configurable pre-made operations while composing complex animations or integrating new types of operations is difficult. PaSe focuses on the creation of complex sequences of events while still providing the ability to embed new animation primitives. We have looked at GSAP as an example of such libraries and some of the limits in combining extensibility with callbacks and inspectability. PaSe is an exercise in improving this combination of features forward in a direction which is more predictable for the user.

Planning-Based Animations. PaSe shares similarities with approaches which specify an animation as a plan which needs to be executed [12,17]. An animation is specified by a series of steps to be executed, the plan of the animation. The coordinator, which manages and advances the animations, is implemented as part of the hosting application. PaSe realizes these plan-based animations with only a few core principles and features the possibility of adding custom operations and inspection. A detailed comparison with these approaches is difficult, since their works are very light on details of the actual implementation aspect.

Inspectable DSLs. Some DSLs for parsing [2,9,15], non-determinism [11], remote execution [5,6] and build systems [19] focus on inspectability aspects, yet none of them provide extensibility and expressiveness in addition to inspection.

10   Conclusion

We have presented PaSe, an extensible and inspectable DSL for micro-animations. PaSe focuses on compositional animations using sequential and parallel animations as basic building blocks. This is in contrast with other animation libraries typically focused on sequential composition and callbacks with implicit effects.

We utilized a to-do list application use case to explain the features of PaSe. In this use case we showed the additional features of PaSe: extensiblity, inspectability and expressivity. We argue that the callback style of providing extensibility hurts the inspectability aspect of animations, which is found in for example the GreenSock Animation Platform. An implementation of the Pac-Man game confirms that this can be a problem even in simple applications.

References

1. Bederson, B.B., Boltman, A.: Does animation help users build mental maps of spatial information? In: INFOVIS 1999, pp. 28–35 (1999). https://doi.org/10.1109/INFVIS.1999.801854
2. Capriotti, P., Kaposi, A.: Free applicative functors. In: MSFP 2014, pp. 2–30 (2014). https://doi.org/10.4204/EPTCS.153.2

3. Carette, J., Kiselyov, O., Shan, C.: Finally tagless, partially evaluated: tagless staged interpreters for simpler typed languages. J. Funct. Program. **19**(5), 509–543 (2009). https://doi.org/10.1017/S0956796809007205
4. Elliott, C., Hudak, P.: Functional reactive animation. In: ICFP 1997, pp. 263–273 (1997). https://doi.org/10.1145/258948.258973
5. Gibbons, J.: Free delivery (functional pearl). In: Haskell 2016, pp. 45–50 (2016). https://doi.org/10.1145/2976002.2976005
6. Gill, A., et al.: The remote monad design pattern. In: Haskell 2015, pp. 59–70 (2015). https://doi.org/10.1145/2804302.2804311
7. Gonzalez, C.: Does animation in user interfaces improve decision making? In: CHI 1996, pp. 27–34 (1996). https://doi.org/10.1145/238386.238396
8. Heer, J., Robertson, G.G.: Animated transitions in statistical data graphics. IEEE Trans. Vis. Comput. Graph. **13**(6), 1240–1247 (2007). https://doi.org/10.1109/TVCG.2007.70539
9. Hughes, J.: Generalising monads to arrows. Sci. Comput. Program. **37**(1–3), 67–111 (2000). https://doi.org/10.1016/S0167-6423(99)00023-4
10. Jones, M.P.: Functional programming with overloading and higher-order polymorphism. In: Jeuring, J., Meijer, E. (eds.) AFP 1995. LNCS, vol. 925, pp. 97–136. Springer, Heidelberg (1995). https://doi.org/10.1007/3-540-59451-5_4
11. Kiselyov, O.: Effects without monads: non-determinism - back to the meta language. In: ML/OCaml 2017, pp. 15–40 (2017). https://doi.org/10.4204/EPTCS.294.2
12. Kurlander, D., Ling, D.T.: Planning-based control of interface animation. In: CHI 1995, pp. 472–479 (1995). https://doi.org/10.1145/223904.223968
13. van Laarhoven, T.: CPS-Based Functional References (2009). https://www.twanvl.nl/blog/haskell/cps-functional-references
14. Liang, S., Hudak, P., Jones, M.P.: Monad transformers and modular interpreters. In: POPL 1995, pp. 333–343 (1995). https://doi.org/10.1145/199448.199528
15. Lindley, S.: Algebraic effects and effect handlers for idioms and arrows. In: WGP 2014, pp. 47–58 (2014). https://doi.org/10.1145/2633628.2633636
16. McBride, C., Paterson, R.: Applicative programming with effects. J. Funct. Program. **18**(1), 1–13 (2008). https://doi.org/10.1017/S0956796807006326
17. Mirlacher, T., Palanque, P.A., Bernhaupt, R.: Engineering animations in user interfaces. In: EICS 2012, pp. 111–120 (2012). https://doi.org/10.1145/2305484.2305504
18. Mokhov, A., Lukyanov, G., Marlow, S., Dimino, J.: Selective applicative functors. In: ICFP 2019, pp. 90:1–90:29 (2019). https://doi.org/10.1145/3341694
19. Mokhov, A., Mitchell, N., Peyton Jones, S.: Build systems à la carte. In: PACMPL (ICFP 2018), vol. 2, pp. 79:1–79:29 (2018). https://doi.org/10.1145/3236774
20. Wadler, P.: Comprehending monads. In: LFP 1990, pp. 61–78 (1990). https://doi.org/10.1145/91556.91592
21. Yallop, J.: Abstraction for web programming. Ph.D. thesis, University of Edinburgh, UK (2010)

BinderAnn: Automated Reification of Source Annotations for Monadic EDSLs

Agustín Mista$^{(\boxtimes)}$ and Alejandro Russo

Chalmers University of Technology, Gothenburg, Sweden
{mista,russo}@chalmers.se

Abstract. Embedded Domain-Specific Languages (EDSLs) are an alternative to quickly implement specialized languages without the need to write compilers or interpreters from scratch. In this territory, Haskell is a prime choice as the host language. EDSLs in Haskell, however, are often incapable of reifying useful static information from the source code, namely variable binding names and source locations. Not having access to variable names directly affects EDSLs designed to generate low-level code, where the variables names in the generated code do not match those found in the source code—thus broadening the semantic gap among source and target code. Similarly, many existing EDSLs produce poor error messages due to the lack of knowledge of source locations where errors are generated.

In this work, we propose a simple technique for enhancing monadic EDSLs expressed using **do** notation. This technique employs *source-to-source plugins*, a relatively new feature of GHC, to annotate every **do** statement of our EDSLs with relevant information extracted from the source code at compile time. We show how these annotations can be incorporated into EDSL designs either directly inside values or as monadic effects. We provide *BinderAnn*, a GHC source plugin implementing our ideas, and evaluate it by enhancing existing real-world EDSLs with relatively minor modification efforts to contemplate the source-level static information related to variables names and source locations.

Keywords: Embedded domain-specific languages · Haskell

1 Introduction

Embedded Domain-Specific Languages (EDSLs) are ubiquitous in Haskell. Its powerful type system and extensible syntax are among the reasons making it a very suitable programming language for implementing EDSLs [14]. Especially, monads [25] and monadic **do** notation [17] are part of programmers' toolbox to implement all sorts of EDSLs. Monadic **do** notation enables users to write domain-specific code in a sequential-like manner that it is easy to adopt by programmers not familiar to Haskell's syntax or even to functional programming languages.

© Springer Nature Switzerland AG 2020
A. Byrski and J. Hughes (Eds.): TFP 2020, LNCS 12222, pp. 25–46, 2020.
https://doi.org/10.1007/978-3-030-57761-2_2

```
semaphore = do
  green   ← node
  yellow  ← node
  red     ← node
  green  .->. yellow
  yellow .->. red
  red    .->. green
```

```
digraph G
{
  n0; n1; n2;
  n0 -> n1;
  n1 -> n2;
  n2 -> n0;
}
```

```
digraph G
{
  green; yellow; red;
  green -> yellow;
  yellow -> red;
  red -> green;
}
```

(a) EDSL code describing a semaphore color cycle.

(b) Generated code without source information.

(c) Generated code using the BinderAnn plugin.

Fig. 1. Enhancing the `dotgen` code generating EDSL with source information.

As a result of being embedded, Haskell EDSLs often lack the ability of reflecting some of the static source information that is intrinsic and available to the host language (Haskell) but not in guest (the embedded DSL), namely bound names and source locations. These limitations are especially known by designers of EDSLs which generate low-level code, e.g., FeldSpar [3], Ivory [8], or Copilot [22]. In these EDSLs, developers adopted, as the best-case scenario, ad-hoc measures to enforce that variables names in the generated code match those in the host language. In this paper, we instead propose a systematic solution to such problems as a *source-to-source* plugin [21] called *BinderAnn*. We will illustrate the aforementioned limitations of Haskell EDSLs using a series of real-world examples of code generation, while we will show in tandem how our approach can be used to overcome it.

1.1   Motivating Examples

We consider as motivating example the monadic EDSL from the `dotgen` package for generating DOT code[1] from inside Haskell [10]. This EDSL creates new graph nodes and connects them using **do** notation. A simple example of this is shown in Fig. 1a, where we create a graph of the alternating colors of a street semaphore.

Internally, this EDSL sequentially creates a fresh node name for each invocation of the **node** combinator, i.e, n0, n1, and so on. Then, the corresponding DOT code is generated referring to these generated names, as it is shown in Fig. 1b. Sadly, the generated code does not quite reflect the nature of our particular graph: *sequential names are of little help for interpreting the semantics of the generated code*. To make things worse, this is not a just limitation of this particular EDSL. The variable names to the left of binds (←) do not belong to an EDSL itself, but to the host language in which it is embedded—thus, such EDSL cannot make use of this useful source information directly.

Common Practices. To address this recurrent limitation, some EDSLs resolve in using redundant strings to indicate variable names when synthesizing

---

[1] DOT is a graph description language used by many open source applications.

```
1 genAddSub = do                         genAddSub = do
2    x ← cgInput "x"                         x ← cgInput
3    y ← cgInput "y"                         y ← cgInput
4    cgOutput "diff" (x − y)                 diff ← cgOutput (x − y)
5    cgReturn (x + y)                        cgReturn (x + y)
```

(a) EDSL code with redundant string   (b) Simplified EDSL where names are ex-
names for generating terms.   tracted automatically by BinderAnn.

Fig. 2. Avoiding redundant string names in the sbv EDSL via source annotations.

code [2,9,22]. For instance, consider the EDSL for synthesizing C programs via
SMT solvers in the sbv package [9]. This EDSL enables to express relationships
between the inputs and outputs of a function, and based on that, it generates
its C body accordingly. Figure 2a presents a very simple example of this, where
we use the cgInput combinator to bind the function inputs "x" and "y" to the
Haskell variables x and y, respectively, and then we specify how the outputs are
calculated based on them. In this example, the function will simply return the
sum of both inputs (line 5), while storing their difference in the output pointer
"diff" (line 4). Then, the EDSL will generate the following C code:

```
SInt32 AddSub(SInt32 x, SInt32 y, SInt32 *diff){
    ...
    *diff = x - y;
    return (x + y);
}
```

where ... simply indicates the rest of the generated code which is not relevant
to the point being made here. Notice how the EDSL expects the users to give
strings denoting variable names to the expressions they already bind with the
same variable name but using **do** notation. While this common technique works
in practice, this added redundancy requires maintenance and might be hard to
keep in sync with the concrete Haskell bind variable names they replicate.

1.2   BinderAnn

In this paper, we present a novel technique to enhance existing (and future)
EDSLs with the static information that is missing to generate faithful code,
and without relying on redundant string names. In essence, our approach consists of automatically transforming the syntactic representation of our Haskell
code to make the static information related to bound names explicitly available
to EDSLs. This is now possible due to the recent addition of *source-to-source*
plugins [21] to the GHC Haskell compiler.

Recalling our dotgen example, our approach can be used to generate DOT
code that accurately reflects the one written by the user of the EDSL—see Fig. 1c
Furthermore, Fig. 2b shows how our approach can simplify the sbv EDSL by not
requiring string names to be passed around while generating the same C code.

1.3 Beyond Bindings

In practice, bound names are not the only kind of useful static information that can be extracted from EDSL code. Many EDSLs lack descriptive error messages which could be improved by having access to the source locations. To illustrate this point, we consider the EDSL provided by the shellmate package for executing shell scripts from Haskell [7]. With this EDSL, we can create computations capturing the output of existing shell commands:

```
cpuinfo = capture (run "cat" ["/proc/cpuinfo"])
meminfo = capture (run "cat" ["/proc/meminfo"])
```

And use them to build complex shell-like scripts:

```
1 saveInfo = do
2    cpu ← cpuinfo
3    mem ← meminfo
4    output "info.txt" (cpu ++ mem)
```

Let us suppose that we mistype the "/proc/meminfo" path. If we run our saveInfo script, the mangled path given to the command cat will produce a runtime exception that will be captured by the EDSL and printed to the user simply as:

```
Command "cat" failed with error code 1
```

This error message is hardly helpful for debugging the problem of our shell script, especially considering that many functions may be defined in terms of capturing the output of the cat command.

By using BinderAnn, it is also possible to extract the exact position in the user code where the error is triggered. In this light, we can enhance this EDSL to support more precise and useful error messages. For instance, the error message above can be improved to:

```
Exception raised at src/MyScript.hs:(3,3):
The value "mem" produced the following error:
Command "cat" failed with error code 1
```

Note how this error message now includes not only the name bound to the problematic command (mem), but also its position in the code.

The examples presented so far have motivated the development of BinderAnn to improve the capabilities of monadic EDSLs considerably. To summarize, the contributions of this paper are:

- We propose a simple yet powerful syntactic transformation technique for annotating monadic computations expressed using **do** notation with useful source information (Sect. 2).

- We propose two different *annotation styles* depending on how EDSLs can consume the static information provided to them, i.e., binding names and source locations (Sect. 3).
- We extend our simple transformation technique with support for annotating monadic computations returning and pattern matching against tuples, as well as a mechanism for controlling the transformation scope (Sect. 4).
- We provide an implementation of our ideas, in the shape of a GHC source-to-source plugin called BinderAnn.[2] With our plugin in mind from the beginning, we develop a complete case study from scratch, demonstrating how the ability of reifying source information automatically might unlock attractive new features in future EDSLs (Sect. 5).
- We discuss other possible approaches to fill the static information gap between hosts and guests embedded languages and their implications. Additionally, we reflect on the limitations of BinderAnn, as well as possible extensions to make it applicable to a larger space of EDSL (Sect. 6).

2   Generating Source Annotations Using Source Plugins

This section briefly describes *source-to-source plugins* (or source plugins for short), a new mechanism included in the GHC compiler for inspecting and transforming the parsed representation of the compiled code before any other transformation is performed. Moreover, we show how it is possible to take advantage of this mechanism to transparently enhance monadic code written using **do** notation with useful source information.

Essentially, a GHC plugin is a Haskell function that can be inserted into the compilation pipeline to transform the output of the compiled code in different ways [20,21]. These transformations can alter the compiled code at different stages, where each stage defines a different interface for its corresponding kind of plugin, dependent on the representation of the code used by the compiler at that point. Historically, this mechanism only allowed plugins to be inserted during type-checking, and after the code was transformed to GHC's Core intermediate representation [15]. Recently, GHC 8.6.1 also added support for plugins to be inserted after parsing and after renaming, and this work focuses on the former kind.

In GHC, the plugin interface is condensed in a record data type `Plugin`, containing a field for each of the transformation stages available. In particular, source-to-source plugins are given by the record field `parsedResultAction` of this data type:

```
data Plugin = Plugin {
  parsedResultAction :: [CommandLineOption] → ModSummary
                        → HsParsedModule → Hsc HsParsedModule
  ...
}
```

---

[2] Available at https://github.com/OctopiChalmers/BinderAnn.

This field exposes the interface of a transformation function over the abstract syntax tree of the module under compilation (of type `HsParsedModule`). This abstract syntax tree includes relevant static information not available to the programmer, such as the variable name of every binding, as well as the source location of every syntactic object in the module—two valuable resources that one might want to have access to when implementing EDSLs in Haskell.

Using this interface, we can implement our source plugin by providing a module exporting a value `plugin :: Plugin`, which executes our code transformation:

```
module BinderAnn (plugin) where
import GhcPlugins
plugin :: Plugin
plugin = defaultPlugin {parsedResultAction =  <our code here>}
```

Later, our plugin can be enabled by passing the name of its module as a flag to the GHC compiler (`-fplugin=BinderAnn`), or using a compiler-options pragma in the module we want our plugin to transform:

```
{-# OPTIONS_GHC -fplugin BinderAnn #-}
```

Next subsection introduces a simple syntactic transformation procedure based on source plugins for transposing useful static information from the source code representation into the internal state of our EDSLs automatically.

2.1   Enhancing EDSLs with Source Information

We have seen that it is possible to expose static source information from our code using source plugins. However, for our EDSLs to take advantage of this information, we need to transform the user code so that it explicitly communicates this information to the EDSL after our plugin runs at compile time.

In this work, we propose a simple transformation over **do** statements: we will *annotate* each statement with the static information that can be extracted from the parsed representation of the code, which we will simply refer to as a *source annotation*. To achieve this, the first step consists of defining a concrete representation for source annotations, which will be used both by our plugin and by the target EDSLs it annotates. For this purpose, we will rely on a new data type `SrcInfo` to hold the static information relative to a **do** statement:

```
data SrcInfo = Info (Maybe String) (Maybe Loc)
```

This data type stores the name bound to the statement (if any), and the location in the source code where it is defined, being the latter a conjunction of a file path, and a row and column within such file:

```
type Loc = (FilePath, Int, Int)
```

The option type used for the location information in the definition of `SrcInfo` is required to represent the fact that the GHC compiler might not know the specific source location of a statement. A situation that might occur, for instance, if such statement was automatically generated by another source plugin.

Later, our source plugin can easily populate a source annotation (of type `SrcInfo`) for each **do** statement it finds. However, we still need to insert each annotation into our EDSL in a predictable way. For this purpose, we will define a function `annotateM`, taking a monadic computation and a source annotation, and returning a new monadic computation which internalizes such annotation:

$$\text{annotateM} :: \text{Monad m} \Rightarrow \text{m a} \rightarrow \text{SrcInfo} \rightarrow \text{m a}$$

Note how this function refers neither to a specific monadic type (m) nor to a specific return type of the monadic computation (a). This generality lets our plugin blindly transform every **do** statement it finds in the user code in a type-safe manner. To do so, it simply wraps every statement with its static information using our generic annotation function. For instance, our plugin will transform the semaphore example from Sect. 1 to the following concrete code:

```
1 semaphore = do
2    green   ← node      `annotateM` Info (Just "green")  (Just ("Main.hs", 2, 3))
3    yellow  ← node      `annotateM` Info (Just "yellow") (Just ("Main.hs", 3, 3))
4    red     ← node      `annotateM` Info (Just "red")    (Just ("Main.hs", 4, 3))
5    green  .->. yellow `annotateM` Info Nothing          (Just ("Main.hs", 5, 3))
6    yellow .->. red    `annotateM` Info Nothing          (Just ("Main.hs", 6, 3))
7    red    .->. green  `annotateM` Info Nothing          (Just ("Main.hs", 7, 3))
```

Notice, for instance, how the bound name **red** is reflected in the source annotation for the **red** ← **node** statement with the value `Just "red"`, whereas the **green .->. yellow** statement in the next line is not given any name, which gets represented by the `Nothing` constructor on its corresponding source annotation.

Additionally, each annotation carries the source location within the user code of its corresponding statement—assuming here that the first **do** statement is defined in line number 2 of the file *Main.hs*.

After this transformation is automatically applied, the user will be able to make use of this useful source information, which is now explicit in the source code—and without the burden of maintaining manually written annotations.

Even though this transformation is rather mechanical, the behavior of the annotating function `annotateM` is not trivial, and is subject to *which* types of our EDSLs are expected to be annotated, and *how* the source annotations should be consumed by them. The next section addresses the challenges of implementing this function in depth.

3   Consuming Source Annotations

In the previous section, we demonstrated how it is possible to annotate expressions written using **do** notation with source information via source plugins. Such annotations rely on a generic function **annotateM** to produce the annotation effect. This section explores the details of this function in two possible variants.

Haskell gives the programmer the freedom to implement EDSLs in many ways, depending on the nature of the embedded language. As a consequence, a concrete solution for annotating EDSLs would likely not fit many use cases. In this light, our approach supports two different *annotation styles* that the programmer can use depending on the particular implementations of their EDSLs:

- *Effect-free annotations:* the annotations are stored directly on the values they refer to, e.g, using a specialized data constructor, or an option type.
- *Effect-full annotations:* the annotations are kept in a monadic context as a side effect, e.g., using a mapping from values to annotations inside a state monad.

On one hand, the effect-free style lets us annotate values in place, regardless of the monadic context producing them, which might come in handy if our EDSL defines several monadic types to be used by the end-user. On the other hand, the effect-full style lets us insert the source annotations in the monadic context without having to modify the return value of each computation. This style might be useful if our EDSL already carries an internal monadic state, or if the source annotations should not be available to the end-user.

Both annotation styles are *independent* of each other and provide different interfaces to interact with BinderAnn. Programmers will then have to choose the most suitable one depending on the nature of their EDSLs, and adapt their code to be able to consume the annotations generated by our plugin.

The rest of this section addresses each annotation style in detail.

3.1   Effect-Free Annotations

The simplest way to annotate a value with source information is given when its type already supports annotations. For instance, suppose that the graph-building EDSL from Sect. 1 defines graph nodes as having an identifier, and an associative list of attributes as payload:

```
data Node = Node Id [(Attr, Value)]
```

With this in place, the rest of the EDSL combinators can be implemented in terms of nodes as inputs and outputs:

```
node   :: Dot Node
(.->.) :: Node → Node → Dot ()
```

where **Dot** is the main monad defined by this EDSL, whose details are not very relevant for this annotation style. To support generating faithful code, we can extend the definition of the **Node** data type to also carry an optional field representing the name of each node:

```
data Node = Node Id (Maybe String) [(Attr, Value)]
```

Then, we need to somehow specify that every monadic computation returning a Node should (potentially) be annotated with its bound name. To encode this, we can define a new *type class* [13] Annotated, representing types (of type a) that can be annotated directly:

```
class Annotated a where
    annotate :: a → SrcInfo → a
```

The function annotate simply takes a value and an annotation and returns an annotated value of the same type. Then, we can specify how the source bound names can be inserted into nodes by giving an appropriate Annotated instance:

```
instance Annotated Node where
    annotate (Node id _ attrs) (SrcInfo name loc) = Node id name attrs
```

where we simply extract the bind name from the source annotation and use it as the node name—for simplicity, we discard the location information here.

Using this type class, we can finally implement our desired annotateM function which transforms **do** statements by unwrapping the return value from the monadic computation and returning the corresponding annotated one:

```
annotateM :: (Monad m, Annotated a) ⇒ m a → SrcInfo → m a
annotateM ma ann = do
    a ← ma
    return (annotate a ann)
```

This is an extensible mechanism that lets us support automatic annotations over the return types of our interest. We simply need to provide an instance of the Annotated type class for every return type of a **do** statement we want to annotate using our plugin.

While simple, this transformation is not safe (yet). Recalling from Sect. 2, our plugin knows nothing about the return type of a **do** statement. Hence, it transforms every statement it finds under the assumption that this transformation will not produce a type error—as annotateM universally quantifies over any possible return type of the monadic computation it transforms. However, our annotateM function now carries an additional Annotated constraint! In practice, this means that our plugin will break the well-typedness of our EDSL if it happens to find a monadic computation returning a value of a type without an Annotated instance. And even though we could potentially provide an Annotated instance for every type used by our EDSL, a user could always write a statement returning a value of a type not known by our EDSL:

```
x ← return False
```

Here, the lack of an instance for `Annotated Bool` will break the module during type checking.

To attenuate this problem, we can make every type trivially annotatable by simply discarding the annotation altogether:

```
instance {-# INCOHERENT #-} Annotated a where
   annotate a _ = a
```

This generic instance works as a default trivial annotation method, where any concrete `Annotated` instance written by the programmer will take precedence against this one [16]. Furthermore, note how this default instance requires to be declared as *incoherent*. This ensures that the type checker will pick a concrete instance written by the user whenever possible, but it will conservatively use the default one in case of an overlapping arising from annotating fully-polymorphic functions—we discuss this in detail in Sect. 6.4.

3.2   Effect-Full Annotations

EDSLs might also be implemented in a fully stateful manner, where the important data is kept in the monadic context, and the user only gets a reference to handle it. For instance, suppose that our graph-building EDSL from Sect. 1 does not return nodes directly, but references to them instead:

```
data NodeRef = NodeRef Id
node :: Dot NodeRef
(.->.) :: NodeRef → NodeRef → Dot ()
```

Here, the node payload will be kept in an internal state of the `Dot` monad defined by the EDSL, which could be defined on terms of a state monad:

```
newtype Dot a = Dot (State DotState a)
data DotState = DotState {
   node_attrs :: Map NodeRef [(Attr, Value)]
}
```

In this case, we might as well want our annotation mechanism to follow the same pattern, inserting the annotations in the monadic context instead of directly in the value they refer to. For this purpose, we can extend our `DotState` type to also carry the source names given to the bound nodes (if any) using a partial mapping:

```
data DotState = DotState {
   node_attrs :: Map NodeRef [(Attr, Value)],
   node_names :: Map NodeRef String
}
```

Similarly as before, we can define a new type class to specify how to annotate values of different types, except that this time we also need to quantify over the specific monadic context in which the annotation takes place:

```
class Monad m ⇒ AnnotatedM m a where
  annotateM :: m a → SrcInfo → m a
```

Notice that this new type class defines our desired **annotateM** function directly. In contrast to the previously seen **Annotated** type class from the previous subsection, this type class let us specify how **do** statements can be annotated depending not only on their result type but also on their specific monadic type. In this light, computations returning new node references can be annotated within the Dot monad by inserting the bound names in the extended internal state:

```
instance AnnotatedM Dot NodeRef where
  annotateM mref (Info name loc) = do
    ref ← mref
    when (isJust name) $ modify $ λs →
      s {node_names = Map.insert ref (fromJust name) (node_names s)}
    return ref
```

As before, we also need to provide a default instance for our new type class, to ensure that our plugin will not break the well-typedness of the user code:

```
instance {-# INCOHERENT #-} Monad m ⇒ AnnotatedM m a where
  annotateM ma _ = ma
```

All in all, the two annotation styles presented in this section cover a wide variety of EDSL implementation patterns.

4 Extensions

This section describes two useful extensions to our annotation approach that are currently supported by our plugin.

4.1 Annotating Computations Returning Tuples

The syntactic transformation described so far contemplates monadic computations with and without bound names. However, in principle we could only use it to extract the names bound to complete resulting values, i.e, when the pattern at the left hand side of (←) is a plain variable pattern. In practice, a computation could produce multiple values and return them in a tuple. For instance, suppose that our graph-building EDSL example from Sect. 1 provides a combinator **nodes** returning multiple new nodes at once:

$(\texttt{green}, \texttt{yellow}, \texttt{red}) \leftarrow \texttt{nodes}$

For this common programming practice, we would want to insert an annotation for each element of this tuple, following the same pattern as we did before. However, our source annotations can only associate a single name bound to a complete result value of a monadic computation.

Fortunately, we can extend our plugin to support tuple results by inserting a function that lifts our annotation mechanism to each element of the resulting tuple:

```
(green, yellow, red) ← nodes
  `annotateM3`
    (Info (Just "green")  (Just ("Main.hs", 2, 4)),
     Info (Just "yellow") (Just ("Main.hs", 2, 10)),
     Info (Just "red")    (Just ("Main.hs", 2, 18)))
```

where `annotateM3` simply extracts each tuple element from the monadic computation, annotates it using the ordinary annotation function, and returns a new tuple containing each annotated value:

```
annotateM3 :: Monad m ⇒ m (a, b, c) → (SrcInfo, SrcInfo, SrcInfo) → m (a, b, c)
annotateM3 mabc (ia, ib, ic) = do
  (a, b, c) ← mabc
  a' ← return a `annotateM` ia
  b' ← return b `annotateM` ib
  c' ← return c `annotateM` ic
  return (a', b', c')
```

It is easy to see how this lifting primitive can be trivially generalized to tuples of any fixed size.

4.2   Specifying the Annotation Scope

By default, our annotation plugin will transform *every* **do** expression present on the module it runs over. Even though a module can contain **do** expressions of different monadic types, we have shown in Sect. 3 how this transformation can effectively affect only those expressions of the types the user is interested in.

Nonetheless, for a given type to be annotated with source information, a user might still want to limit the scope of the annotations to a certain subset of **do** expressions. To support this, our plugin can also be set to work in a selective mode, where the user specifies which **do** expressions should be transformed.

On one hand, if the target expression is bound to a top-level name, we can use a GHC *annotation pragma* to specify that we are interested in annotating it:

```
{-# ANN semaphore SrcInfo #-}
semaphore = do
  <annotated do statements>
```

This way, BinderAnn will begin by reifying all the annotation pragmas defined in the module, and will proceed to transform only those **do** expression for which a corresponding annotation pragma exists.

However, annotation pragmas can only refer to top-level bindings, limiting the applicability of this technique. In practice, writing **do** expressions at the right hand side of the ($) infix function application operator is quite common. For instance, a user might define a graph and render its DOT code right away:

```
semaphoreCode = showDot $ do
  <do statements>
```

There is no top-level name we can use to specify our plugin to annotate this nested **do** expression. To solve this, we can introduce an *infix annotation operator*. This is, we can replace the infix function application operator ($) with a new syntactic operator, e.g., (|$|), that can be sought within the user's code in order to transform nested **do** expressions:

```
semaphoreCode = showDot |$| do
  <annotated do statements>
```

Then, our plugin will transform every **do** expression at the right hand side of a (|$|) operator to include the appropriate source annotations, replacing it with normal function application in the process. In practice, the programmer can specify the annotation operator to be any valid infix operator name using a plugin option in BinderAnn (`-fplugin-opt BinderAnn:infix=|$|`).

This gives us the freedom to choose the most appropriate operator according to the nature of the embedded language. Additionally, the infix annotation operator can be defined as a synonym to the actual function application operator:

```
(|$|) :: (a → b) → a → b
(|$|) = ($)
```

This way, the behavior of our code does not change when the plugin is disabled.

Next section develops a complete case study, exploring some interesting features that our plugin enables and can aid in implementing in future EDSLs.

5   Case Study: Theorem Proving EDSL

So far we have seen how source annotations can be automatically extracted from the source code using a GHC source plugin (Sect. 2), as well as consumed to our EDSLs in different ways depending on how they are implemented (Sect. 3).

Using this approach, we enhanced several existing EDSLs [1,7,9,10] (including the ones presented in Sect. 1) to support source annotations, obtaining attractive results[3] with relatively small effort.

---

[3] Available at http://github.com/OctopiChalmers/BinderAnn-examples.

To demonstrate the full potential of our automated transformation technique, this section introduces a novel case study we designed from scratch having source annotations in mind. In this light, we implemented a simple proof assistant EDSL for propositional logic formulas,[4] based on Coq's [4] tactic style, i.e., our proofs will consist of a series of monadic commands (the tactics) which will manipulate our goals and hypotheses to construct a proof for a given target formula.

Despite not being academically enlightening, this EDSL uses the effect-full annotation style to take advantage of the source information present in the user code, in order to provide useful interactive (modulo recompilation time) proof-state reports—an attractive feature that was not possible to achieve before using monadic EDSLs. To give an example of this, Fig. 3a shows a proof of *Modus ponens* discharged using our EDSL. Firstly, we use the combinator `variables` to create two new propositional variables p and q (line 3). These variables are used immediately in line 4, where the `proof` combinator establishes the current proof goal $(p \wedge (p \Rightarrow q) \Rightarrow q)$ and we can proceed to prove it using the **do** expression starting after the (**$**) operator.

```
1 modus_ponens :: Proof Prop
2 modus_ponens = do
3    (p,q) ← variables
4    proof (p ∧ (p ⇒ q) ⇒ q) $ do
5       hand ← intro
6       (hp,hpq) ← destruct hand
7       hq ← apply hp hpq
8       exact hq
9    qed
```

```
At Proofs.hs:(7,5):
1 subgoal left
p, q: Prop
hand: p ∧ (p ⇒ q)
hp: p
hpq: p ⇒ q
hq: q
===================
q
```

```
Incomplete proof:
1 subgoal left
V0, V1: Prop
H0: V0 ∧ (V0 ⇒ V1)
H1: V0
H2: V0 ⇒ V1
H3: V1
===================
V1
```

(a) A proof of Modus Ponens using do notation in our EDSL.

(b) Proof state using source annotations.

(c) Proof state using internal names.

Fig. 3. User interface of our Coq-like, tactics-based proof assistant EDSL.

The proof itself uses a series of tactic combinators to progressively manipulate our goal and hypotheses in order to prove our goal. In the first place, we introduce the left hand side of the top-level implication goal as a new hypothesis named hand using the `intro` combinator (line 5), leaving us with the responsibility of proving its consequence, i.e., q. From here, we use the `destruct` combinator to split our conjunction hypothesis hand into two new hypotheses named hp and hpq, representing each side of the conjunction (line 6). Having the hypotheses p and $p \Rightarrow q$ now in scope, we use the `apply` tactic to eliminate the latter applying it the former, obtaining a new hypothesis hq which represents our goal (line 7). Our proof concludes in line 8 by telling the EDSL to use the specific hypothesis hq as a proof of our goal, using the `exact` combinator. The final qed command at line 9 simply asserts that the proof given matches the current goal, and returns the proven proposition.

---

[4] Available at http://github.com/OctopiChalmers/PropProver.

While writing this proof, our EDSL assists the user with a report of the current proof state on each step. For instance, by removing the last tactic we apply (line 8), the corresponding proof state given to the user is the one shown in Fig. 3b. Notice how this report reflects the same variable and hypothesis names introduced by the user in the proof code, i.e., p, q, hand, and so on. Additionally, it indicates the current proof position within our file, which is also used to emit a precise error message whenever some tactic is applied incorrectly—all these features being now possible thanks to our plugin.

To illustrate how helpful this information is for our EDSL, Fig. 3c illustrates the same proof state report we would obtain without reified source annotations (by disabling our plugin for instance). There, both variable and hypothesis names are just printed out using their internal names. Moreover, the current proof-state source position is not available either. Together, these two compromises limit the attractiveness of implementing elegant embedded proof assistants in Haskell.

Implementation. To implement our EDSL, we will start by defining our main monadic data type Proof by stacking two monads: a StateT transformer to keep an implicit proof state, on top of an Except monad to raise and catch proof-related errors:

```
newtype Proof a = Proof (StateT ProofState (Except ProofError a))
```

The most interesting bit here is how we define our proof state. In essence, we will keep a set of propositional variables in scope, along with a stack of subgoals (propositional formulas to construct) and their corresponding context:

```
data ProofState = ProofState {
  ps_vars     :: Set Var,
  ps_subgoals :: [(Prop, Context)]
}
```

Here, variables are represented simply as numbers, whereas contexts are mappings from hypotheses (also represented as numbers) to propositions:

```
newtype Var = Var Int
newtype Hyp = Hyp Int
type Context = Map Hyp Prop
```

Finally, propositions are represented using a simple recursive data type encoding each logical connective:

```
data Prop = Var Var | Prop ∧ Prop | Prop ⇒ Prop | ···
```

The machinery introduced so far is enough to implement the core logic of our EDSL and its proof tactics. However, to take advantage of the source information extracted by our plugin using the effect-full annotation style, we will further extend our proof state with three additional fields to keep track of the source information relevant to our proofs:

```
data ProofState = ProofState {
  . . .
  ps_var_names :: Map Var String,
  ps_hyp_names :: Map Hyp String,
  ps_curr_pos  :: Maybe Loc
}
```

These new fields will help us keeping track of: the source name given to each propositional variable (introduced by the `variables` combinator); the source name given to each new hypothesis (introduced by our different tactics); and the location in the source code of the last command evaluated by the EDSL (if any).

Then, to connect this internal state to the source annotations generated by our plugin, we need to consider the different result types that each combinator of our EDSL produces. In first place, our `variables` combinator is used to instantiate new propositional variables (of type `Var`). In this light, we can create an annotation rule (using an `AnnotatedM` instance) to store the source name each variable is given by the user (if any) into the internal names mapping of our proof state:

```
1  instance AnnotatedM Proof Var where
2    annotateM mvar (Info name loc) = do
3      updateCurrentPosition loc
4      var ← mvar
5      when (isJust name) (recordVarName var (fromJust name))
6      return var
```

where `recordVarName` (line 5) inserts the bind name (if any) coming from the source annotation into the internal variable names mapping:

```
recordVarName :: Var → String → Proof ()
recordVarName var name = modify $ λs →
  s {ps_var_names = Map.insert var name (ps_var_names s)}
```

Additionally, the function `updateCurrentPosition` (line 3) simply updates the location in the code of the last command executed by the EDSL (if any):

```
updateCurrentPosition :: Maybe Loc → Proof ()
updateCurrentPosition loc = modify $ λs → s {ps_curr_pos = loc}
```

The next thing we need to consider is how the result of each tactic affects the source information collected in the internal proof state. In principle, proof tactics can return either a new hypothesis (or a tuple of them), when they cause new hypotheses to appear in the proof state, e.g., `intro` or `apply` tactics; or a unit value, when they transform the proof state without introducing any new hypothesis, e.g., the `exact` tactic. With this in mind, we will provide two additional annotation rules to be executed whenever a proof tactic returns either a new hypothesis (of type `Hyp`) or nothing (of type `()`):

```
1 instance AnnotatedM Proof Hyp where
2   annotateM mhyp (Info name loc) = do
3     updateCurrentPosition loc
4     hyp ← mhyp
5     when (isJust name) (recordHypName hyp (fromJust name))
6     return hyp
7 instance AnnotatedM Proof () where
8   annotateM munit (Info name loc) = do
9     updateCurrentPosition loc
10    munit
```

The first `AnnotatedM` instance (line 1) will store the source name each hypothesis is given by the user (if any) into the internal proof state—the function `recordHypName` from line 5 works analogously as `recordVarName`. As before, we keep track of the last command evaluated by the EDSL in case of a proof error.

For the case of the second `AnnotatedM` instance (line 7), tactics not producing new hypotheses will not bring new source names to store into the internal proof state. However, this instance makes sure that if such a tactic fails, we have its position logged into our internal proof state in order to report a precise error message (line 9).

With these `AnnotatedM` instances in place, our plugin will seamlessly interact with them, keeping track automatically of source names introduced by the users in their code, as well as the location of each tactic invocation in case of having to report a proof-related error.

6   Discussion

We have presented a simple mechanism based on source plugins for enhancing Haskell EDSLs with source information. This section reflects on other approaches for supporting the extraction of source information without relying on source plugins. Moreover, we discuss limitations and possible extensions to our approach.

6.1   Preprocessing Haskell Code

Our approach is based on transforming the user code adding explicitly some of the useful information that gets lost during compilation. The main advantage of source plugins is that they provide a simple way of doing so without relying on external machinery. Before their existence, achieving the same kind of functionality would have required a substantial amount of effort.

For an overview of other possible (and arguably less pleasant) solutions of this problem, we refer the reader to the work of Dévai et al. [5]. There, the authors propose different indirect techniques for enhancing Haskell EDSLs with static information, e.g., using *cpphs*, the Haskell implementation of the C preprocessor; as well as transforming the Haskell source AST using existing parsers and pretty printers before feeeding it to the actual compiler.

6.2   Implementing EDSLs Using QuasiQuotation

In contrast to preprocessing our Haskell code to include static information, it is also somewhat possible achieve the same goal using meta-programming.

Template Haskell [23] is the Haskell meta-programming framework bundled in the GHC compiler. This tool can be used to inspect the typing information present in the user's codebase and synthesize new code depending on it but, for technical reasons, inspecting term definitions or modifying existing Haskell code is not possible, making this framework unsuitable for implementing a transformation-based approach. Nonetheless, a useful feature of Template Haskell used by many existing EDSLs [8, 11, 12, 19, 24] is the support for *quasiquotation* [18]. Essentially, quasiquotation allows to embed code written using arbitrary, domain-specific syntax into our Haskell code. To do so, this approach relies on implementing *quasi quoters*, i.e., interpretations from arbitrary strings to their corresponding Haskell expressions:

```
data QuasiQuoter = QuasiQuoter {
  quoteExp :: String → Q Exp,
  ...
}
```

where Q is the quasiquotation monad defined by Template Haskell.

Using this approach, it would be possible to implement our Coq-like EDSL from Sect. 5 as a quasi quoter coq :: QuasiQuoter accepting concrete Coq syntax. Then, we could use it to embed Coq proofs into our Haskell EDSL using quasiquotation brackets syntax ([| ··· |]):

```
1  modus_ponens :: Proof Prop
2  modus_ponens = [coq|
3    Variables P Q.
4    Theorem (P ∧ (P → Q) → Q).
5      Proof.
6      intro hand.
7      destruct hand as [hp hpq].
8      apply hp hpq as hq.
9      exact hq.
10   Qed.
11 |]
```

An advantage of this approach is that the arbitrary code written inside of the quasiquotation brackets has (almost) no syntactic restrictions. Hence, it can be used to embed domain-specific code written using the syntax that fits best the nature of a given EDSL, as opposed to the syntactic restrictions imposed by the use of Haskell syntax and **do** notation—which are exploited by BinderAnn.

However, all this flexibility does not come for free. Implementing a quasi quoter for a language with a novel syntax implies writing a lexer and a parser from a plain string to a Haskell expression—a task that might overcome the benefits of having a new specialized syntax. Moreover, the interaction between quasiquoters and native Haskell code tends to be intricate. In particular, enabling quasiquoters to support embedding native Haskell code inside quasiquotation brackets (something known as *antiquotation*) requires a considerable amount of work and knowledge [18]—without this feature, our quasiquoters can only accept constant EDSL expressions inside the quasiquotation brackets.

Extracting bound names becomes possible using quasi quoters, since, as we mention above, we have access to the literal string written by the user. Source locations, on the other hand, are more tricky to infer. By default, quasi quoters will only be able to recognize source locations relative to where the quasiquotation brackets are interpolated in our Haskell code (line 2 in our example above), difficulting the task of giving the end-user error messages referring to absolute locations within their code.

6.3   Source Annotations for Non-monadic EDSLs

In this work, we decided to focus only on automatically annotating monadic EDSLs expressed using **do** notation. Although it may seem arbitrary, the reason behind this decision is simple: **do** notation gives us a good level of granularity. Our plugin perform statement-wise transformations, matching the natural notion of having one domain-specific command or instruction per **do** statement. This symmetry lets us annotate EDSL very transparently for the end-user.

On the other hand, there exists many remarkable non-monadic EDSLs written in Haskell and not supporting them by default constitutes a noticeable limitation of our current approach. In principle, we could use the pure annotation style introduced in Sect. 3 to insert annotations into pure values. However, it is the lack of a well-defined statement structure what complicates deciding *where* to insert source annotations. On one hand, annotating only top-level bindings might be too sporadic for practical purposes, while doing so for every subexpression within a value might blow up the size of our transformed code exponentially, so an acceptable annotation granularity would seem to lay somewhere in between of these two extremes—an intriguing problem to drive our future work.

6.4   Use of Incoherent Instances

As mentioned in Sect. 3, our approach let us inject source annotations into the values of certain types of interest, and relies on default instances to provide trivial implementations of the annotation functions for any other possible value.

Instead of having to provide concrete annotation instances for each possible type present in the user code, these default instances are a convenient feature that allows doing so on a per-case basis while preserving the type-correctness of the user code after it is transformed by our plugin. Sadly, this convenience has as a limitation that *annotations inserted into fully-polymorphic functions will be systematically discarded.* To illustrate this, consider for example the following function that duplicates the output of a monadic computation:

```
twice :: Monad m ⇒ m a → m (a, a)
twice ma = do
  x ← ma
  return (x, x)
```

If written by the user of the EDSL, and then annotated by our plugin, this function will trigger a type error when there exists at least a single more concrete `Annotated` or `AnnotatedM` instance. The reason behind this is simple: while type checking the annotated statement x ← ma, only the default annotation instance is polymorphic enough to match the type of ma, however, it cannot be chosen directly, as the existence of other more concrete ones would make this choice inconsistent, e.g, using the default instance even when `twice` is instantiated in the user code with a type that has a more concrete one. Then, declaring our default instances as incoherent loosens this constraint, allowing the compiler to choose the default instance whenever it has to solve an overlap while compiling fully-polymorphic functions like `twice`, but leaving us with the aforementioned limitation as a result of this conservative behavior.

The complexity around the use of overlapping instances is well known by the Haskell community. In this light, this problem has been solved using more sophisticated approaches relying on type-level programming, e.g., using *closed type families* [6]. Adopting them in our plugin without sacrificing its transparency and ease of use is an ambitious problem that we keep as future work.

7   Conclusions

We developed a simple mechanism to facilitate the automatic extraction of useful source code information that is otherwise lost during compilation. Having access to such information when implementing embedded domain-specific languages is extremely valuable, making possible to implement attractive features such as faithful code generation and precise error messages. In the past, such features were more complicated if not impossible to achieve without involving undesirable trade-offs like repeated code or quasiquotations.

In the future, we aim to investigate how to extend our approach to a wider set of EDSL programming patterns, especially to those implemented using non-monadic combinators, and for which the use of **do** notation is not available. Additionally, we intend to evaluate how our annotation framework could be extended using generic programming techniques, so programmers should not need to adapt their existing EDSL data type definitions to work with it.

Acknowledgment. We want to thank Koen Claessen for the useful feedback given throughout the development of this work. This work was funded by the Swedish Foundation for Strategic Research (SSF) under the project Octopi (Ref. RIT17-0023) and WebSec (Ref. RIT17-0011) as well as the Swedish research agency Vetenskapsrådet.

References

1. Algehed, M., Jansson, P., Einarsdóttir, S.H., Gerdes, A.: Saint: an API-generic type-safe interpreter. In: Pałka, M., Myreen, M. (eds.) TFP 2018. LNCS, vol. 11457, pp. 94–113. Springer, Cham (2019). https://doi.org/10.1007/978-3-030-18506-0_5
2. Axelsson, E.: Compilation as a typed EDSL-to-EDSL transformation. arXiv preprint arXiv:1603.08865 (2016)
3. Axelsson, E., et al.: Feldspar: a domain specific language for digital signal processing algorithms. In: Eighth ACM/IEEE International Conference on Formal Methods and Models for Codesign (MEMOCODE 2010), pp. 169–178. IEEE (2010)
4. Barras, B., et al.: The Coq proof assistant reference manual: version 6.1 (1997)
5. Dévai, G., Leskó, D., Tejfel, M.: The EDSL's struggle for their sources. In: Zsók, V., Horváth, Z., Csató, L. (eds.) CEFP 2013. LNCS, vol. 8606, pp. 300–335. Springer, Cham (2015). https://doi.org/10.1007/978-3-319-15940-9_7
6. Eisenberg, R.A., Vytiniotis, D., Peyton Jones, S., Weirich, S.: Closed type families with overlapping equations. ACM SIGPLAN Not. **49**(1), 671–683 (2014)
7. Ekblad, A.: shellmate: Simple interface for shell scripting in Haskell (2014). https://hackage.haskell.org/package/shellmate
8. Elliott, T., et al.: Guilt free ivory. In: ACM SIGPLAN Notices, no. 12. ACM (2015)
9. Erkok, L.: SBV: SMT based verification: symbolic Haskell theorem prover using SMT solving (2010). https://hackage.haskell.org/package/sbv
10. Gill, A.: dotgen: A simple interface for building.dot graph files (2008). https://hackage.haskell.org/package/dotgen
11. Giorgidze, G., Grust, T., Schreiber, T., Weijers, J.: Haskell boards the ferry. In: Hage, J., Morazán, M.T. (eds.) IFL 2010. LNCS, vol. 6647, pp. 1–18. Springer, Heidelberg (2011). https://doi.org/10.1007/978-3-642-24276-2_1
12. Giorgidze, G., Nilsson, H.: Embedding a functional hybrid modelling language in Haskell. In: Scholz, S.-B., Chitil, O. (eds.) IFL 2008. LNCS, vol. 5836, pp. 138–155. Springer, Heidelberg (2011). https://doi.org/10.1007/978-3-642-24452-0_8
13. Hall, C.V., Hammond, K., Peyton Jones, S.L., Wadler, P.L.: Type classes in Haskell. ACM Trans. Program. Lang. Syst. (TOPLAS) **18**(2), 109–138 (1996)
14. Hudak, P., et al.: Building domain-specific embedded languages. ACM Comput. Surv. **28**(4es), 196 (1996)
15. Jones, S.L.P., Santos, A.M.: A transformation-based optimiser for Haskell. Sci. Comput. Program. **32**(1–3), 3–47 (1998)
16. Jones, S.P., Jones, M., Meijer, E.: Type classes: an exploration of the design space. In: Haskell Workshop, pp. 1–16 (1997)
17. Launchbury, J.: Lazy imperative programming. In: Workshop on State in Programming Languages, Copenhagen, Denmark. ACM (1993)
18. Mainland, G.: Why it's nice to be quoted: quasiquoting for Haskell. In: Proceedings of the ACM SIGPLAN Workshop on Haskell Workshop, pp. 73–82. ACM (2007)
19. Mainland, G., Morrisett, G.: Nikola: embedding compiled GPU functions in Haskell. In: ACM SIGPLAN Not, vol. 45, pp. 67–78. ACM (2010)
20. Marlow, S., Jones, S.P., et al.: The Glasgow Haskell compiler (2004)

21. Pickering, M., Wu, N., Németh, B.: Working with source plugins. In: Proceedings of the 12th ACM SIGPLAN International Symposium on Haskell. ACM (2019)
22. Pike, L., Goodloe, A., Morisset, R., Niller, S.: Copilot: a hard real-time runtime monitor. In: Barringer, H., et al. (eds.) RV 2010. LNCS, vol. 6418, pp. 345–359. Springer, Heidelberg (2010). https://doi.org/10.1007/978-3-642-16612-9_26
23. Sheard, T., Jones, S.L.P.: Template meta-programming for Haskell. SIGPLAN Not. **37**(12), 60–75 (2002)
24. Snoyman, M.: Developing web applications with Haskell and Yesod. O'Reilly Media Inc, Sebastopol (2012)
25. Wadler, P.: Monads for functional programming. In: Jeuring, J., Meijer, E. (eds.) AFP 1995. LNCS, vol. 925, pp. 24–52. Springer, Heidelberg (1995). https://doi.org/10.1007/3-540-59451-5_2

Generating Next Step Hints for Task Oriented Programs Using Symbolic Execution

Nico Naus[1]([✉]) [iD] and Tim Steenvoorden[2] [iD]

[1] Open University, Heerlen, The Netherlands
nico.naus@ou.nl
[2] Radboud University, Nijmegen, The Netherlands
tim@cs.ru.nl

Abstract. Software that models business workflows is omnipresent in today's society. These systems coordinate collaboration in hospitals, companies, and military institutions. Unfortunately, workflow systems may obfuscate the influence of current user actions on the desired end result. In order to make the right decision, users need to oversee the full process and all information available, both of which are usually buried in the system. We have developed a way to automatically generate next step hints for task oriented programs. Task oriented programming provides programmers with an abstraction over workflow software, while still being expressive enough to describe real world collaboration. By leveraging symbolic execution, we can calculate these hints without modification of the original program. To our knowledge, this is the first time that symbolic execution is used to automatically generate next step hints for end users. We prove the generated hints to be sound and complete, and also demonstrate that the symbolic execution semantics we employ is correct for sequential input. In addition, we have developed a Haskell implementation of our automatic next step hint generation system. By providing next step hints, the chance of human error is reduced, while still allowing end users to intervene if required. The overall performance is raised, since the quality of decisions will improve.

Keywords: Task-oriented programming · Next step hint generation · Symbolic execution

1 Introduction

Software that supports people working together is used in most workplaces nowadays. Its aim is to automate business workflows, in order to simplify processes, to improve service, or to contain cost. In settings like hospitals, first responders and military operations, these systems could even prevent the loss of lives.

Automation and digitalisation of workflows and business processes comes at a cost. For end users it can be hard to see how an action influences their desired goal. They are unable to oversee the complete flow of the process and there might be an abundance of data that they are not fully aware of. End users might wonder if checking a box may prevent them, or someone else, from reaching their goal, or ask themselves if they have taken all information into consideration before making a decision.

© The Author(s) 2020
A. Byrski and J. Hughes (Eds.): TFP 2020, LNCS 12222, pp. 47–68, 2020.
https://doi.org/10.1007/978-3-030-57761-2_3

To overcome these difficulties, we propose to integrate a next step hint system into workflow software. By combining previous research on symbolic execution for Task-Oriented Programming [16] and end-user feedback systems for rule based problems [15], we develop a next step hint end-user feedback system for the Task-Oriented Programming language TopHat ($\widehat{\text{TOP}}$) [20]. Our solution, which we call Assistive $\widehat{\text{TOP}}$, generates next step hints from existing code, and does not require extra work by the programmer. To our knowledge, this is the first work employing symbolic execution to automatically generate next-step hints for end users.

Providing next step hints to end users will provide them with a quick insight in to their situation. It reduces the chance of human error, while still allowing the user to intervene if required. The quality of decisions will improve, raising the overall performance.

In this paper we will introduce Task-Oriented Programming and the $\widehat{\text{TOP}}$ language for readers unfamiliar with either of them, followed by some illustrative examples. Building further on this foundation we show how we use symbolic execution to automatically generate next step hints for end users. It is crucial that these hints are valid, meaning they allow users to reach the desired goal. Therefore we prove correctness of the automatic hint generation system. Our hint generation system relies on symbolic execution as presented in earlier work [16]. There, we proved correctness for the symbolic semantics for single user inputs. Here, we prove the entire symbolic system to be correct, for any sequence of user inputs.

1.1 Contributions

This paper makes the following contributions.

- We describe an automatic end user next step feedback system for $\widehat{\text{TOP}}$, called Assistive $\widehat{\text{TOP}}$, based on a previously presented symbolic semantics.
- We prove the symbolic execution semantics of $\widehat{\text{TOP}}$ to be correct for sequential inputs.
- We change the definition of simulation of $\widehat{\text{TOP}}$ programs to accommodate above proof.
- We prove soundness and completeness of next step hints generated by this system.
- We present an implementation of the end user feedback system in Haskell.

1.2 Structure

Section 2 first introduces the Task-Oriented Programming (TOP) paradigm and the Task-Oriented Programming language $\widehat{\text{TOP}}$. Section 3 lists three example programs to illustrate how $\widehat{\text{TOP}}$ works and to show what we like to achieve with Assistive $\widehat{\text{TOP}}$. In Sect. 4 we briefly introduce the symbolic execution semantics for $\widehat{\text{TOP}}$, followed by a description of Assistive $\widehat{\text{TOP}}$. In Sect. 5 soundness and completeness of the assistive system are shown. Section 6 gives an overview of related work, and finally Sect. 7 concludes.

2   The TopHat Language

The Task-Oriented Programming (TOP) paradigm was first introduced by Plasmeijer et al. [19]. It is created to improve the development and quality of software that coordinates collaboration between users. TOP provides programmers with a high level of programming abstraction, while still being expressive enough to describe real world collaborations. It does so by using features from higher-order functional programming languages, combined with the notion of *tasks*. Tasks model units of work, which can be performed by a human or by a computer. From a task specification, a TOP implementation generates a distributive multi-user (web) application.

Tasks have a couple of properties, listed below.

- Tasks model *collaboration*.
  Programmers describe what work needs to be done, by who and in what way.
- Tasks are *interactive*.
  Users can enter or update information into the system by using *editors*. They can progress to the next task, or choose between tasks.
- Tasks can be *observed*.
  Therefore, other users or the system itself can make decisions based on the observed progress of the task.
- Tasks are *modular*.
  They can be combined into bigger tasks by using *combinators*. The basic combinators are chosen in such a way, that they represent basic collaboration patterns. New combinators can be created by making use of basic combinators and the (higher order) facilities of the host language.
- Tasks *share information*.
  Information is passed along control flow, or, in order for tasks to exchange information, across control flow via references. In particular to share data between parallel tasks.
- Tasks are *typed*.
  This is not just to ensure safety at runtime, but also to automatically derive common program elements. TOP systems automatically generate user interfaces and manage persistent storage of information.

Currently, there are three systems implementing the TOP paradigm. The reference implementation is the iTasks framework [19], which is an embedded domain specific language in the non-strict functional programming language Clean [18]. mTasks [13] is a TOP implementation specifically designed for embedded systems. A formalisation of TOP, called $\widehat{TOP}$ (TopHat), has been created by Steenvoorden, Naus, and Klinik [20]. Assistive $\widehat{TOP}$ builds on $\widehat{TOP}$ and its symbolic counterpart Symbolic $\widehat{TOP}$ [16].

$\widehat{TOP}$ implements TOP by embedding a task language in the simply typed lambda calculus with references, conditionals, and pairs. Note the omission of any fixed point language constructs, which make $\widehat{TOP}$ a total language. Symbolic $\widehat{TOP}$ extends this with built in operators, lists, and most importantly symbols. References are used to model the shared data component of TOP. The complete syntax and semantics can be found in previous work [20]. An overview can be found in the appendix[1]. In the next

---

[1] https://github.com/timjs/assistive-tophat/raw/master/appendix.pdf.

subsections we describe the basic constructs of the $\widehat{\text{TOP}}$ language. Section 4.1 details Symbolic $\widehat{\text{TOP}}$.

2.1 Editors

Editors form the entry points for interaction and communication with the outside world. They are the most basic tasks and can be seen as an abstraction over widgets in a GUI library or forms on a webpage. Users can change the value held by an editor, in the same way they can manipulate widgets in a GUI.

When a TOP implementation generates an application from a task specification, it derives user interfaces for the editors. The appearance of an editor depends on its type. For example, editors of type string can be represented by simple input fields, dates by calendars, and locations by pins on a map.

There are three different editors in $\widehat{\text{TOP}}$.

$\square\,v$ Valued editor.
  This editor holds a value v of a certain type. The user can replace the value by new values of the same type.
$\boxtimes\,\tau$ Unvalued editor.
  This editor holds no value, and can receive a value of type τ. When that happens, it turns into a valued editor.
$\blacksquare\,l$ Shared editor.
  This editor refers to a store location l. Its observable value is the value stored at that location. When it receives a new value, this value will be stored at location l.

2.2 Combinators

Editors can be combined into larger tasks using combinators. The order in which editors and tasks are executed is specified with combinators. Tasks can be performed in sequence, in parallel or a choice can be made between tasks. These combinators originate from basic collaboration patterns.

The following combinators are available in $\widehat{\text{TOP}}$. Here, t stands for tasks and e for expressions.

$t \blacktriangleright e$ Step.
  Users can work on task t. As soon as t has an observable value, as defined in the next section, that value is passed on to the right hand side e. The expression e is a function, taking the value as an argument, resulting in a new task.
$t \rhd e$ User Step.
  Users can work on task t. When t has an observable value, the step becomes enabled. Then, users can send a continue event to the combinator. When that happens, the value of t is applied to the right hand side function e, with which it continues in the same way as normal steps do.
$t_1 \bowtie t_2$ Pair.
  Users can work on tasks t_1 and t_2 in at the same time.

$t_1 \blacklozenge t_2$ Choice.

The system chooses between t_1 or t_2, based on which task first has an observable value. If both tasks have a value, the system chooses the left one. When neither of the two tasks has an observable value, users can continue to work on both tasks until one of them does.

$e_1 \lozenge e_2$ User choice.

A user has to make a choice between either the left or the right hand side. After picking a side, the user can work on that task.

In addition to editors and combinators, $\widehat{\text{TOP}}$ also contains the fail task ($\maltese$). Programmers can use this task to indicate that a task is not reachable or viable. When the right hand side of a step combinator evaluates to $\maltese$, the step will not proceed to that task.

2.3 Observations

Several observations can be made on tasks. These observations are used by the system to determine the progress of combinators, and to draw the user interface. They will also be used by Assistive $\widehat{\text{TOP}}$ to provide next step hints.

Using the value function $\mathcal{V}$, the current value of a task can be determined. The value function is a partial function, since not all tasks have a value. For example empty editors do not have a value. The value of tasks composed of parallel and internal choice combinators, depends on the value of the subtasks. Parallel only has a value if both tasks have an observable value. Internal choice has a value if either of the two tasks has an observable value.

One can also observe whether or not a task is failing, by means of the failing function $\mathcal{F}$. A task is considered to be failing if, after normalisation, a user cannot interact with it. For example, the valued editor is not failing, since the user can update it with a new value. The task $\maltese$ is failing, as is a parallel combination of failing tasks $\maltese \bowtie \maltese$, since both the left and the right task cannot be interacted with. Both observation definitions can be found in Fig. 1.

The step combinators make use of both functions in order to determine if they can step to the right hand side. First, $\mathcal{V}$ determines if the left hand side produces a value. If that is the case, $\mathcal{F}$ checks if stepping to the right hand side is successful.

2.4 Input

Input events drive the evaluation of tasks. Because tasks are typed, input is typed as well. Editors only accept input of the correct type. For example, an editor can only be updated with a new value, if it has the same type as the old value. When the system receives a valid event, it applies this event to the current task, which evaluates to a new task. Everything in between two events is evaluated atomically with respect to inputs. This means that tasks are normalised up to the point where they await new user interactions.

Input events are synchronous, which means that the order of execution is completely determined by the order of the events. In particular, the order of input events determine the progression of parallel branches.

$\mathcal{V}$: Tasks × States ⇀ Values

$\mathcal{V}(\square\,v,\sigma) \quad = v$

$\mathcal{V}(\boxtimes\,\tau,\sigma) \quad = \bot$

$\mathcal{V}(\blacksquare\,l,\sigma) \quad = \sigma(l)$

$\mathcal{V}(\text{\textreferencemark},\sigma) \quad = \bot$

$\mathcal{V}(t_1 \blacktriangleright e_2, \sigma) = \bot$

$\mathcal{V}(t_1 \triangleright e_2, \sigma) = \bot$

$\mathcal{V}(t_1 \bowtie t_2, \sigma)$

$\quad = \begin{cases} \langle v_1, v_2 \rangle & \text{when } \mathcal{V}(t_1,\sigma) = v_1 \wedge \mathcal{V}(t_2,\sigma) = v_2 \\ \bot & \text{otherwise} \end{cases}$

$\mathcal{V}(t_1 \blacklozenge t_2, \sigma)$

$\quad = \begin{cases} v_1 & \text{when } \mathcal{V}(t_1,\sigma) = v_1 \\ v_2 & \text{when } \mathcal{V}(t_1,\sigma) = \bot \wedge \mathcal{V}(t_2,\sigma) = v_2 \\ \bot & \text{otherwise} \end{cases}$

$\mathcal{V}(t_1 \lozenge t_2, \sigma) \quad = \bot$

$\mathcal{F}$: Tasks × States → Booleans

$\mathcal{F}(\square\,v,\sigma) \quad = \text{False}$

$\mathcal{F}(\boxtimes\,\tau,\sigma) \quad = \text{False}$

$\mathcal{F}(\blacksquare\,l,\sigma) \quad = \text{False}$

$\mathcal{F}(\text{\textreferencemark},\sigma) \quad = \text{True}$

$\mathcal{F}(t_1 \blacktriangleright e_2, \sigma) = \mathcal{F}(t_1,\sigma)$

$\mathcal{F}(t_1 \triangleright e_2, \sigma) = \mathcal{F}(t_1,\sigma)$

$\mathcal{F}(t_1 \bowtie t_2, \sigma) = \mathcal{F}(t_1,\sigma) \wedge \mathcal{F}(t_2,\sigma)$

$\mathcal{F}(t_1 \blacklozenge t_2, \sigma) = \mathcal{F}(t_1,\sigma) \wedge \mathcal{F}(t_2,\sigma)$

$\mathcal{F}(e_1 \lozenge e_2, \sigma) = \mathcal{F}(t_1,\sigma_1') \wedge \mathcal{F}(t_2,\sigma_2')$

$\quad\quad\quad\quad \text{where } e_1,\sigma \Downarrow t_1,\sigma_1'$

$\quad\quad\quad\quad \text{and } e_2,\sigma \Downarrow t_2,\sigma_2'$

Fig. 1. Observations on task t. $\mathcal{V}$ gets the value of t, $\mathcal{F}$ observes if it is unsafe to step to t. Note that $\mathcal{V}$ is a partial function.

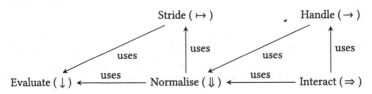

Fig. 2. Semantic functions defined in this report and their relation.

2.5 Semantics

The semantics of $\widehat{\text{TOP}}$ are defined in three layers. Figure 2 contains an overview of these semantics and their relations. The first layer consists of the standard big step semantics for the simply typed λ-calculus. We call this semantics evaluation (↓). All task specific language constructs, as described previously in Sects. 2.1 and 2.2, are normalised using a dedicated big step semantics (⇓) in the second layer. Normalisation can be regarded as preparing tasks for user input. It makes use of a helper small step semantics called striding (↦).

The above semantics are internal to the system and do not take any user interaction into account. On the third level, the small step interaction semantics (⇒) first handles any user input i using the handle semantics (→) and then normalises the resulting task so it is ready to handle the next user input.

The semantic rules can be found in the appendix[2]. For a thorough explanation of all rules, we refer to previous work [20].

3 Examples

This section introduces three example $\widehat{\text{TOP}}$ programs. Each example illustrate different functionality of the $\widehat{\text{TOP}}$ language. Section 3.1 demonstrates the step combinator,

---

[2] https://github.com/timjs/assistive-tophat/raw/master/appendix.pdf.

Sect. 3.2 includes the parallel and choice combinators, and finally Sect. 3.3 demonstrates the use of shares in order for tasks to communicate with each other. The examples will be used in Sect. 4 to demonstrate how Assistive $\widehat{\text{TOP}}$ works, and are included in the implementation.

3.1 Vending Machine

Using the editors and combinators described in Sect. 2, we can create a vending machine that dispenses a biscuit for one coin and a chocolate bar for two coins as follows:

```
let vend : TASK SNACK = □0 ▷ λn.                        1
    if n ≡ 1 then □Biscuit                              2
    else if n ≡ 2 then □ChocolateBar                    3
    else ⌇                                              4
```

Listing 1.1. Vending machine dispensing biscuits or chocolate.

This example demonstrates the usage of a user step guarded by a branching expression (Line 2) using the failure task (Line 4). The editor $\square 0$ asks the user to enter an amount of money. It simulates a coin slot in a real machine that freely accepts and returns coins. There is a continue button, generated by the user step combinator $\triangleright$. Only when the user has inserted exactly 1 or 2 coins will the continue button become enabled. Other cases will result in the failure task $\frac{1}{2}$, and stepping to it is prohibited by definition. When the user presses the continue button, the machine dispenses either a biscuit or a chocolate bar, depending on the amount of money. Snacks are modelled using a custom type.

3.2 Tax Subsidy Request

The example program listed in this section is taken from our previous work on symbolic execution for $\widehat{\text{TOP}}$ [20]. It models a simplified tax subsidy application process for citizens who have installed solar panels. This was first described by Stutterheim et al. [21], who worked on modelling a fictional but realistic law about solar panel subsidies.
    A subsidy is only given under the following conditions.

– The roofing company has confirmed that they installed solar panels for the citizen.
– The tax officer has approved the request.
– The tax officer can only approve the request if the roofing company has confirmed, and the request is filed within one year of the invoice date.
– The amount of the granted subsidy is at most €600.

Listing 1.2 gives the $\widehat{\text{TOP}}$ code for this example. To enhance readability of the example, we omit type annotations and make use of pattern matching on tuples. The program works as follows.
    In parallel, the citizen has to provide the invoice documents of the installed solar panels, while the roofing company has to confirm that they have actually installed solar panels at the citizen's address (Line 6). Once the invoice and the confirmation are there,

```
let today = 13 Feb 2020 in                                                    1
let provideDocuments = ⊠Amount ⋈ ⊠Date in                                      2
let companyConfirm = □True ◊ □False in                                         3
let officerApprove = λinvoiceDate. λtoday. λconfirmed.                         4
   □False ◊ if (today - invoiceDate < 365 days ∧ confirmed)  then □True else ↯ in  5
provideDocuments ⋈ companyConfirm ▶ λ⟨⟨invoiceAmount, invoiceDate⟩ , confirmed⟩ .  6
officerApprove invoiceDate today confirmed ▶ λapproved.                        7
let subsidyAmount = if approved then min 600 (invoiceAmount / 10) else 0 in    8
□⟨subsidyAmount, approved, confirmed, invoiceDate, today⟩                      9
```

Listing 1.2. Subsidy request and approval workflow at the Dutch tax office.

the tax officer has to approve the request (Line 7). The officer can always decline the request, but they can only approve it if the roofing company has confirmed and the application date is within one year of the invoice date (Line 5). The result of the program is the amount of the subsidy, together with all information needed to prove the required properties (Line 9).

In previous work, we have shown that this code indeed adheres to the requirements listed above. There we focussed on assisting the developer by proving the program correct. In this work we focus on supporting the end user that is requesting a subsidy. The end user wants the outcome of this program to be a subsidy amount larger than zero. In Sect. 4.4 we will show how to generate hints for the end user to reach this goal.

3.3 Dining Computer Scientists Problem

The dining philosophers problem is a classic concurrency problem in computer science. A number of philosophers sit at a round table with a meal in front of them. In between the plates lies a fork. In order to eat their meal, each philosopher has to acquire two forks. Only after eating his or her meal, is a philosopher allowed to place the two forks back on the table. This, of course, means that the philosophers cannot eat at the same time, since there are not enough forks. Deadlock can occur when all philosophers pick up the fork to their right (or left). Then, everybody has one fork. This means that each philosopher cannot start his or her meal. Next to that, is also not allowed to put his fork back on the table.

We look at dining computer scientists instead. Figure 3 shows a visual representation of the problem. Listing 1.3 lists an implementation in T͡OP for this problem, with three computer scientists. The forks are represented by references containing Booleans (Lines 1 to 3). Using references allows tasks to communicate with each other across control flow. The value True indicates that the fork is available, False indicates that the fork is being used.

Picking up a fork is only possible when the fork is available, i.e. reading the reference results in True (Line 5). This fork is then marked as being used (Line 6). Reading a reference l is denoted as $!l$, assigning a new value v to a reference l is written as $l := v$.

The use of references ensures that the neighbouring scientist cannot pick up this fork: this choice will be disabled. After that, one can press continue if the second fork is also available (Line 7). For the sake of simplicity, one returns the first fork, rather than setting the second fork to False, and then setting both to True again.

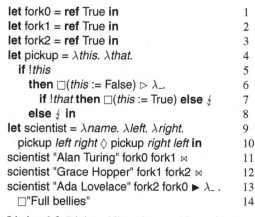

```
let fork0 = ref True in                              1
let fork1 = ref True in                              2
let fork2 = ref True in                              3
let pickup = λthis. λthat.                           4
    if !this                                         5
        then □(this := False) ▷ λ_.                  6
            if !that then □(this := True) else ↯     7
        else ↯ in                                    8
let scientist = λname. λleft. λright.                9
    pickup left right ◊ pickup right left in        10
scientist "Alan Turing" fork0 fork1 ⋈              11
scientist "Grace Hopper" fork1 fork2 ⋈             12
scientist "Ada Lovelace" fork2 fork0 ▶ λ_ .         13
    □"Full bellies"                                 14
```

Listing 1.3. Dining philosophers problem with three computer scientists.

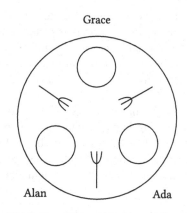

Fig. 3. Rendering with three philosophers.

Each computer scientist takes as arguments a name and references to the two forks that he or she can reach (Line 9). They have a choice to take either the left or the right fork. This is represented with an user choice (◊, Line 10).). The last lines instantiate three computer scientists sitting next to each other (Lines 11 to 13). In TOP terms, this means they collaborate in parallel (⋈) while eating their dinner, sharing some resources, in this case fork0, fork1, and fork2.

By design of $\widehat{\text{TOP}}$, the events of picking up a fork are performed sequentially. That is, when one computer scientist decides to pick up his right fork, we will handle that event first. After that, we will handle the choices from the other scientists. So, the order of the events is explicitly determined by the scientists themselves.

In Sect. 4.5 we will analyse this example. Our goal is to provide each scientist with a hint on which choice to make, in order to reach the common goal of full bellies. When the scientists follow these hints, no deadlock will occur.

4   Generating Next Step Hints

This section introduces our Assistive $\widehat{\text{TOP}}$ system. The aim of Assistive $\widehat{\text{TOP}}$ is to automatically provide next step hints. When users follow these hints, they can be sure that they will reach the goal they described beforehand. Users can, however, still decide to deviate from the given hints.

During the execution of $\widehat{\text{TOP}}$ programs, users are presented with input fields, choices and continue buttons. The way in which tasks progress and the resulting task value depend on these inputs. At any point during execution, we would like to present users with all possible inputs that leads users to the goal they have selected. These inputs are either concrete actions, like continue, pick the left task, pick the right task; or a restricted set of values to be entered into an editor. This set is restricted, since concrete values potentially influence the flow of the program. To give a concrete example, the user should enter an integer, but this integer must be larger than zero to reach the end goal.

To come to these concrete actions and restricted values, we make use of symbolic execution. In the next two sections, we briefly describe how symbolic execution for $\widehat{\text{TOP}}$ works and recap its symbolic semantics presented in earlier work [16]. Thereafter, we show how to turn symbolic execution results into next step hints. In Sects. 4.4 and 4.5, we study what these automatically generated hints look like for the examples from Sect. 3.

All examples have been tested in our implementation. We added Assistive $\widehat{\text{TOP}}$ to our existing implementation of Symbolic $\widehat{\text{TOP}}$, which is written in Haskell.[3] It uses the z3 SMT solver under the hood. By defining the formal hints function directly on top of the symbolic execution semantics, we can leverage the already existing symbolic execution for Symbolic $\widehat{\text{TOP}}$ in the practical implementation.

4.1 Symbolic Execution

A symbolic execution semantics [4, 12] aims to execute a program without knowing its input. Instead, symbols are fed into the program. During evaluation, the influence of values is recorded in the path condition. The resulting symbolic value together with the path conditions can be used to prove properties of the program.

$$⊠\text{INT} ⋈ ⊠\text{INT} \blacktriangleright \lambda\langle x,y\rangle \,.\, \textbf{if } x > y \textbf{ then } □\langle y, x\rangle \textbf{ else } □\langle x, y\rangle$$

Listing 1.4. Ordering of tuple elements.

Consider the tiny example in Listing 1.4. This program asks for two integer values. After the user has entered this information, the function to the right of the step combinator makes sure the result will be an editor containing a pair, where the second element is larger then the first. When we run this program symbolically, we have to create fresh symbols to be entered in either of the two editors, say s_0 and s_1. After entering both symbolic values and then normalising the task, there are two possible outcomes, namely

- $\langle s_1, s_0\rangle$, provided that the path condition $\varphi_1 = s_0 > s_1$ holds; or
- $\langle s_0, s_1\rangle$, with path condition $\varphi_2 = \neg(s_0 > s_1)$.

Now, the property that we want to prove for this program is that no matter what the input is, the second element should always be larger than the first. We write this property as $\psi(\langle a, b\rangle) = a \leq b$. Looking at the two symbolic runs, we first need to verify that the symbolic runs are indeed viable. This is done by checking that both φ_1 and φ_2 are satisfiable, written $\mathcal{S}(\varphi_1)$ and $\mathcal{S}(\varphi_2)$. Symbolic runs with a path condition that is not satisfiable are discarded. Finally, we check that both path conditions conform to the goal property ψ, which is the case. Therefore, we can conclude that the property holds. When applying this technique to larger programs, it is a powerful tool to show that a program behaves as expected.

---

[3] https://github.com/timjs/symbolic-tophat-haskell.

4.2 Symbolic Semantics

To support symbolic execution in $\widehat{\text{TOP}}$, we extend our host language with symbols. In addition, we also need to modify the semantics described in Sect. 2.5, to accommodate symbolic execution. The observation functions from Sect. 2.3 are extended in a similar way. These new semantic relations operate on expressions which may contain symbols. Instead of stepping to one result, they lead to a set of possible symbolic results, accompanied with a path condition φ.

Table 1. Overview of meta variables and semantic relations for concrete and symbolic evaluations.

	Concrete	Symbolic
Expressions	e	$\tilde{e}$
Tasks	t	$\tilde{t}$
States	σ	$\tilde{\sigma}$
Inputs	i	$\tilde{\imath}$
Evaluation	$e, \sigma \downarrow v, \sigma'$	$\tilde{e}, \tilde{\sigma} \; \wr \; \overline{\tilde{v}, \tilde{\sigma}', \varphi}$
Normalisation	$e, \sigma \Downarrow t, \sigma'$	$\tilde{e}, \tilde{\sigma} \; \wr\wr \; \overline{\tilde{t}, \tilde{\sigma}', \varphi}$
Striding	$t, \sigma \mapsto t', \sigma'$	$\tilde{t}, \tilde{\sigma} \rightsquigarrow \overline{\tilde{t}', \tilde{\sigma}', \varphi}$
Handling	$t, \sigma \xrightarrow{i} t', \sigma'$	$\tilde{t}, \tilde{\sigma} \rightsquigarrow \overline{\tilde{t}', \tilde{\sigma}', \tilde{\imath}, \varphi}$
Interacting	$t, \sigma \overset{i}{\Rightarrow} t', \sigma'$	$\tilde{t}, \tilde{\sigma} \approx\!\!\!\!\Rightarrow \overline{\tilde{t}', \tilde{\sigma}', \tilde{\imath}, \varphi}$

We denote entities containing symbols with an additional tilde, and symbolic semantic relations with squiggly arrows instead of straight ones. So $\tilde{t}$, $\tilde{\sigma}$, and $\tilde{\imath}$ are respectively tasks, states, and inputs containing symbols. Table 1 gives an overview of the entities in the concrete world, and their symbolic counterparts. Concrete expressions are a subset of symbolic expressions. Therefore, symbolic semantic relations can be applied on concrete expressions, as well as symbolic expressions.

The symbolic interaction semantics ($\approx\!\!\!\!\Rightarrow$) results in a set of symbolic runs, each of them just containing one symbolic input. In other words, the symbolic interaction semantics just looks ahead one symbolic interaction. To be able to reason about an end state after multiple symbolic interactions, we introduce the notion of *simulation*. Informally, simulation performs multiple symbolic interactions after each other, until the rewritten task has an observable value. I.e. if n is the number of interactions needed to be done, $\mathcal{V}(t'_i, \sigma'_i)$ has a result for $i = n$ but is undefined for all $i < n$. Apart from this restriction, we want to permit only viable executions. This is enforced by validating the satisfiability ($\mathcal{S}$) of the conjunction of all sequential path conditions. More formally, simulating a task for multiple user inputs is defined as follows.

Definition 1 (Simulation ($\approx\!\!\!\!\Rightarrow^*$)). *Let t and σ be a concrete task and concrete state. We define the simulation relation*

$$t, \sigma \; \approx\!\!\!\!\Rightarrow^* \; \overline{\tilde{v}, \tilde{I}, \Phi}$$

to be the set of results after performing symbolic interaction n times:

$$t, \sigma \approx\!\!\!\Rightarrow \tilde{t}_1, \tilde{\sigma}_1, \tilde{\imath}_1, \varphi_1 \approx\!\!\!\Rightarrow \cdots \approx\!\!\!\Rightarrow \tilde{t}_n, \tilde{\sigma}_n, \tilde{\imath}_n, \varphi_n$$

where:

- *the nth task has a value:* $\mathcal{V}(\tilde{t}_n, \tilde{\sigma}_n) = \tilde{v}$;
- *all tasks before do not have a value:* $\mathcal{V}(\tilde{t}_{i<n}, \tilde{\sigma}_{i<n}) = \bot$;
- $\tilde{I} = \tilde{\imath}_1 \cdots \tilde{\imath}_n$ *is the concatenation of all symbolic inputs generated along the way;*
- $\Phi = \varphi_1 \wedge \cdots \wedge \varphi_n$, *is the conjunction of all path conditions encountered.*

Furthermore we require that:

- *the resulting predicate is satisfiable:* $\mathcal{S}(\Phi)$.

The simulation definition used in this paper differs from the one in previous work [16]. Previously, infinite symbolic executions were filtered out by allowing two steps look-ahead in case of idempotent executions. The definition above only allows finite executions by definition.

4.3   Next Step Hints Observation

As we have seen in Definition 1, a symbolic task $\tilde{t}$ is considered done as soon as it has an observable value $\tilde{v}$. In order to calculate next step hints, one needs to formulate a goal over this resulting value. Only then, we can calculate next step hints for end users.

$$\mathcal{H} : \text{Tasks} \times \text{States} \times (\text{Values} \rightarrow \text{Booleans}) \rightarrow \mathcal{P}(\text{Inputs} \times \text{Predicates})$$
$$\mathcal{H}(t, \sigma, g) = \{\langle \tilde{\imath}, \Phi \wedge g(\tilde{v}) \rangle \mid (t, \sigma \approx\!\!\!\Rightarrow^* \tilde{v}, \tilde{\imath} \cdot \tilde{I}, \Phi), \mathcal{S}(\Phi \wedge g(\tilde{v}))\}$$

Fig. 4. Definition of next step hint function.

Hints are calculated by means of the $\mathcal{H}$ function listed in Fig. 4. As input, it receives a concrete task t and concrete state σ together with a goal predicate g. The hints observation simulates t starting in σ. This results in a set of symbolic values $\tilde{v}$, together with a list of symbolic inputs $\tilde{\imath} \cdot \tilde{I}$ and a condition Φ to reach this path. We only want to use the symbolic executions that satisfy the goal g when applied to $\tilde{v}$. Since $\tilde{v}$ could contain symbols, it might be the case that $g(\tilde{v})$ is symbolic and would clash with the path condition Φ. Therefore, we require that the conjunction of the path condition with the goal is satisfiable ($\mathcal{S}(\Phi \wedge g(\tilde{v}))$). From the executions that fulfill this requirement, we return the first symbolic input $\tilde{\imath}$ from the complete list of inputs $\tilde{\imath} \cdot \tilde{I}$, together with the full condition that must hold ($\Phi \wedge g(\tilde{v})$). The resulting set contains pairs of symbolic inputs guarded by this condition.

To get a better understanding how $\mathcal{H}$ works, we study it more concretely in the next subsections. Section 4.4 demonstrates on the basis of the tax example listed in Sect. 3.2, how the results of the symbolic execution are used to construct automatic next step hints. Section 4.5 shows how hints can be generated during the execution of the example $\widehat{\text{TOP}}$ program listed in Sect. 3.3.

4.4   Tax Subsidy Request

Recall the Tax example program in $\widehat{\text{TOP}}$ from Sect. 3.2, which models the application for a solar panel tax refund. The user enters the invoice date and invoice amount, the installation company confirms, and finally the tax officer either approves or denies the request.

Table 2. The results of simulating the program from Listing 1.2.

Symbolic value ($\tilde{v}$)	Symbolic input ($\tilde{I}$)	Path condition (Φ)
$\langle \min(600, s_a/10), \text{True}, \text{True}, s_i, 13 \text{ Feb } 2020 \rangle$	$FF\,s_a \cdot FS\,s_i \cdot SL \cdot S$	$(13 \text{ Feb } 2020 - s_i) < 365 \text{ days}$
$\langle \min(600, s_a/10), \text{True}, \text{True}, s_i, 13 \text{ Feb } 2020 \rangle$	$FS\,s_i \cdot FF\,s_a \cdot SL \cdot S$	$(13 \text{ Feb } 2020 - s_i) < 365 \text{ days}$
$\langle \min(600, s_a/10), \text{True}, \text{True}, s_i, 13 \text{ Feb } 2020 \rangle$	$SL \cdot FF\,s_a \cdot FS\,s_i \cdot S$	$(13 \text{ Feb } 2020 - s_i) < 365 \text{ days}$
$\langle \min(600, s_a/10), \text{True}, \text{True}, s_i, 13 \text{ Feb } 2020 \rangle$	$SL \cdot FS\,s_i \cdot FF\,s_a \cdot S$	$(13 \text{ Feb } 2020 - s_i) < 365 \text{ days}$
$\langle \min(600, s_a/10), \text{True}, \text{True}, s_i, 13 \text{ Feb } 2020 \rangle$	$FS\,s_i \cdot SL \cdot FF\,s_a \cdot S$	$(13 \text{ Feb } 2020 - s_i) < 365 \text{ days}$
$\langle \min(600, s_a/10), \text{True}, \text{True}, s_i, 13 \text{ Feb } 2020 \rangle$	$FF\,s_a \cdot SL \cdot FS\,s_i \cdot S$	$(13 \text{ Feb } 2020 - s_i) < 365 \text{ days}$
$\langle 0, \text{False}, \text{True}, s_i, 13 \text{ Feb } 2020 \rangle$	$FF\,s_a \cdot FS\,s_i \cdot SL \cdot F$	True
$\langle 0, \text{False}, \text{True}, s_i, 13 \text{ Feb } 2020 \rangle$	$FS\,s_i \cdot FF\,s_a \cdot SL \cdot F$	True
$\langle 0, \text{False}, \text{True}, s_i, 13 \text{ Feb } 2020 \rangle$	$SL \cdot FF\,s_a \cdot FS\,s_i \cdot F$	True
$\langle 0, \text{False}, \text{True}, s_i, 13 \text{ Feb } 2020 \rangle$	$SL \cdot FS\,s_i \cdot FF\,s_a \cdot F$	True
$\langle 0, \text{False}, \text{True}, s_i, 13 \text{ Feb } 2020 \rangle$	$FS\,s_i \cdot SL \cdot FF\,s_a \cdot F$	True
$\langle 0, \text{False}, \text{True}, s_i, 13 \text{ Feb } 2020 \rangle$	$FF\,s_a \cdot SL \cdot FS\,s_i \cdot F$	True
$\langle 0, \text{False}, \text{False}, s_i, 13 \text{ Feb } 2020 \rangle$	$FF\,s_a \cdot FS\,s_i \cdot S \cdot F$	True
$\langle 0, \text{False}, \text{False}, s_i, 13 \text{ Feb } 2020 \rangle$	$FS\,s_i \cdot FF\,s_a \cdot S \cdot F$	True
$\langle 0, \text{False}, \text{False}, s_i, 13 \text{ Feb } 2020 \rangle$	$SS \cdot FF\,s_a \cdot FS\,s_i \cdot F$	True
$\langle 0, \text{False}, \text{False}, s_i, 13 \text{ Feb } 2020 \rangle$	$S \cdot FS\,s_i \cdot FF\,s_a \cdot F$	True
$\langle 0, \text{False}, \text{False}, s_i, 13 \text{ Feb } 2020 \rangle$	$FS\,s_i \cdot S \cdot FF\,s_a \cdot F$	True
$\langle 0, \text{False}, \text{False}, s_i, 13 \text{ Feb } 2020 \rangle$	$FF\,s_a \cdot S \cdot FS\,s_i \cdot F$	True

In this section, we will demonstrate what symbolic execution looks like for this example, and how we generate next step hints from the symbolic execution results. First, we call the simulate function $\leadsto^*$ on the program, with an empty state. The resulting set of symbolic executions is listed in Table 2. Each line represents one symbolic execution. In the first column, the resulting symbolic value $\tilde{v}$ is listed. The second column lists the symbolic input $\tilde{I}$ that was produced to arrive at that value, followed by the path condition Φ in the third column. The symbolic values that are produced are s_i for the invoice date and s_a for the invoice amount.

The definition of $\mathcal{H}$ describes how these results should be used in order to calculate next step hints. First of all, we need a goal g to select the symbolic runs that we are interested in. The most straight forward goal would be that we want to end up in a situation where we get a subsidy amount larger than zero. This goal can be formulated as $g(\langle v, \_, \_, \_, \_ \rangle) = v > 0$.

The first six symbolic runs listed in Table 2 fulfill this goal condition. From those runs, we then take the first symbolic input, together with the path condition conjugated with the goal. After removing duplicates and redundant information, the result of $\mathcal{H}$ is as follows.

$$\langle \mathsf{F\,F}\,s_a\ ,\ \min(600, s_a/10) > 0\rangle$$
$$\langle \mathsf{F\,S}\,s_i\ ,\ (13\ \text{Feb}\ 2020 - s_i) < 365\ \text{days}\rangle$$
$$\langle \mathsf{S\,L}\quad ,\ \mathsf{True}\rangle$$

This means that, at this stage, users have three possible options.[4]

1. The applicant may enter an amount s_a for which $\min(600, s_a/10) > 0$ should hold.
2. The applicant may enter an invoice date s_i for which $(13\ \text{Feb}\ 2020 - s_i) < 365$ days should hold.
3. The company should take the left choice (L) to confirm they installed the solar panels.

4.5 Dining Computer Scientists

Recall the example program Dining Computer Scientists from Sect. 3.3. Three computer scientist sit at a table and have to coordinate their eating. We want to calculate all possible next steps that lead to the goal. The goal in this example is for all computer scientists to finish their meal. In terms of the resulting task value, this means that we want to reach the value "Full bellies". Witten as a predicate, we get $g(v) = v \equiv$ "Full bellies".

Let us assume that both Grace Hopper and Ada Lovelace have already picked up the forks to their left (fork2 and fork0 respectively). We then find ourselves in the situation shown in Fig. 5.

$t =$ (scientist "Alan Turing" fork0 fork1 ⋈

     □⟨⟩ ▷ λ_.

        if!fork2 then fork1 := True else ↯ ⋈

     □⟨⟩ ▷ λ_.

        if!fork0 then fork2 := True else ↯)

    ▶ λ_. □ "Full bellies"

$\sigma = \{\text{fork0} \mapsto \text{False}, \text{fork1} \mapsto \text{True}, \text{fork2} \mapsto \text{False}\}$

Fig. 5. Task, state and visual representation of dining computer scientists after two moves.

Calling $\mathcal{H}(t, \sigma, g)$ will result in just one hint, namely

$$\langle \mathsf{S\,F\,C}, \mathsf{True}\rangle$$

This means that the only step towards goal g is for the second scientist,[5] which is Grace Hopper, to pick up the right fork. Although it is also possible for Alan Turing to pick up the fork to his left, this step is not a valid hint and performing this action will result in deadlock.

---

[4] Note that the first branch, entering an amount, is denoted by $\mathsf{F\,F}$; the second branch, entering the invoice date, is denoted by $\mathsf{F\,S}$; and the third branch, making a left/right choice, is denoted by S.

[5] The second branch is denoted by $\mathsf{S\,F}$. The action C means pushing the continue button.

5   Properties

In this section, we want to validate our approach by proving correctness. For the hints function, which forms the heart of Assistive $\widehat{TOP}$, we want to prove that its results are both sound and complete. Since the hints function relies on Symbolic $\widehat{TOP}$, and more specifically, the updated definition of the simulate relation, we first prove correctness of simulate.

5.1   Correctness of Simulate

The symbolic execution semantics is correct when all symbolic runs relate to a concrete run, and the other way around, when all concrete runs are contained in the set of all symbolic executions. These properties are, respectively, soundness and completeness.

The simulation applies symbolic interaction multiple times. In order to prove certain properties with respect to the concrete semantics, we need a concrete analog of simulation. Therefore, we define *execution*, which applies concrete interaction multiple times.

Definition 2 (Execution ($\Rightarrow^*$)). *Let t be a concrete task, σ a concrete state, and $I = i_1 \cdots i_n$ a list of n concrete inputs. We define the execution relation*

$$t, \sigma \stackrel{I}{\Rightarrow}^* v$$

to be the value of task t after performing concrete interaction for each input i in I:

$$t, \sigma \stackrel{i_1}{\Rightarrow} t_1, \sigma_1 \stackrel{i_2}{\Rightarrow} \cdots \stackrel{i_n}{\Rightarrow} t_n, \sigma_n$$

where

- *v is the value of t_n: $\mathcal{V}(t_n, \sigma_n) = v$; and*
- *all tasks before t_n do not have a value: $\mathcal{V}(t_{i<n}, \sigma_{i<n}) = \bot$.*

Using execution, we can state soundness and completeness for simulation as follows.

Lemma 1 (Soundness of simulate). *For all tasks t and states σ such that $t, \sigma \rightsquigarrow^* \tilde{v}, \tilde{I}, \Phi$ where $\tilde{I} = \tilde{i}_0 \cdots \tilde{i}_n$, for each triple of results $\langle \tilde{v}, \tilde{I}, \Phi \rangle$ there exists a concrete input I with the same length as the symbolic input $\tilde{I}$ such that $t, \sigma \stackrel{I}{\Rightarrow}^* v$ with $[s_i \mapsto c_i]\tilde{v} = v$ and $[s_i \mapsto c_i]\Phi$ where $SymOf(\tilde{i}_i) = s_i$ and $ValOf(i_i) = c_i$.*

Lemma 2 (Completeness of simulate). *For all tasks t, states σ, and lists of input I such that $t, \sigma \stackrel{I}{\Rightarrow}^* v$, there exists a symbolic value $\tilde{v}$ and a symbolic input $\tilde{I}$ with the same length as I, such that $(\tilde{v}, \tilde{I}, \Phi) \in t, \sigma \rightsquigarrow^*$, with $\tilde{i}_i \sim i_i$, $[s_i \mapsto c_i]\tilde{v} = v$ and $[s_i \mapsto c_i]\Phi$, where $SymOf(\tilde{i}_i) = s_i$ and $ValOf(i_i) = c_i$.*

Where $\tilde{i} \sim i$ is defined as follows.

Definition 3 (Input simulation). *A symbolic input $\tilde{i}$ simulates a concrete input i denoted as $\tilde{i} \sim i$ in the following cases.*

$s \sim a$, *where s is a symbol and a a concrete action.*

$\tilde{i} \sim i \supset \mathsf{F}\tilde{i} \sim \mathsf{F}i$

$\tilde{i} \sim i \supset \mathsf{S}\tilde{i} \sim \mathsf{S}i$

And $SymOf(\tilde{i}) = s$ and $ValOf(i) = c$ are defined as follows.

Definition 3 (Value from input).

$ValOf :$ Inputs $\rightarrow$ Values
$ValOf(\mathsf{F}i) = ValOf(i)$
$ValOf(\mathsf{S}i) = ValOf(i)$
$ValOf(c) = c$
$ValOf(\_) = \bot$

Definition 4 (Symbol from input).

$SymOf :$ Symbolic Inputs $\rightarrow$ Symbolic Values
$SymOf(\mathsf{F}i) = SymOf(i)$
$SymOf(\mathsf{S}i) = SymOf(i)$
$SymOf(s) = s$
$SymOf(\_) = \bot$

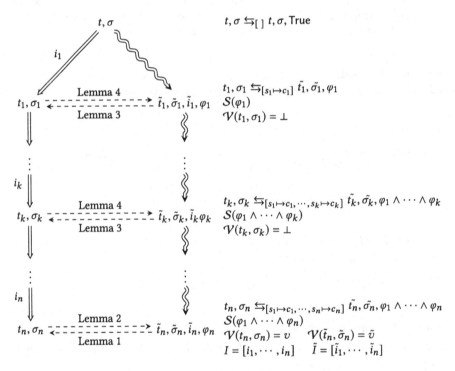

Fig. 6. Proof structure

Our strategy to prove these two lemma's is outlined in Fig. 6. At the top, we start out with any task t and state σ. The left side of the diagram is an overview of the evaluate function. Inputs i_1 until i_n are sequentially applied, until the task has an observable value.

On the right side, symbolic execution is performed. One step of the symbolic inter-action semantics is taken, which results in a symbolic task, state, input and a path condition. Provided that the path condition holds, interaction is executed sequentially until the symbolic task has an observable symbolic value.

Proving soundness and completeness of simulation now comes down to relating the left and right side of the diagram. From symbolic to concrete (right to left) is soundness, as stated in Lemma 1. From concrete to symbolic (left to right) is completeness, as stated in Lemma 2.

Since simulation and execution rely on the (symbolic) handling semantics, we prove soundness and completeness of those semantics first. Looking at Fig. 6, there are two different settings in which the (symbolic) handling semantics are applied. At the top, both symbolic and concrete execution start out with the same task and state. But further down, the task and state differ for both semantics. The task and state are related to each other however. The symbolic semantics introduces symbols, the concrete semantics handles concrete values. This relation is expressed by the consistence relation listed in Definition 5.

Definition 5 (Consistence relation $\leftrightarrows$). *A concrete task t and concrete state σ are considered to be consistent with a symbolic task $\tilde{t}$, symbolic state $\tilde{\sigma}$ and path condition Φ under a certain mapping $M = [s_1 \mapsto c_1, \cdots, s_n \mapsto c_n]$, denoted as $t, \sigma \leftrightarrows_M \tilde{t}, \tilde{\sigma}, \Phi$ if and only if $M\tilde{t} = t$, $M\tilde{\sigma} = \sigma$ and $M\Phi$.*

Now Lemma 3 and Lemma 4 express soundness and completeness of interacting respectively.

Lemma 3 (Soundness of interacting). *For all concrete tasks t, concrete states σ, symbolic tasks $\tilde{t}$, symbolic states $\tilde{\sigma}$ path conditions Φ and mappings M, we have that $t, \sigma \leftrightarrows_M \tilde{t}, \tilde{\sigma}, \Phi$ implies that for all pairs $(\tilde{t}', \tilde{\sigma}', \tilde{\imath}, \varphi)$ in $\tilde{t}, \tilde{\sigma} \rightsquigarrow \overline{\tilde{t}', \tilde{\sigma}', \tilde{\imath}, \varphi}$, $S(\Phi \wedge \varphi)$ implies that there exists an input i such that $\tilde{\imath} \sim i$, $t, \sigma \xrightarrow{i} t', \sigma'$ and $t', \sigma' \leftrightarrows_{M.[s \mapsto c]} \tilde{t}', \tilde{\sigma}', \Phi \wedge \varphi$ where $SymOf(\tilde{\imath}) = s$ and $ValOf(i) = c$.*

Lemma 4 (Completeness of interacting). *For all concrete tasks t, concrete states σ, symbolic tasks $\tilde{t}$, symbolic states $\tilde{\sigma}$ path conditions Φ and mappings M, we have that $t, \sigma \leftrightarrows_M \tilde{t}, \tilde{\sigma}, \Phi$ implies that for all inputs i such that $t, \sigma \xrightarrow{i} t', \sigma'$, there exists a symbolic input $\tilde{\imath}$, $\tilde{\imath} \sim i$ such that $\tilde{t}, \tilde{\sigma} \rightsquigarrow \overline{\tilde{t}', \tilde{\sigma}', \tilde{\imath}, \varphi}$, $S(\Phi \wedge \varphi)$ and $t', \sigma' \leftrightarrows_{M.[s \mapsto c]} \tilde{t}', \tilde{\sigma}', \Phi \wedge \varphi$ where $SymOf(\tilde{\imath}) = s$ and $ValOf(i) = c$.*

In other words, if a symbolic and concrete task and state are related, they will still be related after (symbolic) handling. The top case, where both the symbolic and concrete semantics start out with the same task and state, can be seen as a special case of the consistence relation. Obviously a task and state are consistent with themselves, using the empty mapping and the path condition True.

The full proof of all four lemma's is listed in the appendix online[6].

---

[6] https://github.com/timjs/assistive-tophat/raw/master/appendix.pdf.

5.2 Correctness of Hints

Now that soundness and completeness of simulate have been proven, we can prove that our hints function produces correct hints. Intuitively, for a next step hint to be correct, it should adhere to the following requirements:

- it leads to concrete input users can actually insert; and
- when users follow the hint, the end goal is still reachable.

Moreover, a set of next step hints is correct when:

- each hint it contains is correct; and
- it covers all possible inputs that lead to the end goal.

We separate these requirements into two lemma's, namely soundness and completeness.

Theorem 1 (Soundness of hints). *For all tasks t, states σ, and goals g, for every next step hint $\langle \tilde{\imath}, \Phi \rangle$ in $\mathcal{H}(t, \sigma, g)$, there exists a sequence of concrete inputs I and a concrete input i such that $\tilde{\imath} \sim i$, $S([s \mapsto c]\Phi)$, $t, \sigma \overset{i}{\Rightarrow} t', \sigma' \overset{I}{\Rightarrow}^* v$ and $g(v)$.*

Theorem 2 (Completeness of hints). *For all tasks t, states σ, lists of input $i \cdot I$, and goals g, if $t, \sigma, \overset{i \cdot I}{\Rightarrow}^* v$ and $g(v)$, then there exists a symbolic input $\tilde{\imath}$ and path condition Φ such that $\langle \tilde{\imath}, \Phi \rangle \in \mathcal{H}(t, \sigma, g)$ with $\tilde{\imath} \sim i$ and $S([s \mapsto c]\Phi)$ with $ValOf(i) = c$ and $SymOf(\tilde{\imath}) = s$.*

The proofs of these two threorems are quite straight forward.

Proof (Theorem 1). Theorem 1 follows from the definition of $\mathcal{H}$ and Lemma 1 as follows.

The definition of $\mathcal{H}$ gives us that for every pair $\langle \tilde{\imath}, \Phi \rangle$ produced by $\mathcal{H}$, there exists a triple $\langle \tilde{v}, \tilde{\imath} : \tilde{\imath}s, \Phi \rangle$ with $S(\Phi \wedge g(\tilde{v}))$. Then by Lemma 1 we have that there exists a sequence of concrete inputs I such that $t, \sigma \overset{I}{\Rightarrow}^* v$ and $g(v)$.

Proof (Theorem 2). In order to prove that i is contained in $\mathcal{H}(t, \sigma, g)$, we need to show that $t, \sigma \rightsquigarrow^* \langle \tilde{v}, \tilde{\imath} \cdot \tilde{I}, \Phi \rangle$, with $\tilde{\imath} \sim i$ and $S([s_0 \mapsto c_0, \cdots, s_n \mapsto c_n] \wedge g(\tilde{v}))$, where $ValOf(i_0) = c_0, \cdots, ValOf(i_n) = c_n$ and $[c_0, \cdots, c_n] \in i \cdot I$ and $SymOf(\tilde{\imath}_0) = s_0, \cdots, SymOf(\tilde{\imath}_n) = s_n$.

By Lemma 2, we directly obtain that this indeed exists. Therefore we know that $\tilde{\imath}$ and Φ exist.

6   Related Work

In previous work, we have attempted to provide end users with next step hints by viewing workflows as rule based problems [15]. By abstracting over workflows, reasoning about them becomes simpler. A standard search algorithm can be run to find a path to the desired goal state. Two drawbacks of this approach however are that only very general hints can be given, that range over multiple steps, and that a programmer needs to augment existing workflows with extra information in order to convert it to a rule-based problem.

Stutterheim et al. [22] have developed Tonic, a task visualiser for iTasks with limited path prediction capabilities. The main goal is not to provide hints to end users, but the system is able to handle the complete task language, and visualise the effects of user input on the progression of tasks.

In order to overcome the problems of our own previous research and the limited use of Tonic for end user hints, we have combined symbolic execution, together with workflow modelling and next step hint generation. To our knowledge, this is the first work describing the combination of these techniques in this way. The different components coming together in this paper have been studied extensively. The following sections give an overview of the work done in those areas.

6.1   Symbolic Execution

Symbolic execution [4, 12] is typically being applied to imperative programming languages, but in recent years it has been used for functional programming languages as well. Ongoing work by Hallahan et al. [8, 9] aims to implement a symbolic execution engine for Haskell. Giantsios et al. [7] use symbolic execution for a mix of concrete and symbolic testing of Erlang programs. Their goal is to explore all execution paths up to a certain depth. Chang et al. [5] present a symbolic execution engine for a typed lambda calculus with mutable state where only some language constructs recognise symbolic values. They claim that their approach is easier to implement than full symbolic execution and simplifies the burden on the solver, while still considering all execution paths.

6.2   Workflow Modelling

Workflow modelling has been studied extensively from different viewpoints. Since many software exists that automates workflows, it is a research topic that potentially has a huge impact on society.

Workflow patterns are regarded as special design patterns in software engineering. Similar to the combinators in TOP, they describe recurring patterns in workflow systems. Van der Aalst et al. [3] identifies common patterns, and examines their availability in industry workflow frameworks.

Workflow nets allow for the modelling an analysis of business processes [2]. Workflow Nets are a subclass of Petri nets, and are therefore graphical in nature. Research on workflow nets includes verification of models [1] and complexity analysis [14], just to name a few.

iTasks [19] is an implementation of TOP in the programming language Clean. It differs from the above mentioned modelling techniques, since it is not graphical in nature. iTasks supports higher order workflows, and leverages techniques from functional and generic programming.

6.3   Automatic Hint Generation in Intelligent Tutoring Systems

The intelligent tutoring systems (ITS) research community is very elaborate. Work that is most relevant to our own is the research into automatic hint generation. More traditional ITSs rely heavily on experts to write dedicated hints for every specific case of an exercise. Automatic hint generation attempts to overcome this burden by calculating a hint rather than having every case specified.

Heeren et al. [10] develop a framework for so called domain reasoners that allow for automatic hint generation. Feedback is calculated automatically from a high-level description of an exercise class. Their approach is applicable to domains like logic, mathematics and linear algebra. Paquette et al. [17] present a different automatic next step hint ITS, that is used to provide hints to students in a programming exercise.

Based on the work mentioned above by Heeren et al., an ITS for Haskell exercises has been developed by Gerdes et al. [6]. It tuns out that programming exercises is a popular area for automatic hint generation. Keuning et al. [11] have written an excellent literature study of this research area.

7 Conclusion

In this paper, we have demonstrated how to apply symbolic execution to automatically generate next step hints for $\widehat{TOP}$ programs. We have proven the symbolic execution to be sound and complete with regards to sequential inputs. Based on this property, we have also shown that the generated next step hints are correct. Furthermore, we have presented an implementation of the end user feedback system in Haskell.

7.1 Future Work

As future work, we are very interested in bringing the theory presented in this paper into practice. We feel that there are three possible angles to pursue this interest.

Presenting Hint Information. The information calculated by the current hints function cannot directly be presented to the end user. The set of calculated hints contains duplicates. This is due to the fact that there might be several different paths to the goal, that start out with the same symbolic input. Another source of redundant information is the path conditions. The path conditions contained in the hint tuple contains information about the complete execution, while the symbolic input is only concerned with the immediate next step. Therefore, the path condition may contain references to future inputs and constraints, which offer no information for the end user. In a future implementation of Assistive $\widehat{TOP}$, we would like to filter out both sources of redundancy, in order to present the user with more concise information.

Hint Generation in iTasks. Since iTasks is currently the biggest TOP framework, it would be the next logical step to integrate automatic hint generation into the framework. This would allow a wide range of applications to immediately benefit from automatic next step hint generation. The iTasks framework is shallowly embedded in the purely functional programming language Clean, which means that programmers can leverage the full power of the host language. This makes implementing symbolic execution non-trivial.

Measuring Impact of Hints. Finally, we would like to test the impact of next step hints in workflow systems in an empirical study. TOP research has been applied and studied in the field at the Royal Netherlands Sea Rescue Institution and the Royal Netherlands Navy, which would be ideal testing grounds for Assistive $\widehat{\text{TOP}}$.

Acknowledgements. This research is supported by the Dutch Technology Foundation STW, which is part of the Netherlands Organisation for Scientific Research (NWO), and which is partly funded by the Ministry of Economic Affairs.

References

1. Aalst, W.M.P.: Verification of workflow nets. In: Azéma, P., Balbo, G. (eds.) ICATPN 1997. LNCS, vol. 1248, pp. 407–426. Springer, Heidelberg (1997). https://doi.org/10.1007/3-540-63139-9_48
2. van der Aalst, W.M.P.: The application of petri nets to workflow management. J. Circuits Syst. Comput. **8**(1), 21–66 (1998)
3. van der Aalst, W.M.P., ter Hofstede, A.H.M., Kiepuszewski, B., Barros, A.P.: Workflow patterns. Distrib. Parallel Databases **14**(1), 5–51 (2003)
4. Boyer, R.S., Elspas, B., Levitt, K.N.: Select - a formal system for testing and debugging programs by symbolic execution. In: Proceedings of the International Conference on Reliable Software, pp. 234–245. ACM, New York (1975)
5. Chang, S., Knauth, A., Torlak, E.: Symbolic types for lenient symbolic execution. In: PACMPL 2(POPL), pp. 40:1–40:29 (2018)
6. Gerdes, A., Heeren, B., Jeuring, J., van Binsbergen, L.T.: Ask-Elle: an adaptable programming tutor for haskell giving automated feedback. Int. J. Artif. Intell. Educ. **27**(1), 65–100 (2016). https://doi.org/10.1007/s40593-015-0080-x
7. Giantsios, A., Papaspyrou, N., Sagonas, K.: Concolic testing for functional languages. Sci. Comput. Program. **147**, 109–134 (2017)
8. Hallahan, W.T., Xue, A., Bland, M.T., Jhala, R., Piskac, R.: Lazy counterfactual symbolic execution. In: McKinley, K.S., Fisher, K. (eds.) Proceedings of the 40th ACM SIGPLAN Conference on Programming Language Design and Implementation, PLDI 2019, Phoenix, AZ, USA, 22–26 June 2019, pp. 411–424. ACM (2019)
9. Hallahan, W.T., Xue, A., Piskac., R.: Building a symbolic execution engine for haskell. In: Proceedings of TAPAS, vol. 17 (2017)
10. Heeren, B., Jeuring, J.: Feedback services for stepwise exercises. Sci. Comput. Program. **88**, 110–129 (2014)
11. Keuning, H., Jeuring, J., Heeren, B.: A systematic literature review of automated feedback generation for programming exercises. TOCE **19**(1), 3:1–3:43 (2019)
12. King, J.C.: A new approach to program testing. SIGPLAN Notices **10**(6), 228–233 (1975)
13. Koopman, P., Lubbers, M., Plasmeijer, R.: A task-based DSL for microcomputers. In: Proceedings of the Real World Domain Specific Languages Workshop, RWDSL@CGO 2018, Vienna, Austria, 24–24 February 2018, pp. 4:1–4:11. ACM (2018)
14. Lassen, K.B., van der Aalst, W.M.P.: Complexity metrics for workflow nets. Inf. Softw. Technol. **51**(3), 610–626 (2009)
15. Naus, N., Jeuring, J.: Building a generic feedback system for rule-based problems. In: Van Horn, D., Hughes, J. (eds.) TFP 2016. LNCS, vol. 10447, pp. 172–191. Springer, Cham (2019). https://doi.org/10.1007/978-3-030-14805-8_10
16. Naus, N., Steenvoorden, T., Klinik, M.: A symbolic execution semantics for tophat. In: IFL 2019 (accepted for publication) (2019)

17. Paquette, L., Lebeau, J.-F., Beaulieu, G., Mayers, A.: Automating next-step hints generation using ASTUS. In: Cerri, S.A., Clancey, W.J., Papadourakis, G., Panourgia, K. (eds.) ITS 2012. LNCS, vol. 7315, pp. 201–211. Springer, Heidelberg (2012). https://doi.org/10.1007/978-3-642-30950-2_26
18. Plasmeijer, R., van Eekelen, M., van Groningen, J.: Clean language report version 2.1 (2002)
19. Plasmeijer, R., Lijnse, B., Michels, S., Achten, P., Koopman, P.W.M.: Task-oriented programming in a pure functional language. In: Principles and Practice of Declarative Programming, PPDP 2012, Leuven, Belgium, 19–21 September 2012, pp. 195–206 (2012)
20. Steenvoorden, T., Naus, N., Klinik, M.: Tophat: a formal foundation for task-oriented programming. In: Proceedings of the 21st International Symposium on Principles and Practice of Programming Languages, PPDP 2019, Porto, Portugal, 7–9 October 2019, pp. 17:1–17:13 (2019)
21. Stutterheim, J., Achten, P., Plasmeijer, R.: Maintaining separation of concerns through task oriented software development. In: Wang, M., Owens, S. (eds.) TFP 2017. LNCS, vol. 10788, pp. 19–38. Springer, Cham (2018). https://doi.org/10.1007/978-3-319-89719-6_2
22. Stutterheim, J., Plasmeijer, R., Achten, P.: Tonic: an infrastructure to graphically represent the definition and behaviour of tasks. In: Hage, J., McCarthy, J. (eds.) TFP 2014. LNCS, vol. 8843, pp. 122–141. Springer, Cham (2015). https://doi.org/10.1007/978-3-319-14675-1_8

Debugging and Testing

Scaling Up Delta Debugging
of Type Errors
Category: Research

Joanna Sharrad$^{(\boxtimes)}$ and Olaf Chitil

University of Kent, Canterbury, UK
{jks31,oc}@kent.ac.uk

Abstract. Type error messages of compilers of statically typed functional languages are often inaccurate, making type error debugging hard. Many solutions to the problem have been proposed, but most have been evaluated only with short programs, that is, of fewer than 30 lines. In this paper we note that our own tool for delta debugging type errors scales poorly for large programs. In response we present a new tool that applies a new algorithm for segmenting a large program before the delta debugging algorithm is applied. We propose a framework for quantifying the quality of type error debuggers and apply it to our new tool demonstrating substantial improvement.

Keywords: Type error · Error diagnosis · Blackbox · Delta debugging · Haskell

1 Introduction

Type errors in statically typed functional languages such as Haskell, ML and OCaml are difficult to understand and repair. The type error message of a compiler gives a location in the ill-typed program, but this location is often far from the defect that needs to be repaired. In over 30 years numerous solutions have been proposed, but none has been widely adopted.

In our opinion the major reason for this non-adoption is the effort required for implementing proposed solutions for full programming languages and maintaining them in the face of evolving languages and compilers. Proposed solutions usually require new compiler front-ends, including new type inference implementations, or substantial modifications of existing compilers. We believe that a small improvement that requires little implementation and maintenance effort is much better than a big improvement that requires substantial effort. Hence it has been our goal to develop a type error debugger that uses the compiler as a true black box, that is, it calls the compiler as an external program.

In an earlier paper we presented and evaluated such a type error debugger [18]. Our debugger implements the *isolating delta debugging* algorithm [28] to locate the defective line in an ill-typed program. Our debugger works solely on a line-based principle, directly adding and removing the lines of the source code

---

J. Sharrad—PhD Student.

A. Byrski and J. Hughes (Eds.): TFP 2020, LNCS 12222, pp. 71–93, 2020.
https://doi.org/10.1007/978-3-030-57761-2_4

to generate configurations. These configurations, that is variants of the ill-typed program, are tested by calling the compiler. Our debugger does not duplicate compiler work such as parsing, instead it uses minimal information from the outcome of the compiler call; in particular, the only information the debugger uses is whether compilation succeeded (passed), failed with a type error (fail), or failed with some other error (unresolved). As a consequence such a debugger is mostly programming language agnostic.

We showed that our debugger yields good locations in reasonable time for a data-set sample of 121 ill-typed programs, named the CE benchmarks, that had been taken from papers on type error debugging [3]. However, unlike delta debugging of run-time failures, which was evaluated with large programs, successfully finding a fault in a 178,000 line program, all these programs are short; the longest has 23 lines [27]. So for many type error debugging methods proposed in the literature that use this and other data-sets, including our own debugger, it is unknown from their evaluations whether they scale for larger programs. To counter this we introduce a new data-set, named the *scalability* benchmarks, of 80 type errors that we introduced into the large program Pandoc. This data-set provides a starting point for evaluating the scalability of type error solutions.

1.1   Brief Example of the Line-Based Problem

As our debugger is line-based it is affected by where the *isolating delta debugging* algorithm chooses to split the source code. The *isolating delta debugging* algorithm tests a logarithmic[1] number of configurations if no outcome is unresolved. For example, an ill-typed program containing just one line will immediately locate the fault on that line from the first configuration whereas an ill-typed program containing 6 lines of code can take three configurations to locate the type error. However, as we have previously said we do not replicate parsing and so every line combination can be a possible configuration. This has the detrimental effect of causing many ill-formed variants; producing a significant number of unresolved results.

Take as a brief example this Haskell program from Stuckey et al. [21] that we used in our previous paper[18]:

```
1 insert x [] = x
2 insert x (y:ys) | x > y     = y : insert x ys
3                 | otherwise = x : y : ys
```

The program is ill-typed. The first line is incorrect the x should be a list of x. The Glasgow Haskell compiler[2] gives us line 2 as the incorrect line, whereas our previous debugger correctly points out line 1. However, even in this three line program we still receive unresolved results from the *isolating delta debugging* algorithm. For example the following configuration returns a parse error:

---

[1] With respect to the number of lines of the original ill-typed program.

[2] https://www.haskell.org/ghc, version 8.4.3.

```
1
2
3          | otherwise = x : y : ys
```

The more outcomes are unresolved, the less efficient *isolating delta debugging* becomes, up to a quadratic number of configurations. "When using ... [isolating delta debugging], it is thus wise to keep unresolved test outcomes to a minimum, as this keeps down the number of tests required" [28]. All applications implementing *isolating delta debugging* try to minimise the number of configurations with unresolved test outcomes. In our application the root cause of most unresolved outcomes are parse errors. Building some kind of parser for our debugger would contradict our goals. Hence here we present an algorithm, Moiety, that calls the compiler as a black box. Moiety detects the lines within an ill-typed program that are valid splitting points. A moiety is a configuration of the original program that consists of consecutive lines that should not be split. If a moiety is split, then compilation will produce a parse error. In summary, the moiety information guides the *isolating delta debugging* algorithm to reduce unresolved test outcomes and thus reduce the time taken for the algorithm to run.

We implemented the new type error debugger, Elucidate20. It combines the new moiety algorithm with an *isolating delta debugging* algorithm that uses moiety information. The debugger locates a defective line of an ill-typed Haskell program, using the Glasgow Haskell compiler as black box. To debug large programs, Elucidate20, unlike our previous debugger, also supports multi-module programs and a standard project build tool.

In this paper we make the following contributions:

- We present the moiety algorithm, which generates, using the compiler as a black box, a set of moieties of the ill-typed program. That set determines the configurations for the *isolating delta debugging* (Sect. 3).
- We propose a framework for quantifying the quality of type error debuggers (Sect. 4).
- We introduce a new data-set of 80 ill-typed variants of the program Pandoc (Sect. 5)
- We evaluate Elucidate20 to see whether the moiety algorithm reduces unresolved results and thus the run-time of the *isolating delta debugging* algorithm. We use our new framework and scalability data-set (Sect. 5).

2   The Problem

2.1   Delta Debugging Type Errors

Let us briefly review what delta debugging is and how we applied it to type error debugging [18].

To locate the defect in an ill-typed program, many programmers simply remove (or comment out) some parts of the program and compile the smaller program. If the smaller program is also ill-typed, the procedure is repeated.

If the smaller program is not ill-typed, a different part of the previous program is removed. This shrinking by trial and error repeats until the program cannot shrink further, that is, no smaller program is ill-typed.

Simplifying delta debugging [27,28] is a greedy algorithm that automates this method. Simplifying delta debugging divides the program into two halves and tests each one. If one half is ill-typed, the algorithm calls itself recursively for that half. If neither half is ill-typed, it divides the program into four parts and tests each one. Again the algorithm calls itself recursively for any ill-typed part, but if none is ill-typed, it tries again by dividing the program into eight parts. When the program cannot be divided further, the algorithm stops with the last ill-typed program as result.

Recall that testing a program yields one of *three outcomes*: *fail* (ill-typed), *pass* (well-typed) or *unresolved* (any other error such as parse error or unbound identifier). For the simplifying delta debugging algorithm it does not matter whether an outcome is pass or unresolved, but for the *isolating delta debugging* algorithm, which we actually use, the difference is essential.

A program variant that may be tested is called a *configuration*. For type error debugging we made the same choice of configurations as many other implementations of delta debugging: we chose to always remove whole lines of the ill-typed program[3]. Hence a configuration is the original ill-typed program with some lines replaced by empty lines[4]. A configuration being a subconfiguration of another configuration is a natural partial order on configurations, with the empty configuration, consisting of many empty lines, being the minimum and the original ill-typed program being the maximum.

A minimal ill-typed program is often still big, because for every function or type that it uses it has to includes its definition, which is usually well-typed. To isolate a cause of the type error we want to exclude these well-typed definitions. Therefore we decided to use the *isolating delta debugging* algorithm for type error debugging.

The *isolating delta debugging* algorithm [6,28,29] works with a pair of configurations, a passing and a failing configuration, the former being a subconfiguration of the latter. The algorithm starts with the empty configuration as passing configuration and the ill-typed program as failing configuration. The algorithm divides the difference between the two configurations into two parts and tests the passing configuration with each of these parts added and the failing configuration with each of these parts removed. If any tested configuration yields a passing outcome, it can become the new passing configuration, if any tested configuration yields a failing outcome, it can become the new failing configuration; then the algorithm calls itself recursively with a new pair of configurations. If all of the tested configurations yield unresolved outcomes, the difference is divided instead into four, eight, etc. parts, similar to the simplifying delta debugging algorithm, until eventually a passing or failing configuration is found; if no further division

---

[3] Removing single characters is another choice presented by Zeller [28].

[4] Instead of removing the lines completely we still keep the empty lines to avoid undesirable changes of program layout.

is possible, the algorithm terminates. The algorithm does not specify how the difference between two configurations is divided into parts and there may be several passing and failing outcomes; thus the algorithm is non-deterministic; however, like any other implementation, ours makes a choice and thus is deterministic [1, 12]. In every recursive call the passing configuration is a subconfiguration of the failing configuration (and both are subconfigurations of the original ill-typed program). Every recursive call reduces the difference between the two configurations, until the difference cannot be reduced any further.

The final result of *isolating delta debugging* is a pair of configurations, where the first configuration is a passing subconfiguration of the second failing configuration, such that there exists no passing or failing configuration between the two configurations. The algorithm is greedy to limit run-time and it is not guaranteed to return a pair of configurations with minimal difference.

The final pair of configurations is the result of the *isolating delta debugging* algorithm. The difference between the two configurations, which may be neither a passing nor a failing configuration, isolates a failure cause. This difference is the result of our type error debugger.

2.2   The Effect of Unresolved Outcomes

Because our definition of configuration is based on program lines, all complexity measures of type error debugging are with respect to the number of lines of the ill-typed program. For a given ill-typed program there exists an exponential number of configurations. Already finding a failing configuration of minimal size is known to be NP-complete [11].

In type error debugging nearly all run-time is spent in the tests made by the compiler. In general, the run-time of delta debugging is proportional to the number of tests made.[5]

We see from the description of delta debugging that if no test outcome is unresolved, it is basically a binary search. In contrast, frequent unresolved outcomes cause the algorithm to repeatedly divide (differences of) configurations into four, eight, etc. parts and make more tests. If every configuration is unresolved the algorithm starts to generate configurations that contain a single line until all lines of the program have been checked[6]. So as we already stated in the introduction, the *isolating delta debugging* algorithm has logarithmic time complexity if no outcome is unresolved and becomes less efficient, up to a quadratic time complexity, with many unresolved outcomes. Therefore any successful application of delta debugging makes some effort to avoid unresolved outcomes.

The issue with many unresolved outcomes can be shown more clearly within our earlier results [18]. These 900 programs were generated by concatenating pairs of some of the original small CE benchmark programs. For space reasons, we have ordered the 900 programs by number of lines and put them into 4 groups: the shortest 225 in the first group, the next 225 in the second group, etc.

---

[5] This assumes similar run-time for every test, which may not be the case.

[6] A proof is available on page 408 of 'Why Programs Fail' [28].

Table 1 on the left shows the average outcomes and indicates that the number of unresolved results grows substantially with program size which can be seen more clearly with the a graphically representation on the right.

Table 1. Average number of unresolved outcomes compared to number of lines of code.

# lines	# unresolveds
10	2
17	4
22	7
25	14

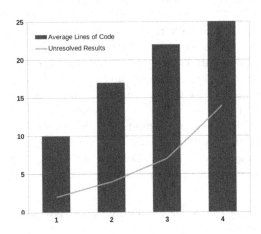

However, we noted in the introduction that ill-typed programs that have been used to evaluate type error debuggers are short. The longest program in the CE benchmark suite [3] of 121 programs has just 23 lines. Such programs are good for studying how a type error debugger works and many of these programs are representative for the first programs written by novices learning a functional programming language. But they do not show us how a type error debugger will scale as not just novices need help with type error debugging, but also more experienced functional programmers who build useful, real-world programs.

In October 2019 we measured the top 100 Haskell programs on the popular public repository GitHub[7]. On average each program has 31872 lines of code, 138 modules, and 229 lines of code per module, far from the 23 lines mentioned above. Even though our type error debugger processes small programs in a few seconds, when applied to programs such as these that contain on average a few hundred lines, due to a hefty number of unresolved results, it could take substantially longer, which is unacceptable [18].

As already stated there is an obvious suspect for the high number of unresolved outcomes in larger programs: although splitting multiple equations of a single function definition yields well-formed definitions in Haskell, splitting a multi-line equation into half usually yields ill-formed programs; the same holds for multi-line type declarations, which often appear in larger programs, and case expressions with a branch per line. Many configurations are simply unparsable!

---

[7] https://github.com/search?l=Haskell&q=Haskell&s=stars&type=Repositories.

Table 2. Number of error messages giving unresolved outcome.

Error message	#
The last statement in a 'do' block must be an expression	4
Variable not in scope	4
Not in scope:	5
Empty 'do' block	5
Parse error (incorrect indentation or mismatched brackets)	7
Empty list of alternatives in case expression	8
The type signature...lacks an accompanying binding	16
Parse error on input	77
Total	126

To test our suspicion, we chose the most popular software from our Github results Pandoc, to initiate our *scalability* data-set. As a initial test we introduced a single type error in a single module. The ill-typed module has 87 lines and our debugger had 126 unresolved outcomes, which we categorise by error message of the Glasgow Haskell compiler in Table 2. Most error messages are related to parsing and "parse error on input" is by far the most frequent one.

3   The Moiety Algorithm and Delta Debugging

We always obtain a configuration that does not parse, if we split the original ill-typed program at certain consecutive lines. Given its dominance, we solely focus on the "parse error on input" error message. These indicate that parsing failed somewhere inside the configuration, whereas for example "parse error (incorrect indentation or mismatched brackets)" indicates that parsing fails at the end of the configuration. Concentrating on the former means our algorithm has the ability to distinguish between the two. So we use this information to first determine which lines that should never be separated as they will cause a "parse error on input" and then apply the delta debugging algorithm such that it never splits in these places.

We name our pre-processing algorithm *Moiety*; according to the Merriam-Webster dictionary a moiety is "one of the portions into which something is divided".[8] Moiety divides the ill-typed program into moieties, that is, what position in the source code we can split the lines. This is represented as a tuple, with the starting and ending points of the splits.

---

[8] https://www.merriam-webster.com/dictionary/moiety.

3.1 Illustration of the Algorithm

The moiety algorithm is designed to reduce unresolved, "parse error on input", results from large programs. However, to present how moiety works concisely we have to consider the following small ill-typed program[9]:

```
1 f x = case x of
2    0 -> [0]
3    1 -> 1
4 plus :: Int -> Int -> Int
5 plus = (+)
6 fib x = case x of
7    0 -> f x
8    1 -> f x
9    n -> fib (n-1) `plus` fib (n-2)
```

To limit runtime, the algorithm may only traverse the program once from beginning to end to produce its set of moieties; no line in the program is submitted to the compiler duplicate times. Moiety calls the compiler to test a program for whether it yields "parse error on input" or not. We show the tested program on the left and the test outcome and resulting moicty set on the right. We note that line 1 never yields "parse error on input" so start with line 2.

```
1
2        0 -> [0]          "parse error on input"
3
4                          moieties: ()
5
6
7
8
9
```

As line 2 produces a "parse error on input" it cannot be the starting line for a plausible split; and so we continue with line 3:

```
1
2                          "parse error on input"
3    1 -> 1
4                          moieties: ()
5
6
7
8
9
```

---

[9] It should be noted when we talk about small programs in type error debugging we are discussing those that are used for evaluation and not those used for examples.

Like line 2, line 3 also cannot start a new moiety; we continue with line 4:

```
1
2
3
4 plus :: Int -> Int -> Int
5
6
7
8
9
```

not "parse error on input"

moieties:(3,4)

Line 4 is not a "parse error on input" so we can create a new moiety. We can successfully split line 4 from line 3; and so line 3 is our starting point and line 4 is our finishing points of our first moiety. Next line 5:

```
1
2
3
4
5 plus = (+)
6
7
8
9
```

not "parse error on input"

moieties:(3,4) (4,5)

Likewise, line 5 starts a new moiety as it can be split from line 4. We move on to line 6:

```
1
2
3
4
5
6 fib x = case x of
7
8
9
```

not "parse error on input"

moieties:(3,4) (4,5) (5,6)

So line 6 starts a new moiety too. We continue with line 7:

```
1
2                                    "parse error on input"
3
4                                    moieties:(3,4) (4,5) (5,6)
5
6
7    0 -> f x
8
9
```

At this point it is hopefully obvious that lines 8 and 9 each also gives the outcome "parse error on input" and so the algorithm finishes with the moieties (3,4) (4,5) (5,6).

Working through the example shows how simple the moiety algorithm is: The algorithm tests every single line of the original ill-typed program whether it yields "parse error on input" or not. In case of the former, the line cannot be split from the preceding lines so no moiety can be generated. Otherwise it does start a new moiety. The result is an ordered set of moieties, two lines that can be successfully split.

3.2 Example of Isolating Delta Debugging with Moieties

In the subsequent *isolating delta debugging* algorithm moieties are never split, simply by redefining a configuration as a subset of moieties.

So in our example we have the moiety list (3,4) (4,5) (5,6).

We start *isolating delta debugging* with the passing configuration {} and the failing configuration {[1,2,3],[4],[5], [6,7,8,9]}. As we can see our failing configuration, of source code line numbers, is now split using the moieties.[10] We divide the difference between the two configurations by two and hence test the configurations {[1,2,3],[4]} and {[5],[6,7,8,9]}. Both configurations give the outcome unresolved. Hence we have to divide the difference between our passing and failing configuration by four and test the configurations {[1,2,3]}, {[4]}, {[5]}, {[6,7,8,9]} and the configurations {[4],[5],[6,7,8,9]}, {[1,2,3],[5],[6,7,8,9]}, {[1,2,3],[4],[6,7,8,9]}, {[1,2,3],[4],[5]}. Our implementation happens to test {[5]} first and the test gives outcome pass.

Next, *isolating delta debugging* calls itself recursively with the new passing configuration {[5]} and the failing configuration {[1,2,3],[4],[5],[6,7,8,9]}. We divide the difference, which is 3 moieties, by two and hence test the configurations {[1,2,3],[4],[5]} and {[5],[6,7,8,9]}. The first configuration gives outcome fail.

Next, *isolating delta debugging* calls itself recursively with the old passing configuration {[5]} and the new failing configuration {[1,2,3],[4],[5]}.

---

[10] {[1],[2], [3],[4],[5],[6],[7],[8],[9]} represents the non-moiety failing configuration. Every line is an acceptable splitting location.

We divide the difference by two and hence test the configurations $\{$[1,2,3] , [5]$\}$ and $\{$[4] , [5]$\}$. The first configuration gives outcome fail.

Finally, *isolating delta debugging* calls itself recursively with the old passing configuration $\{$[5]$\}$ and the new failing configuration $\{$[1,2,3] , [5]$\}$. Because the difference between the two configurations is only one moiety, the algorithm terminates with the these two configurations as result. Our type debugger returns the difference between these two configurations as the location of the defect: $\{1, 2, 3\}$. The actual type error is in line 2, but our type debugger can return at best a single moiety and its preceding lines.

3.3 Time Complexity

We designed the moiety algorithm to return a list of moieties in the shortest time possible, that is linear in the number of lines of the ill-typed program. We know that *isolating delta debugging* takes between logarithmic and quadratic time, now in the number of moieties. Because moieties avoid the most common type of unresolved outcome, we hope that overall the time complexity of type error debugging is close to linear.

4 A Framework for Type Error Debugging

In data science using model metrics such as Accuracy, Precision, and Recall are an accepted standard [19,26]. Yet within type error debugging evaluations only recall, whether a type error has been located correctly or not, run-time, and the authors personal goals are deemed important [4,16]. We disagree with using only one metric as it can bias results, and in later works authors seem to agree [17,30]. However, even though we are slowly seeing other metrics joining recall in type error debugging evaluations they are not representing the same formulas, and so we are proposing the following as a framework for future evaluations to allow for ease of solution comparison (Table 3).

Table 3. Terminology

Shorthand	Longhand	Equivalents
Data science		
TP	True Positive	
TN	True Negative	
FP	False Positive	
FN	False Negative	
Our terms		
R_L	Reported lines (number of lines returned)	TP + FP
R_E	Reported errors (number of correct errors)	TP
U_R	Unreported lines (number of correct unreported lines)	TN
L	Lines of code (total source code)	TN + TP + FN + FP
E	Errors (number of errors in the code)	TP + FN

4.1   The Metrics

Accuracy tells us the typical distance from a measure to the optimum value. For our domain, number of lines correctly excluded plus correctly reported lines containing a type error. However, this is problematic as we receive a high number of True Negative answers, number of correct lines ignored, and so this is generally ignored in the type error debugging domain in favour of recall.

$$Accuracy = \frac{TN + TP}{TN + TP + FN + FP} = \frac{U_R + R_E}{L} \tag{1}$$

Recall, aka sensitivity, is the measure of the quantity of elements correctly returned.

$$Recall = \frac{TP}{TP + FN} = \frac{R_E}{E} \tag{2}$$

For type errors this measures the number of errors that are reported correctly compared to the number of errors within the source code. As already noted, this metric is most used in type error debugging evaluations. It shows if a debugger can successfully discover the correct number of type errors within an ill-typed program. However, like Accuracy, it is not without fault as the following example will show.

Lets us assume we have an ill-typed program containing 8 lines (L = 8) and 1 type error (E = 1). We run a debugger and it returns all 8 lines of code as containing the type error ($R_L = 8$) and, obviously, returns the correct line location within this ($R_E = 1$). Most type error debugging evaluations do not mention the amount of lines returned, only if their debugger located the line correctly. If recall is used as the only metric in evaluations we end up being able to state that this example shows our debugger is 100% correct.

$$Recall = \frac{R_E}{E} = \frac{1}{1} = 100\% \tag{3}$$

This, to us, is obviously incorrect, yet the metric proves it to be true. To counter this issue Data Science employs another metric.

Precision, also known as positive predictive value, is the number of elements within the entire returned set of results.

$$Precision = \frac{TP}{TP + FP} = \frac{R_E}{R_L} \tag{4}$$

Mapped to our domain it is the number of correct lines of code reported by the debugger compared to the total number of lines returned. Precision allows us to see if we have returned the correct location as one single line versus returning a correct location within several lines.

Applying precision to our ongoing example we receive:

$$Precision = \frac{R_E}{R_L} = \frac{1}{8} = 12.5\% \tag{5}$$

As can be seen this is a significant difference from our results from recall, however it is also not practical to use Precision as a singular metric either due its reliance on False Positives, some of the lines returned do not contain a type error. This is where the Data Science domain employs the F_1 Score.

F_1 *Score* is calculated from the harmony mean of the two metrics *Recall* and *Precision*. This produces an accuracy measure that accounts for the imbalance of data within type error debugging, meaning the F_1 score is crucial in showing the true results of evaluations.

$$F_1 = 2\frac{Precision \cdot Recall}{Precision + Recall} = 2\frac{R_E}{E + R_L} \tag{6}$$

Now with our example we can see meaningful feedback for evaluation.

$$F_1 = 2\frac{R_E}{E + R_L} = 2\frac{1}{1 + 8} = 22\% \tag{7}$$

With this framework we can now generate easily comparable evaluations for future work in the type error debugging domain.

5 Evaluating Our Method

We now apply our method on a single real-world program to test scalability; Pandoc is a Haskell library for markup conversion, it has a total of 64,467 lines of code with an average of 430 lines of code per module in 150 modules. We place within Pandoc 80 individual type errors into 40 of its modules (using each module twice) of which each contain between 32 and 2305 lines of code (Table 4).

Table 4. Lines of code per module with associated errors

Errors	LoC	Errors	LoC	Errors	LoC	Errors	LoC
{1, 2}	32	{21, 22}	73	{41, 42}	156	{61, 62}	238
{3, 4}	37	{23, 24}	77	{43, 44}	167	{63, 64}	240
{5, 6}	45	{25, 26}	79	{45, 46}	187	{65, 66}	258
{7, 8}	48	{27, 28}	83	{47, 48}	192	{67, 68}	261
{9, 10}	48	{29, 30}	86	{49, 50}	204	{69, 70}	266
{11, 12}	52	{31, 32}	86	{51, 52}	205	{71, 72}	271
{13, 14}	58	{33, 34}	91	{53, 54}	212	{73, 74}	275
{15, 16}	58	{35, 36}	94	{55, 56}	213	{75, 76}	278
{17, 18}	65	{37, 38}	140	{57, 58}	214	{77, 78}	287
{19, 20}	68	{39, 40}	155	{59, 60}	227	{79, 80}	2305

The modules chosen were the first 39 in size order that contained code that could be made ill-typed. The last module was the largest module Pandoc contained at 2305 lines. The placement of the error was decided upon by a random

Table 5. Type error categories

Category	Errors total
Couldn't match...	**79**
Rigid type variable bound by the type signature ..	5
In the ? field of a record ..In the expression ..	3
...In the expression:?...	**22**
In an equation ? ..	7
In a stmt of a 'do' block ? ..	3
In a case alternative ? ..	7
In the expression: ? ..	5
...In the ? argument of ?...	**20**
In the expression ? In an equation for ? ...	7
In a stmt of a 'do' block ? ..	11
In the ? argument of ?..	2
...In the pattern: ?...	**3**
In a case alternative ? In the expression ? ..	2
In equation ? ..	1
...is applied to...arguments ...	**26**
Possible cause ? is applied to too many arguments ..	3
Probable cause ? is applied to too few arguments ..	11
The function ? is applied to ? argument/s ..	12
Couldn't deduce...	**1**
Arising from a use of ? from the context ? bound by the type signature	1

number generator. If the line suggested was unsuitable for type error placement the generator was re-run. The type errors were inserted manually with no prior planning on the category of type error. The categories, listed by the individual error message presented by GHC, can be seen in Table 5. To note, all of the type errors inserted are Equality Errors as according to *TcErrors*[11].

We compare our debugger, Elucidate20, with Gramarye19. Gramarye19 is a modified version of our previous debugger Gramarye; and like Elucidate20 now supports the following features:

Modular Programs. The type error location of a compiler is unreliable, but our type error debugger assumes that the first module identified by the compiler as ill-typed does contain the type error location; our type error debugger works solely on that module. If a module causes the first compiler type error, then all modules directly or indirectly imported are well-typed. An identifier defined in an imported module may have a type that contradicts with how the identifier is used in the ill-typed module. However, even when both definition and use are

---

[11] TcErrors is part of the Glasgow Haskell Compiler and states that type errors fall into one of 4 groups; more information about this can be found in: https://github. com/JoannaSharrad/ghcErrorsDoc/blob/master/RoughGuidetoGHCTcErrors.pdf.

in the same module and the definition is typable, delta debugging will always identify the use of the identifier as the cause of the error, not the definition. So our treatment of modules is consistent with our general treatment of definition vs. use.

Haskell Specific Language. There are some language declarations that should be ignored when removing lines as they will always lead to an unresolved result. Hence our type error debugger leaves these declarations in all configurations tested by the delta debugging algorithm. The following are never the location of a type error; import declarations, single line comments, multi-line comments, and module declaration. Unfortunately, recognising lines with these declarations is specific to the programming language Haskell, and thus removes the agnostic status from the delta debugging algorithm.

The Build Tool. When measuring the top 100 Haskell programs on GitHub, we found that they all use Cabal[12] for packaging and building. Therefore our type error debugger has a flag to call the build tool cabal instead of the Glasgow Haskell compiler for testing. When cabal is used, the user has to state the target program instead of the ill-typed module.

Though the above have been added as features to both Gramarye19 and Elucidate20, the latter still keeps delta debugging free of the moiety pre-processing [18].

For this evaluation we ran our benchmarks on an AMD Phenom X4, 32 GB RAM, Samsung SSD 850, PC running Ubuntu 18.04LTS to answer the following questions:

1. Does the Moiety algorithm reduce the number of unresolved results?
2. Does the pre-processing affect the time taken by *Isolating Delta Debugging*?
3. Does applying the new framework quantify the quality of the debugger?

5.1   Reduction of Unresolved Results

Question: Does the Moiety algorithm reduce the number of Unresolved results?

The moiety algorithm produces a set of splitting locations in the source code. Our scalability benchmark contained a total of 16264 lines of code of which 16184 were places that the *isolating delta debugging* algorithm was allowed to split. Pre-processing the source code using the moiety algorithm we see that out of these 7953 (68%) were plausible splitting points. On average 39% of a single benchmark could not be split without causing a "parse error on input".

In Fig. 1 we can see the number of unresolved outcomes, on the y axis, for each of the 80 type errors in the scalability benchmark listed on the x axis. For the desired outcome we want the bar to be close to zero. For ease of reading we have capped Fig. 1 at a maximum of 170 unresolved results, however it is worth noting that Gramarye19 returned seven results higher than this with modules

---

[12] https://www.haskell.org/cabal/.

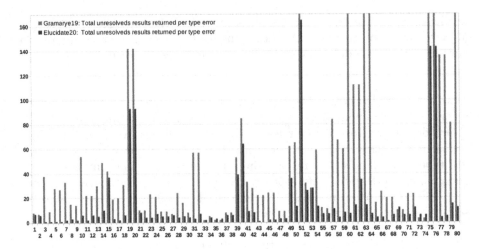

Fig. 1. Unresolved results per introduced type error

51, 60, 63, 64, 75, 76 and 80 returning 265, 395, 1436, 1436, 221, 221, and 504 unresolved results respectively. The highest outcome of unresolveds from Elucidate20 was 165, with its lowest being 0 compared to Gramarye19 with 2.

On average there are 16 unresolved outcomes per type error from Elucidate20 compared to Gramarye19 at 88; meaning a reduction of 72 calls to the blackbox compiler. The importance of reducing calls is seen in benchmark 64 a module with 240 lines of code; here Gramarye19 has 1436 unresolved outcomes and takes just over an hour to run the *isolating delta debugging* algorithm whereas Elucidate20 receives only 7 unresolved results and the time taken drops to just 36 s, a difference of around 52 min.

Elucidate20 has an significant impact, totalling a removal of 5743 unresolved outcomes from the entire benchmark, over Gramarye19. However, though we have seen, with benchmark 64, that the delta debugging Run-Time can be reduced does the Moiety algorithm make a reduction to all of our benchmarks?

5.2   The Run-Time Speeds

Question: Does the pre-processing effect the time taken by Isolating Delta Debugging?

With the unresolved results minimised we hypotheses that the time taken by delta debugging should reduce. In Fig. 2 we show the outcome of just the run-time of delta debugging (excluding pre-processing) in seconds on the y axis, and again each type error on the x axis. As in Sect. 5.1 we have again modified the figure so that we can see the data more clearly by dropping off the most extreme results of Gramarye19 in type errors 60, 63, 64, and 80 who returned run-time results of 1295 s (21 m 35 s), 4299 s (1 h 11 m 39 s), 4201 s (1 h 10 m 1 s), and 1482 s (24 m 42 s) each. The highest result from Elucidate20 is 436 s (7 m 16 s), with the lowest being recorded at 16 s compared to Gramarye19 at 21 s.

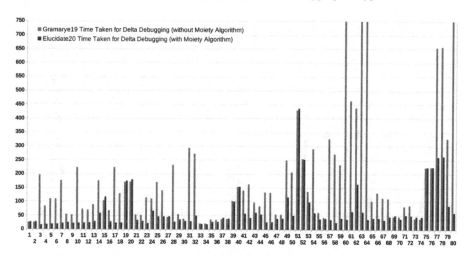

Fig. 2. Delta debugging run-time

On average Gramarye19 took 285 s (4 m 45 s) to run the *isolating delta debugging* algorithm, 219 (3 m 39 s) more than Elucidate20 at 66 (1 m 6 s) showing a clear link between total unresolved outcomes received and the time taken to locate a type error. In total Elucidate20 reduced the time taken by *isolating delta debugging* algorithm for the entire benchmark by 4 h 52 m 8 s.

However, when running a debugger the user experiences the entire process not just the algorithm locating the type errors. Our pre-processing is linear, based on lines of code in the program, and the length equals the amount of calls we need to make to the blackbox compiler. Gramarye19 with its lack of moiety algorithm takes on average 303 (5 m 3 s) compared to Elucidate20 at 419 (6 m 59 s). It is clear to see that when using our moiety algorithm we are around a minute slower than our previous debugger. This issue with pre-processing is down to the calling of the compiler as a blackbox. In the case of the scalability benchmark we are calling the build tool Cabal. As an example, if we take our worst case result, benchmark 79, we can see that we reduce the run-time of the *isolating delta debugging* algorithm from 327 s (5 m 27 s) to 85 s (1 m 25 s), however the user-time is increased from 330 s (5 m 30) to the awful 4888 s (1 h 21 m 28 s). If we look at this benchmark it is 2306 lines of code and every call to Cabal takes around 2 s. If we apply 2 s exactly to every line of code we can see that we get a result of 4612 s (1 h 16 m 52 s) close to our worst case benchmark. However, the pre-processing method does have occasional successes in improving overall debugging time, with Elucidate20 reducing the user-time for some of our benchmarks by over an hour.

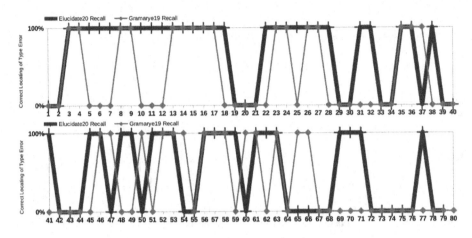

Fig. 3. Recall

5.3 Applying the Framework

In Fig. 3 and Table 6 we present the data from applying the framework to our results. We display the outcome of *recall* in more depth as to mimic other type error debugging evaluations. The two graphs show all 80 modules on the x axis and if the type error they contained were either correctly located (100%) or not (0%) or the y axis.

The framework results table shows the average outcome for all four of our metrics. The higher the percentage the more desirable.

Table 6. Framework results - average

Metric	Gramarye19	Elucidate20
Accuracy	94%	88%
Recall	38%	59%
Precision	16%	14%
F_1 Score	20%	19%

Question: Does applying the new framework quantify the quality of the debugger? Recall shows us if the debugger has returned the correct type error specified. As we only have a single type error per benchmark our result is binary. Elucidate20 correctly locates 59% (47/80) of the type errors compared to Gramarye19 which returns fewer correct type errors at 38% (30/80). This rise in correct results from Elucidate20 is directly linked to the pre-processing of the source code. Firstly, as we are passing a new configuration to delta debugging, setting out how to split our lines, we have the chance to generate an alternative pathway of modifications leading to different results from our Blackbox compiler; as the path that the debugger takes relies on these outcomes an alternative result can happen. Secondly as our method does not allow the splitting of lines outside the moieties we gain the bias of returning a greater set of locations and so increasing our chances of success. As described in Sect. 4 this bias can allow us to return 100 results as suggested locations with an ill-typed program of only 100 lines; we can say that this would not make a suitable solution and so is countered with the precision metric.

In the Table 6 we see that indeed Gramarye19 is more precise than Elucidate20; however overall this only accounts for a difference of 2% points meaning we need to invoke the F_1 score for an accurate reading.

The F_1 score blends our metric results, Recall and Precision, to form a true overview of the results, as already mentioned this is the harmony mean of the two metrics. With this set of benchmarks we receive a 1% difference between the presented debugger Elucidate20 and the previous Gramarye19, with the latter providing a higher F_1 score. This outcome is not surprising; the precision of Elucidate20 is hampered by the moiety algorithm. However, we do not see this as a negative; it was our aim to avoid causing unresolveds and as such these are the most precise result we can currently return for the specific benchmarks utilised in this evaluation. This outcome was also positive evidence that shows the importance of using more than one metric when evaluation debugging solutions, and works well to indicate that many metrics are needed to present the true quality of a type error debugger.

5.4 Summary

Applying the moiety algorithm successfully reduced the number of unresolved outcomes significantly. This in turn reduced the time taken for the *isolating delta debugging* algorithm to run by an average of around 3 min. However, for the actual time the user experiences we must include the pre-processing that moiety provides. In doing so we found that calling the build tool Cabal as our blackbox compiler clearly gave unsatisfying results and that work is needed to reduce the time of each blackbox compiler call. When applying the framework we found that using the de facto recall metric did show improved results for Elucidate20. However, when we added the metrics precision and F_1 score from the framework a more accurate picture was presented with Elucidate20's results being slightly lower than Gramarye19.

In all, we have improved the time taken by *isolating delta debugging*, we have detected further work for reducing the time-taken by calling a Blackbox Compiler, and have shown the need for the framework to quantify the quality of type error debuggers in the future.

6   Related Work

Type Error Debugging research has a long and fruitful history starting in the eighties[25]. It spans many solutions in a variety of categories each specialising on their own core ideas [2,4,5,7,10,13,15,16,20,22,24,30]. However, these solutions rarely contain a through evaluation and when they do it does not attempt to directly evaluate on large programs with type errors. Instead the evaluations aim for success on small programs, typically of the size that first-time programmers would produce. For example from a recent paper *'Learning to blame: localizing novice type errors with data-driven diagnosis'* though the evaluation mentions the usage of both accuracy and recall the authors state; "We acknowledge, of course, that students are not industrial programmers and our results may not translate to large-scale software development..." [17] and in a well-known type error debugging paper *Counter-Factual Typing for Debugging Type Errors* the authors say "...the numbers do not tell much about how the systems would perform in everyday practice." [4]. One general method of debugging that has been applied to a 178,000 line program is Delta Debugging. Defined by Zeller in 1999, delta debugging comes in two forms Simplifying and Isolating and is applied to a general debugging domain rather than specific categories of errors [6,27–29]. In our previous paper we applied Zeller's work specifically to type errors in functional languages employing the compiler as a blackbox [18]. A Blackbox Compiler differs from other Blackbox solutions mentioned in prior literature(Blackbox Type Checkers, Blackbox Type Inference [9,15,23]) as it treats the entire compiler as an external entity rather than a component of it. This method of only taking external cues, such as whether a program is ill or well-typed, avoids users having to patch or download a specific compiler to explicitly improve type error discovery. Though combining a Blackbox Compiler and *isolating delta debugging* to the domain of type errors returned positive results reducing unresolveds was seen to be beneficial future work. One option for reducing the unresolveds was the modification of the delta debugging configuration. Generating Configurations to avoid invalid inputs for delta debugging is not new [11,14]. The closest to our work observes that modifying lines of source code can and will generate broken code that will still need to be sent to the test function causing debugging times to increase [8]. In *Binary Reduction of Dependency Graphs* the authors aim to reduce these invalid inputs by using dependency graphs to map the smallest set of classes that are invalid without each other, reference's to other classes, in Java bytecode. Their dependency analysis is specific for Java and they only use the *simplifying delta debugging* algorithm.

7   Conclusion and Future Work

We presented a method of combining *Isolating Delta Debugging* and a blackbox compiler to locate type errors. Most solutions in type error debugging do not evaluate on large programs, those that have more than 30 lines of code, and so we aimed to target these. However, when applying *isolating delta debugging* to locate type errors in these large programs we can receive outcomes that are unresolved, it can split source code in a way that causes parse errors, that reduce the efficiency. We introduce an algorithm that pre-processes an ill-typed program to eliminate these parse error; in particular 'parse errors on input'. Our pre-processing algorithm, Moiety, presents where in the source code the lines can be split to avoid causing a parse errors. These moieties are then used as a configuration for delta debugging to reduce the unresolveds caused by parse errors, which in turn is linked to the time taken in delta debugging large programs.

To test the success of our solution on locating type errors in large programs we introduced the scalability benchmarks, a set of 80 ill-typed large programs within the real-world program Pandoc, and a framework based on Data Science standards. The evaluation comprised of comparing our original debugger, Gramarye19, that used *isolating delta debugging* to locate type errors and our new debugger, Elucidate20, that also include the pre-processing algorithm moiety. In the first part of the evaluation we saw if a reduction of unresolved results and a decrease in the *isolating delta debugging* algorithms run-time could be achieved. Elucidate20 on average returned 72 fewer unresolveds per benchmark reducing the time taken for *isolating delta debugging* to run by an average of 216 s (3 m 36 s). The best case reduction of time was from over an hour to 7 s, however, the overall time the user experiences was a priority too. Here, with the combination of moiety and *isolating delta debugging*, Elucidate20 did take longer than our previous debugger to locate type errors on average with an increase of 100 s (1 m 40 s), however, when looking at individual benchmarks Elucidate20 did reduce some user-times by more than an hour. In the second part of our evaluation we employed our new suggested framework. We noted that one metric within the framework, recall, is the most commonly used in our domain and showed a positive result for Elucidate20 with a 21% points increase in locating a type error compared to Gramarye19. However, the reason for the framework is to improve the ability to quantify the quality of type error debuggers and when the entire framework is applied it shows that the difference between Elucidate20 and Gramarye19 drops to just 1% point. This significant difference in results shows that just applying the traditional recall metric is not satisfactory for evaluations in this field and the application of the framework on future type error debugging solutions is needed to be able to report clearer results, and comparisons between solutions.

For future work an increase of the categories of parse errors we treat with the pre-processing along with adding other errors such as *Variables not in Scope* is a concrete direction; as the moiety algorithm already works though individual lines adding these will not increase the overheads and has the possibility of reducing the time delta debugging takes further down. It is also clear that though pre-processing speeds up delta debugging it also, on average, slows the overall run-time of the debugger. Reducing the time it takes to generate a list of moieties would be extremely beneficial. We would also want to increase our scalability benchmarks to include more than one core program as this will remove any bias away from how a programmer may specifically layout out their source code. Lastly, though we applied our method to Haskell programs, our debugger is nearly language agnostic. Delta Debugging and the Moiety algorithm are not specific for the programming language, allowing for a reasonable modification towards an agnostic debugger in the future.

Acknowledgements. We would like to thank all of the reviewers for their thorough feedback, which we incorporated into this paper.

References

1. Artho, C.: Iterative delta debugging. STTT - Softw. Tools Technol. Transf. **13**(3), 223–246 (2011). https://doi.org/10.1007/s10009-010-0139-9
2. Bernstein, K.L., Stark, E.W.: Debugging type errors. Technical report, November 1995
3. Chen, S., Erwig, M.: Counter-factual typing for debugging type errors. In: Jagannathan, S., Sewell, P. (eds.) POPL 2014, pp. 583–594. ACM (2014)
4. Chen, S., Erwig, M.: Guided type debugging. In: Codish, M., Sumii, E. (eds.) FLOPS 2014. LNCS, vol. 8475, pp. 35–51. Springer, Cham (2014). https://doi.org/10.1007/978-3-319-07151-0_3
5. Chitil, O.: Compositional explanation of types and algorithmic debugging of type errors. In: Pierce, B.C. (ed.) ICFP 2001, pp. 193–204. ACM (2001)
6. Cleve, H., Zeller, A.: Locating causes of program failures. In: Roman, G., Griswold, W.G., Nuseibeh, B. (eds.) 27th International Conference on Software Engineering, pp. 342–351. ACM (2005)
7. Haack, C., Wells, J.B.: Type error slicing in implicitly typed higher-order languages. Sci. Comput. Program. **50**(1–3), 189–224 (2004)
8. Kalhauge, C.G., Palsberg, J.: Binary reduction of dependency graphs. In: Proceedings of the 2019 27th ACM Joint Meeting on European Software Engineering Conference and Symposium on the Foundations of Software Engineering, pp. 556–566. ACM (2019)
9. Lerner, B.S., Grossman, D., Chambers, C.: Seminal: searching for ML type-error messages. In: Proceedings of the ACM Workshop on ML, pp. 63–73 (2006)
10. McAdam, B.J.: On the unification of substitutions in type inference. In: Hammond, K., Davie, T., Clack, C. (eds.) IFL 1998. LNCS, vol. 1595, pp. 137–152. Springer, Heidelberg (1999). https://doi.org/10.1007/3-540-48515-5_9
11. Misherghi, G., Su, Z.: HDD: hierarchical delta debugging. In: ICSE 2006, pp. 142–151. ACM (2006)
12. Misherghi, G.S., HDD, Z.S.: Hierarchical delta debugging. Ph.D. thesis, University of California, Davis (2007). https://pdfs.semanticscholar.org/a337/e5ba5b18cc45fd4517b90c5ac92e8052b6d3.pdf
13. Rahli, V., Wells, J.B., Pirie, J., Kamareddine, F.: Skalpel: a type error slicer for standard ML. Electron. Notes Theor. Comput. Sci. **312**, 197–213 (2015)
14. Regehr, J., Chen, Y., Cuoq, P., Eide, E., Ellison, C., Yang, X.: Test-case reduction for C compiler bugs. In: PLDI 2012, pp. 335–346. ACM (2012)
15. Schilling, T.: Constraint-free type error slicing. In: Peña, R., Page, R. (eds.) TFP 2011. LNCS, vol. 7193, pp. 1–16. Springer, Heidelberg (2012). https://doi.org/10.1007/978-3-642-32037-8_1
16. Seidel, E.L., Jhala, R., Weimer, W.: Dynamic witnesses for static type errors (or, ill-typed programs usually go wrong). In: ICFP 2016, pp. 228–242. ACM (2016)
17. Seidel, E.L., Sibghat, H., Chaudhuri, K., Weimer, W., Jhala, R.: Learning to blame: Localizing novice type errors with data-driven diagnosis. CoRR abs/1708.07583 (2017). http://arxiv.org/abs/1708.07583
18. Sharrad, J., Chitil, O., Wang, M.: Delta debugging type errors with a blackbox compiler. In: IFL 2018, pp. 13–24. ACM (2018)

19. Shung, K.P.: Accuracy, precision, recall or f1? November 2019. https:// towardsdatascience.com/accuracy-precision-recall-or-f1-331fb37c5cb9
20. Stuckey, P.J., Sulzmann, M., Wazny, J.: Interactive type debugging in Haskell. In: Proceedings of the ACM SIGPLAN Workshop on Haskell, pp. 72–83. ACM (2003)
21. Stuckey, P.J., Sulzmann, M., Wazny, J.: Improving type error diagnosis. In: Nilsson, H. (ed.) Workshop on Haskell 2004, pp. 80–91. ACM (2004). https://doi.org/10. 1145/1017472.1017486
22. Tip, F., Dinesh, T.B.: A slicing-based approach for locating type errors. ACM Trans. Softw. Eng. Methodol. **10**(1), 5–55 (2001)
23. Tsushima, K., Asai, K.: An embedded type debugger. In: Hinze, R. (ed.) IFL 2012. LNCS, vol. 8241, pp. 190–206. Springer, Heidelberg (2013). https://doi.org/ 10.1007/978-3-642-41582-1_12
24. Tsushima, K., Chitil, O.: Enumerating counter-factual type error messages with an existing type checker. In: PPL 2014 (2014)
25. Wand, M.: Finding the source of type errors. In: POPL 1986, pp. 38–43. ACM (1986)
26. Witten, I., Frank, E.: Data Mining: Practical Machine Learning Tools and Techniques. Morgan Kaufmann, Burlington (2005)
27. Zeller, A.: Yesterday, my program worked. Today, it does not. Why? In: Nierstrasz, O., Lemoine, M. (eds.) ESEC/SIGSOFT FSE -1999. LNCS, vol. 1687, pp. 253–267. Springer, Heidelberg (1999). https://doi.org/10.1007/3-540-48166-4_16
28. Zeller, A.: Why Programs Fail Guide to Systematic Debugging, 2nd edn. Academic Press, Cambridge (2009)
29. Zeller, A., Hildebrandt, R.: Simplifying and isolating failure-inducing input. IEEE Trans. Softw. Eng. **28**(2), 183–200 (2002)
30. Zhang, D., Myers, A.C., Vytiniotis, D., Peyton Jones, S.L.: Diagnosing type errors with class. In: Grove, D., Blackburn, S. (eds.) PLDI 2015, pp. 12–21. ACM (2015)

Flexible Formality Practical Experience with Agile Formal Methods

Philipp Kant[1]([✉])⑩, Kevin Hammond[1]⑩, Duncan Coutts[1,2]⑩,
James Chapman[1]⑩, Nicholas Clarke[1,4]⑩, Jared Corduan[1]⑩, Neil Davies[1,3]⑩,
Javier Díaz[1,6]⑩, Matthias Güdemann[1,5]⑩, Wolfgang Jeltsch[1,2]⑩,
Marcin Szamotulski[1]⑩, and Polina Vinogradova[1]⑩

[1] IOHK, Wan Chai, Hong Kong
{philipp.kant,kevin.hammond,duncan.coutts,james.chapman,nicholas.clarke,
jared.corduan,neil.davies,javier.diaz,matthias.gudemann,wolfgang.jeltsch,
marcin.szamotulski,polina.vinogradova}@iohk.io
[2] Well-Typed, London, UK
{duncan,wolfgang}@well-typed.com
[3] PNSol, Stonehouse, UK
neil.davies@pnsol.com
[4] Tweag, Cambridge, UK
nicholas.clarke@tweag.io
[5] University of Applied Sciences Munich, Munich, Germany
matthias.guedemann@hm.edu
[6] Atix Labs, Buenos Aires, Argentina
jdiaz@atixlabs.com

Abstract. Agile software development and Formal Methods are traditionally seen as being in conflict. From an *Agile* perspective, there is
pressure to deliver *quickly*, building vertical prototypes and doing many
iterations/sprints, refining the requirements; from a *Formal Methods* perspective, there is pressure to deliver *correctly* and any change in requirements often necessitates changes in the formal specification and might
even impact all arguments of correctness.

Over the years, the need to "be agile" has become a kind of mantra
in software development management, and there is a prevalent prejudice
that using formal methods was an impediment to being agile. In this
paper, we contribute to the refutation of this stereotype, by providing a
real-world example of using good practices from formal methods and agile
software engineering to deliver software that is simultaneously reliable,
effective, testable, and that can also be iterated and delivered rapidly.
We thus present how a lightweight software engineering methodology,
drawing from appropriate formal methods techniques and providing the
benefits of agile software development, can look like. Our methodology
is informed and motivated by practical experience. We have devised and
adapted it in the light of experience in delivering a large-scale software
system that needs to meet complex real-world requirements: the Cardano
blockchain and its cryptocurrency ada.

The cryptocurrency domain is a rather new application area for which
no clear engineering habit exists, so it is fitting well for agile methods.

© The Author(s) 2020
A. Byrski and J. Hughes (Eds.): TFP 2020, LNCS 12222, pp. 94–120, 2020.
https://doi.org/10.1007/978-3-030-57761-2_5

At the same time, there is a lot of real monetary value at stake, making it a good fit for using formal methods to ensure high quality and correctness. This paper reports on the issues that have been faced and overcome, and provides a number of real-world lessons that can be used to leverage the benefits of both agile and formal methods in other situations.

1   Introduction

There has long been a tension between Software Engineering and Formal Methods. From a *software engineer's* perspective, there is pressure to deliver *quickly*; from a *formal methods* perspective, it is essential to deliver *correctly*. In this paper, we argue that rather than fueling this tension, formal methods not only can, but should, be *fused* with agile software engineering methods. The goal is to promote a *flexible* software engineering methodology that aims to combine the best aspects of both agile and formal methods to deliver properly engineered and correct software solutions quickly and effectively. We illustrate how such a methodology can look like by referring to our experience at IOHK, a company that is using strongly typed and functional programming (specifically Haskell) to deliver a new cryptocurrency.

1.1   Formality Versus Agility

Agile software development [BBvB+01] has, since its inception at the turn of the century, risen to become one of the most prevalent software development methodologies. Agile methodologies are attractive because they promise rapid delivery, and fit normal development approaches. When done well, with a focus on what *needs* to be delivered, rather than what is *easily* delivered, agile techniques allow effort to be focused towards the most important goals, and away from unimportant goals. However, if they are to be used successfully, *discipline is essential* and *management must exercise strong control.*

Agile techniques can appeal to undisciplined developers precisely because they can deflect attention from what *needs* to be done (which is often hard) towards what can *quickly* be done. This allows an *illusion of progress* to be maintained. Management is then happy because they can apparently observe progress, and the software is close to product, or only needs a few more small adaptations; and software developers feel valued because they are producing code that is apparently appreciated, and there are continual exciting challenges that they must overcome. Unfortunately, the software may have little real utility, may be hard to maintain, and may also be unreliable. When this happens, "agile" methods are both costly and ineffective: the precise opposite of the motivation for adopting them.

In contrast, classical formal methods require careful thought and design. It is necessary to first carefully specify a system, then to laboriously translate this into an implementation, and finally to verify the result against some complex and often hard-to-understand semantics. Since a large fraction of the overall time and work is spent on writing specifications, it can be hard to demonstrate progress unless the specifications are accessible to management. Furthermore, changes to the software product require changes in the specification, code, and verification, which can act as a barrier to accepting changes in requirements.

For this reason, commercial product teams can be very wary of adapting formal methods, and startups can feel that they cannot afford the costs. This is a pity, since modern formal methods do not have to suffer from these drawbacks. For example, using executable specifications are a great tool to demonstrate progress, and automated tools like QuickCheck can be used to check correctness of software in a way that is stable against local changes. We hope that by providing our own positive experience, we can help reducing the bad reputation of formal methods being too slow and inflexible for practical things, and ultimately encourage more practitioners to consider using some formal techniques.

1.2   Our Contribution

In this paper, we argue from our own experience that the perceived dichotomy between "being agile" and "being formal" is mostly a consequence of an outdated view on the landscape of formal methods[1], and that using modern formal techniques not only does not contradict the goals of quickly delivering software in the presence of changing requirements, but that they are indeed rather helpful. This paper makes the following contributions:

- We describe the motivation that led to the real-world adoption of formal methods techniques and functional programming technologies within an advanced technology company (IOHK);
- We provide examples of the real-world use of lightweight formal methods and functional programming as part of a large software development process;
- We consider the positive and negative aspects of both formal and agile techniques in the light of experience with both approaches, as well as the gap in left between the methodologies;
- Based on this analysis we outline a *flexible formal* software engineering methodology that provides the most significant benefits of both agile and formal software development;
- We discuss the advantages of functional programming for *flexible formal* software development.

Moreover, there are relatively few reports of real-world experiences of using functional programming technologies as an intrinsic part of large-scale, distributed software development (exceptions include e.g. reports on Erlang). This paper provides another addition to this corpus.

---

[1] In fact, we would go even further and say that the the picture of a waterfall-style development, with a strictly linear succession of gathering requirements, writing specifications, writing code, and proving correctness against the specification, was always more of a caricature of a bad approach than an accurate description of how people were using formal techniques in practice.

2   Cardano: A Proof-of-Stake Cryptocurrency

Cardano (https://www.cardano.org) is a novel decentralised blockchain and cryptocurrency that is being developed by IOHK. cryptocurrencies are distributed systems that contain a public shared transaction *ledger*, which allows participants to track and send funds in a virtual currency. The striking feature is that these systems are permissionless and decentralised, in the sense that anyone can run a node and take part in maintaining the *ledger* without needing to be registered with a central authority.

This poses an immediate problem: since there is no central authority, it is necessary to reach *consensus* on how to progress the construction of the *blockchain*. The consensus algorithm has to be resistant to a malicious actor setting up any number of nodes with the aim of taking over the decision finding process (a so-called *Sybil attack* [Dou02]). Bitcoin [Nak09], the first cryptocurrency, achieves this using a *Proof-of-Work* (PoW) mechanism, where taking part in the consensus requires computational resources that are proportional to the total amount of computational resources in the system. This renders a Sybil attack highly expensive. The cost is in making the whole system ridiculously inefficient: Bitcoin is now at a stage where it consumes as much electrical power as a mid-sized nation state, but can only enter a handful of transactions into its ledger per second. Were it not for the computational cost of the PoW Sybil protection, this could be easily achieved using a single commodity laptop or other small device.

In contrast, Cardano uses an alternative *Proof-of-Stake* mechanism (PoS). Under PoS, the price of participating in the consensus algorithm is not paid in computational power, but instead by having to own some of the virtual currency in the system. The larger your share of the total funds (the higher your stake), the greater is the probability of your being elected as the leader in the next consensus round.

While PoS has many advantages over PoW – it is ecologically sustainable, and automatically incentivises powerful parties in the consensus to behave honestly (since large stakeholders have a lot to lose if the system is found to be manipulated) – it is hard to get right. For this reason, IOHK committed itself to base Cardano on a solid foundation of original peer-reviewed research, and to using formal methods in the development process.

There are already a lot of moving parts to the Cardano cryptocurrency system. In time, it will additionally become a smart contracts platform, running the languages Plutus[2] and Marlowe [LST18], which have been specifically designed to be used on Cardano.

3   Formal and Agile Development of Cardano

While IOHK has always been devoted to getting things right, building upon sound academic research and robust, reliable engineering, the company is also aware of commercial realities, such as the importance of *time-to-market* in a

---

[2] https://github.com/input-output-hk/plutus.

relatively young and quickly evolving sector. For this reason, it set out on a two-pronged approach for Cardano: a team A of energetic developers would quickly develop, in an Agile manner, a Minimal Viable Product (MVP) to release to market. Meanwhile, a second team B would aim for a high-assurance version, using formal methods, that would, once ready, replace the first implementation. Team A would deliver swiftly, and Team B would use the experience from having a working system in production to guide their design and development. Both implementations were done in Haskell.

Some time after releasing the MVP, it became clear that maintaining it and adding new features was much harder than anticipated. The organically grown code, which had been developed under time pressure in an agile style, lacked a proper separation of concerns or good documentation of the design. This resulted in poor testability and extensibility for the codebase. Crucially, the implementation of some key features (namely, a proper system for stake delegation) had been delayed until the very end, and by that time, design choices that had been made while implementing other, simpler, functionality, had made that task more complicated than it would have needed to be. As a consequence, estimated development times for the missing features, as well as for future features, were much longer than they needed to be.

At the same time, team B had achieved a first success, in successfully implementing a wallet[3] for Cardano based on a semi-formal specification. A decision was thus made to pivot, cutting back development effort on the existing implementation to a bare minimum. Team B would scale up and accelerate their efforts, and the next features on the roadmap would be implemented exclusively in the follow-on to the MVP. At this point, Team B faced a number of challenges:

- Since team A was no longer adding new features, they had to accelerate their pace in order to quickly get to a point where the new implementation could be used to deliver new features.
- Compromising on the quality and robustness, or future maintenance costs, was not an option; Cardano has to safely manage and secure large-scale financial transactions, and needs to be fit for that purpose.
- They had to ensure backwards compatibility with the already released code. The lack of good documentation meant that they had to write a specification based on the existing code. Writing specifications and code adhering to them is like time travel, in that one direction is significantly easier than the other.
- As the research and design for the new features were still somewhat in flux, they would need to be flexible to adjust to changing requirements.

To overcome those challenges, the team chose a pragmatic approach – with a well-dosed, non-dogmatic use of *lightweight* formal methods, and a focus on rapid delivery – that we will describe in this paper.

---

[3] A cryptocurrency wallet is a piece of software that allows users to track their balance in the system and submit transactions.

4   "Flexible Formal Development": A Fusion of Formal Methods and Agile Software Engineering

Both agile software development and formal methods aim at helping their practitioners to become "better" at producing software, but they focus on different aspects: agile is all about speed and flexibility; formal methods is all about correctness and method. This is not helped by the number of books, papers and experts that promote specific methods (whether formal or agile) as a complete solution. Examples include Agile Scrum Methodology [SB01]; Lean Software Development [PP03]; Kanban [Bre15]; Extreme Programming (XP) [Bec00]; Feature Driven Development (FDD) [PF01]; Model Checking [CGP99]; Abstract Interpretation [CC77]; Type-Driven Development [Bra16] etc. In this section, we will explore the broad differences, similarities, and potential synergies between formal and agile approaches and aim to understand how their fusion can ensure software that is both high-assurance and reasonably time- and cost-effective to produce.

4.1   What Do We Need?

Fundamentally, software development needs are quite simple. In general, we need to produce software that does what it is supposed to do; is produced quickly; costs no more to produce than is necessary; can be easily maintained, at reasonable cost; and doesn't require expensive support. Other issues are generally secondary or specific to particular domains (e.g. telecommunications applications may have real-time constraints, aerospace applications may have overriding safety concerns, autonomous vehicles may have regulatory concerns, etc). The basic criteria for a successful methodology which is shared by many software development domains is presented in Table 1.

Table 1. Criteria for software engineering methodologies, along with stereotypical expectations of whether agile or formal methodologies satisfy them. This is to be taken with a grain of salt, as there is a large variety of both agile and formal techniques.

Issue	Agile	Formal
Identify the requirements for the software	Y?	Y
Ensure that the software meets these requirements	Y?	Y
Provide usable prototypes rapidly	Y	Y?
Minimise the costs of development	Y?	N?
Ensure that code is high quality	N	Y
Ensure that software is easy to use	N	N
Ensure that changes can be made easily	Y	N
Be easily applied without extensive training	N	N

The details of this table can be argued, of course, mainly because there are many different agile techniques and many different formal methods. Different development teams may also have different levels of experience and be more or less familiar with specific techniques and technologies. They will also have different competencies in terms of e.g. mathematical backgrounds or training in specific development techniques. Effective deployment of either technology, however, needs extensive specific training and practice. We will consider each of the issues from the table in detail, considering how well they are met by agile and formal development techniques.

Identify Requirements. Here, the key issue is to have a strong product vision. Ideally, there should be a dialogue between the *product manager* and the *software developers.* **Agile** developers should then interact with the *product manager* to deliver the capabilities in the software that is needed, and the *product manager* should adapt the capability requirements of the product to make it easier to implement/maintain, without compromising on essential features. In practice, there may be no distinct *product manager*, meaning that the *development team* acts as the designers. This can create a number of problems, including failure to deliver a successful product, repeated non-converging iterations, missing essential features, and included non-essential features. Requirements gathering and design is done on the fly. Because it is easy to change requirements, the software design and implementation will frequently change direction. The final solution will then have no clear design pathway. **Formal methods techniques** on the other hand often require detailed and careful analysis of alternatives, followed by months of painstaking work to laboriously craft out possible solutions, prove that they are sound with respect to some formal model or semantics, and then to verify that the software matches those requirements. Even small changes may require major alterations to the formal specification, and significant effort to re-prove, re-verify and then re-implement the software. In this approach, it is therefore essential for the product owner to be involved in the requirements analysis and problem specification. Unfortunately, they will often lack the technical/mathematical knowledge to be able to understand the implications of the design decision.

Meet Requirements. Since **formal methods** use mathematical techniques to specify requirements, provided that they are properly captured and the process is followed correctly, then the software will always meet these requirements. This is a major strength of a formal approach. When using **agile methods**, on the other hand, the *product owner* – and also users, where early delivery is used – can easily see the current version of the software, identify any mistakes or misunderstandings and feed corrections into the development process.

Provide Prototypes. Good **agile methods** will always ensure that a prototype is available. By using *continuous integration* and *continuous testing*, a non-breaking version will always be available for deployment. Non-breaking means, of course, that the code will compile and that none of the tests have failed, not that the code works perfectly. However, it is easy to observe change, and therefore to measure (real or apparent) progress. Some **formal methods** also allow the production of prototypes. For example, where a modelling approach is used, an *executable specification* might be produced, or where a *refinement process* is used, then successive refinements will produce gradually more detailed prototypes. However, this is not a feature of all formal methods techniques. Because it is usually necessary to formally prove software correctness, there may be long periods when no new software versions are produced. Since there is no observable change, it is difficult to measure progress during such periods.

Minimise Development Cost. A key goal of **agile** (especially *lean*) software development is to minimise software costs by producing precisely the minimal product that is required, and by focusing attention on the most important features. By avoiding implementing unnecessary features or by delaying less useful features, the software can be brought to market more quickly, and at an adequate cost. In practice, achieving this requires strong discipline. It is easy to focus attention instead on short-term, but less important bug fixes, on easy-to-implement features, or on features that are nice-to-have. While daily "stand-up" meetings allow good team communication, they need to be properly organised if a priority task list is to be produced and followed. By using *continuous testing*, software is not accepted that does not pass regression tests, so fewer bugs will enter the code base. However, this same process can also act as a barrier to major change – completely new tests will then be necessary. In contrast, reducing development cost is not usually a major goal of **formal methods** development. If correctness is paramount, then spending effort to ensure correctness is always the right thing to do. Although there has been major progress in e.g. automated proof assistants and model checking, most formal methods tooling is not well integrated into the usual software development process.

Ensure High Quality. The primary aim of **formal methods** is to produce very high quality, high reliability, high assurance software. This is, however, rarely an explicit goal of **agile methods**.

Maximise Ease of Use. Ease of use is not a primary goal for either agile software development or when using formal methods. Rather, it must be layered as an additional concern.

Enable Change. Software is notoriously hard to change. While **agile methods** allow design changes to be incorporated during development, as discussed above, they do not encourage major design changes: any significant change will break not only the existing code, but also testing, documentation, etc. Similarly, traditional **formal methods** do not provide any assistance with major design changes. While small changes can usually be incorporated without major work, large changes will often require significant and laborious specification, verification, proof or other work. In both cases, it is often easier to start with a blank canvas and produce a completely new design. This can also be cheaper and quicker than adapting an existing design. However, it means that significant effort has been wasted.

Do Not Require Extensive Training. There is a major software skills shortage. As evidenced by e.g. salary levels, good software developers are rare and in high demand. It is not cost effective to require them to learn to use new tools and techniques on a regular basis. While they may be highly effective once mastered, mathematical techniques may also require extensive study and practice, which is also costly. Unfortunately, much of the available tooling to support **both agile software development and formal methods** is special-purpose and requires extensive time to learn to use effectively. This creates stickiness: better tooling is not used because it takes time to learn to use (or sometimes, especially in smaller companies, because it costs money). It also means that few people have experience with both kinds of tools or the expertise to move easily between them.

Our Goal: Flexible Formal Software Engineering. Based on the analysis above, we argue for a *flexible formal* approach. Our goal is to combine the best elements of agile and formal software engineering so that we can produce software that meets all of the criteria above. In particular, it should be high quality, quick and cost effective to produce, easy to change, clearly meet the requirements and not require extensive training to develop. This is naturally highly ambitious, and in this paper we will only be able to report on the initial steps that we have taken. However, it is important that the software development community does not simply settle for the *status quo* but strives to achieve these goals. In this way, we will be able to deliver software that is better, less costly, and easier to adapt both *by design* and *by construction*. Modern functional programming is key to helping us achieve this.

5   Key Messages and Lessons

5.1   Approach(es) Taken at IOHK

When rebuilding Cardano, we separated concerns into layers, as is common when dealing with larger projects. This allowed us to parallelise work, test things in isolation, and will allow us to swap out individual components when needed, to produce customised variants. It turns out that there is sufficient difference in nature between the components to make each amenable to a different approach in designing and implementing them. In the following, we will briefly describe each layer, and explain the methodology chosen for each, and why.

Ledger Layer. The ledger layer contains the main logic of the cryptocurrency. It is where all the data is kept, and has to ensure that users' balances are recorded correctly, that money can not be arbitrarily created or destroyed, that no one can spend funds they do not own (or spend their funds twice), etc. Correctness of the ledger is thus of utmost importance to the integrity of the system.

The Cardano ledger is of moderate complexity. It does not have to deal with any concurrency issues – those are contained in the consensus and networking layers – but it is more than just a simple book-keeping device. In addition to listing and ordering transactions, and keeping balances, it has to also keep track of state that is important for the operation of the system itself. Parameters of operation (such as the frequency with which new blocks[4] are created) can be adjusted during operation, by announcing the new value on the ledger. Similarly, new versions of the software itself can be announced via an update mechanism. Another aspect of the ledger is *delegation*: while every stakeholder has the *right* to participate in the consensus algorithm, it is unlikely that each and every user of the system would want to continuously run and maintain a node in the system. In Cardano, users can chose to delegate their stake to people who do run a node, forming a *stake pool*. Rewards that the system pays out for maintaining consensus are automatically shared between operators and participants of such pools.

All of this lead to a rather voluminous design; the informal document describing the mechanisms of delegation and incentives alone [SL-D1] runs at roughly 60 pages, and builds upon two papers of original research conducted for Cardano [KKL18, BKKS18]. While none of the individual parts are rocket science, they can interact in subtle ways. Since the ledger is where the value is being held, correctness has to be on the top of the list of priorities of the development methodology chosen. However, we also needed a flexible approach: commercial reality required us to start work on the implementation before the design and research of the whole ledger was truly finished, so choosing an approach where small changes in the design would require massive amounts of work to be done had to be ruled out.

We decided to simplify the ledger design by defering all stateful operations – in particular data storage and issues related to eventual consistency – to the consensus layer. This allows us to express the whole ledger logic in a purely functional way, in terms of a set of valid state transitions and transition rules. The approach we followed in defining operational semantics is called *small-step semantics* (see [FM-TR-2018-01]). We can use these operational semantics to define valid state transitions in a deterministic way, e.g. what sequences of transactions forms a valid ledger. We will not discuss here the language and rules itself, but instead summarize the principles we follow in constructing rules and types with this approach:

– There should always be a unique way to represent every state transition as a sequence of these "small steps". E.g., to apply a block, the sequence of intermediate states must contain each of the states resulting from applying every transaction in the block individually to the ledger ledger state resulting from preceding.

---

[4] Cryptocurrencies are built on a data structure called blockchain, which are essentially linked lists, where each block contains a page of a transaction ledger.

– There should not be any partial state transition rules or unnecessary data dependencies between state transitions. E.g., we do not want to make separate state transition rules for processing the inputs and the outputs of a transaction.

The first principle requires us to define rules with high granularity, so that we don't miss any intermediate steps. The second principle discourages us from having unnecessary intermediate steps, during which some invariants we expect from the system may not hold.

We call the transition types, together with the transition rules we defined in this way, a *semi-formal* specification, since it is formal, but not machine checked. Translating this specification into valid Haskell code is straightforward and mostly mechanical: every transition rule corresponds to a pure Haskell function, with some pre- and postconditions. This gives us an *executable* specification.

This is a very powerful tool: the typechecker is very good at finding subtle self-consistency errors. Since it is executable, this specification can serve as a prototype and demonstrate tangible progress to stakeholders. You can also start running tests with the executable specification. Lastly, it can either serve as a basis for developing a production implementation through a series of refinement steps, or as a testing oracle for the production implementation (we chose the former here).

We did not, initially, produce any proofs about the emergent properties of the ledger (such as conservation of value, delegating stake properly modifying the stake of a pool, etc.). Instead, we got reasonable confidence by having the executable specification pass the type checker (we got the plumbing right), and by writing the desired properties as QuickCheck properties. Not performing proofs at this stage allowed us to move quickly, and react to changes in the design. Having the type checker and QuickCheck properties allowed us to do so with confidence that the changes were not breaking parts of the system. In that way, the approach combines elements from formal methods and agile practices like test-driven development. As things became more stable, we also started proving a subset of the properties, most of them in a traditional, pen and paper style, and some also formally in Isabelle.

This approach requires two techniques that are not stock items in the repertoire of software engineers: formal specifications, and efficient use of property based testing[5]. We organised a one-week intensive on-site training course in those techniques for our engineers to make up for that, run by Well-Typed, QuviQ, and the IOHK education department. The course was very well-received, and our engineers report that programming from executable specifications was a very pleasant experience.

---

[5] While the use of property based testing has surged in recent years, with QuickCheck clones available in most languages, experience in *efficient* use, including writing good generators and shrinkers, is not common.

Here is a list of the things that we found worked well, or not so well:

+ The language of transition rules in a small-step operational semantics formed a lingua franca to talk about the ledger within the company. While it might look intimidating when unfamiliar, we found that after a little bit of introduction to the framework, we could use it to communicate not only with engineers, but also other stakeholders within the company (researchers, product management, and the CEO). Subtle questions from the researchers were easier to answer by looking at the formal spec than by looking at code. Additionally, we received a lot of very helpful feedback from our auditors, concerning details in the specification.

+ The simple mathematical style of the small-step operational semantics translated extremely well to Haskell. Comparing the two specs side-by-side is very easy to do, therefore strengthening our trust in the translation from paper to machine.

+ In most cases, small-step semantics combined nicely with agile methodology. Adhering to the two principles we stated above encouraged us to maintain the right granularity in our rule definitions. That is, in response to a requirement change, the scope of the type-level changes and associated semantic rule changes was often contained to a single transition type and an (often singular) relevant rule, or at least easily traceable over several rules. Because of this, implementing incremental local changes could be done in a rather a non-disruptive and tractable way. Note, however, that even with this approach, not all small local changes can be made to be non-breaking.

+ Flexibility with confidence, through the type-checker and QuickCheck.

+ Extensibility: even before the first version of the ledger was finished, we had one team member work on integrating the next feature, integration of the smart contract language Plutus, on the level of the specification. This required adding some new types, some new transition rules, and modifications to a few existing rules. We expect a massive reduction in lead times for future features.

+ The formal spec made the job of estimating the work required to implement new features much easier than it would have been with code alone: the spec provided a view on the system that had enough detail to see which parts would have to be changed in order to implement a new feature, while still being concise enough to quickly analyse the impact on the whole system. Similarly, when integration issues made us consider the impact of refactoring, the formal spec was valuable for choosing the path forward.

− We had to keep two versions of essentially the same document − the semi-formal and executable specification − in sync. Performing formal proofs in Isabelle required yet another version of the same specification. Ideally, we would like to derive all of those documents from one single source. While there are some tools available (such as lhs2tex[6], Ott [SZNO+10], and Lem [OBZNS11, MOG+14]), we chose to do this manually on the first project, for pragmatic reasons: we did not have enough time to research the existing tools sufficiently to convince ourselves that we would not run into limitations

---

[6] http://hackage.haskell.org/package/lhs2tex.

along the way. We intend to improve this, by evaluating existing tools, and possibly modifying one, or even writing our own.

Consensus Layer. The consensus layer determines who is allowed to produce a block at which point in time. It is based upon Ouroboros [KRDO17], the first provably secure PoS protocol, and variants [DGKR17, BGK+18]. Ouroboros guarantees – as long as more than half of the participants (weighted by their stake) behave according to the protocol – that transactions submitted to the network will be included in the ledger, and that the ledger stabilises, so that transactions can not be dropped after they have been in the ledger for a certain amount of time. Having those guarantees for Cardano requires a faithful implementation of the consensus protocol.

Unavoidably, the consensus protocol inherently involves concurrency, which is notoriously hard to get correctness guarantees about. While we do want to ultimately get a high-assurance implementation of Ouroboros, we decided that going for that right away was too risky in terms of development time.

So again, we chose an approach of two development streams, with different speeds and levels of formality. But we took a lesson from the past, and asked very experienced and disciplined engineers to do the initial implementation. They would produce code that was well documented, designed with testability in mind, modular, and solid. They would use prototyping to make informed design decisions. Rigorous code review, direct communication with the Ouroboros authors, and extensive property based testing would ensure that the resulting code was of high quality. Extensive use of polymorphism and Haskell type classes was essential in achieving a flexible and testable design (more on that in *Integration* below).

To eventually get the extra bit of assurance that comes with a formal model and proofs, a second group of people is following their traces, and is modelling the resulting design formally in Isabelle, using a process calculus. They should then be able to provide machine-checked proofs about the correctness of aspects of the implementation, or providing a basis for re-implementing parts of the consensus to build on the fully formal core. As a first step towards this goal, we have developed a custom process calculus [Jel19] and proved some properties relating message relaying and broadcast based on it.

The advantage of our approach is that we do not have to make an up-front decision about the final level of formality, but can defer this decision to a point where we have a better understanding of the complexity of the endeavour. The code that we do have is robust enough stay in production for the lifetime of the system. Every step that we go on the formal side increases our confidence in the design, and thus is not wasted, regardless of whether we will go to an actual implementation derived from the formal model. We achieve this incremental confidence by first performing proofs about the *design* that we followed in the implementation. Those are relevant for the implementation even if the code is not derived from the formal model underlying the proofs. The next step is modelling the actual implementation formally and proving more elaborate global properties. This is still much less work than an implementation based on a formal model, since we can abstract over many details (in particular, interactions with other layers). The option of ultimately replacing the implementation with code that builds upon the formal model is still open, but even if we decide not to do that, the confidence we gained during the previous steps is not lost.

For instance, one of the proofs that we did concerns the way that chains of blocks are distributed amongst nodes in the system. In the research paper, there is an abstract and perfect notion of a network where every node can broadcast their chain to every other node, and then each node will pick the "best" one according to certain rules. The proofs of the security of the protocol assume this perfect broadcast, but it is not feasible to directly implement this in a real world system; for one, nodes will already agree on a long prefix of the correct chain, so they should only interchange the latest blocks. Also, in a large network, the abstract broadcast will be implemented in terms of communications of each node with a limited number of peers. We have been able to prove that our design for relaying blocks through the network is a refinement of the abstract whole chain broadcast functionality in the paper.

Networking Layer. A PoS blockchain cryptocurrency like Cardano is very demanding on the networking side. Ouroboros divides time into discrete slots, and elects slot leaders for the consensus in a pseudorandom manner. For this to work, the next block in the blockchain has to traverse the network from one elected leader to the next leader within the available time, and it must do so successfully in the vast majority of cases. This places a hard real-time constraint on the networking layer. At the same time, the network should be decentralised and permissionless, allowing anyone to join the network. Not only is this in tension with ensuring performance, it also increases the attack surface. Nodes in the system must interact with other potentially adversarial nodes, and the design of this interaction has to enable honest nodes to avoid asymmetric resource attacks, which is not simple in PoS designs[7].

The networking design for Cardano consists of nodes engaging in one-to-one protocols. To reduce complexity, this communication is divided into separate concurrent "mini-protocols", each with a narrow focus[8]. The protocols are designed to ensure that honest nodes can work in bounded resources; they all use consumer-driven control flow for example. The construction of the peer-to-peer network aims to ensure rapid dispersion of information across the network,

---

[7] In PoW systems, there is a distinct computational cost advantage for the honest nodes, in that validating a block is very cheap (just hashing the block) but producing a block requires an enormous amount of computational work by an adversary. In PoS, the computational costs are much more finely balanced and the validation checks require the full ledger state, and thus a closer coupling of the networking layer with the rest of the application.

[8] For efficiency and to aid with network resource management complexity, we use multiplexing to just use one network connection for all protocols between a pair of nodes.

and limiting an attacker's ability to spam the network, or slow down the network by intentionally delaying replies. We used simulations to verify that our peer selection algorithm, which takes decisions locally, leads to suitable network topologies globally. The peer selection takes into account both the number of hops to disperse information and the network distance of each hop, relying on local measurements of the network distance to available peers in the ΔQ framework [Ree03, DHT99b, LGPC+16, DHT99a, DHST99].

Networking protocols are hard to get right. Reducing complexity by having dedicated mini-protocols for specific tasks was already very helpful, but we also wanted to reason formally about those protocols. To do that, we used *session types*, modeling the communication between two nodes as state machines. We intentionally restricted the admissible communication patterns, so that in each state, one of the nodes could send a message, and the other had to expect and handle any message by the other node. That restriction ensures that there can be no deadlocks (since it there is no state in which both nodes are expecting a message), and also no race conditions (since there is no state where two nodes send messages at the same time). And those powerful guarantees do not have to be proven manually, but are enforced by the Haskell type checker!

Both the network and consensus layers make significant use of concurrency which is notoriously hard to get right and to test. We use Software Transactional Memory (STM) to manage the internal state of a node. While STM makes it much easier to write correct concurrent code, it is of course still possible to get wrong, which leads to intermittent failures that are hard to reproduce and debug.

In order to reliably test our code for such concurrency bugs, we wrote a simulator that can execute the concurrent code with both timing determinism and giving global observability, producing execution traces. This enables us to write property tests that can use the execution traces, and to run the tests in a deterministic way so that any failures are always reproducible.

The use of the mini-protocol design pattern, the encoding of protocol interactions in session types, and the use of a timing reproducible simulation, has yielded several advantages:

+ Adding new protocols (for new functionality) with strong assurance that they will not interact adversly with existing functionality and/or performance consistency.
+ Consistent approaches (re-usable design approaches) to issues of latency hiding, intra mini-protocol flow control and timeouts/progress criteria.
+ Performance consistent protocol layer abstraction/substitution: construct real world realistic timing for operation without complexity of simulating all the underlying layer protocol complexity. This helps designs/development to maintain performance target awareness during development.
+ Consistent error propagation and mitigation (mini protocols to a peer live/die together) removing issues of resource lifetime management away from mini-protocol designers/implementors.

Integration. Having broken the design into components allowed us to parallelise work, which was crucial to reduce development time. Unless done carefully, however, this can lead to a situation where after each component is finished and working in isolation, integration of the components becomes unexpectedly painful and time intensive.

A common way to avoid that situation is to fix, up front, the interfaces between the components, and ensure that every team works against those unyielding interfaces. But this goes against our goal of flexibility: during the design and development process, we might discover that the interfaces we put in place were not ideal, forcing one or more team to work around those imperfections, making their component(s) clunkier, and the whole system more brittle and inefficient than necessary. Conversely, a laissez-faire attitude to the interfaces is asking for trouble during the integration phase. But we can find a middle ground.

For us, the key to avoiding problems with late integration was to perform large parts of the integration at a very early stage, before any of the components was actually finished.

For the consensus/ledger integration, our design puts the consensus in control. It will access functions provided by the ledger layer for things like transaction validation, evolving the ledger state, or querying the distribution of stake between actors in the system (which is relevant for the consensus itself in a PoS system). To achieve an early integration, the consensus layer is developed against a Haskell type class representing an arbitrary ledger, that provides exactly the functions that consensus needs. The result is a consensus implementation that is polymorphic in the ledger.

When we noticed during development that we needed to change that type class, the team was free to do so – after talking to the ledger team to ensure that there would be nothing preventing writing an instance of the new type class for the real ledger.

The benefits of this approach go well beyond avoiding integration pains, though. Being able to swap components proved to be very useful for running demos, and for testing. The ability to demonstrate continuous progress to stakeholders is a key goal emphasised by agile techniques. Performing demo sessions where we could show working code in different stages of readiness – from a mock implementation, to an executable specification/prototype, through refinements of these, up to the final production code – let us achieve this goal.

We used the same technique to improve the testability of our code. Not only could we run tests for the consensus layer before the ledger was ready, by using a mock ledger. We also wrote a mock implementation for the cryptography layer, that would not perform cryptographic signatures, for testing purposes. Not only are tests using the mock cryptographic layer faster and produce test output that is easier to analyse; it also simplified the process of generating and shrinking test cases in property based testing.

To test resilience of the storage layer against file corruption, we wrote a mock implementation that would simulate a file system. Not only did that allow us to run those tests consistently and reproducibly, it also allowed us to increase the frequency of file system errors during tests, to find bugs during testing that would occur only after years of running in production otherwise.

Finally, being polymorphic in the ledger allows IOHK to reuse the codebase for other blockchain-based products.

+ Avoids both late integration pains and the inflexibility that comes with setting interfaces in stone up front.
+ Better testability: tests can be performed independently of other components. That allows us to run them before those components are ready, can make tests run faster, and test output easier to understand.
+ Continuously assessing progress: we could run an early demo session using mock components, use an executable specification (that would already have the real logic, but might not be efficient, not feature persistence, etc) in another demo, and plug in the production implementation when ready.
+ Facilitates code reuse in other projects.

Upcoming Features: Smart Contracts Languages Plutus and Marlowe. In IOHKs forthcoming smart contract offering Plutus, formal methods have been involved from the outset. Aspects of the design have been prototyped first in Agda before implementation in Haskell [PJGK+19]. This is because the Agda type system and its interactive programming environment provide greater assistance to the programmer that help speed up development on certain tasks. Building on the methodology described in this paper, Plutus Core (the compilation target for the Plutus language) has an executable specification written in Agda [CKNW19]. Plutus is a general purpose language for designing smart contracts that is closely related to Haskell. It is complemented by the Marlowe [LST18] language, a domain specific language specifically targetted at financial smart contracts. In Marlowe, formal methods also play a crucial role; Marlowe programmers can use builtin support for static analysis when programming [IOH]. This functionality makes use of the Z3 SMT solver [DMB08].

5.2   Lessons

We have learned several lessons from our experience.

Lesson 1: Flexibility. One key lesson is about flexibility. By adopting an agile mentality and by using *suitably lightweight* formal methods – most notably, executable specifications in a functional language with a strong type system, and property based testing via QuickCheck, we have been able to quickly and effectively incorporate design changes, even at a late stage in the implementation process, without either breaking code or restarting the development process. Using the type system to bank the consensus between teams - type classes being especially useful in this respect - proved to be an efficient technique for retaining flexibility in a large scale project.

Lesson 2: Communication. A second major lesson that we have learned is about communication. Agile methods are effective partly because they are designed to ensure good internal communication within a team (this may break down in practice, of course), but also, less obviously, because they naturally improve external communication. Agile methods are effective precisely because the results of the development process are visible externally: there should always be a workable fallback once the MVP is produced, and it is easy to evaluate the differences between the current status of the product and what is wanted/needed (the feature list).

In contrast, not all formal methods are suitable for continuously communicating progress. Formal methods development may suffer from a lack of transparency for several reasons. The dense and difficult to parse (for a human) proofs and specifications result, internally, in uncertainty about the amount of effort required to bring them to completion. This is reflected in external communication as well, as it is more difficult to communicate the current state of the formalization to those without a formal methods background.

By enforcing better communication (both internal and external), including by providing regular measurable results, it is possible to bring software projects to a quicker, more successful conclusion, without compromising on software quality. We found prototypes and demonstrations, based on executable specifications, and a refinement approach to development, to be very helpful here.

Lesson 3: No "Big Bang". A third, related, lesson is about iteration. Rather than saving results until a formal process is finished, it is important to share intermediate results, even if they are not fully worked out. This has the key benefit of demonstrating progress, but also has the advantage that it is possible to obtain constructive feedback, that can then be incorporated into new designs and implementations. Sometimes, this reveals that some planned work is not actually necessary, or that some part of the design or implementation can be eliminated, because it is no longer required, or of reduced interest. This is, of course, part of a good agile approach. Refinement-based or gradual approaches, where abstractions are made increasingly concrete, can be highly effective. An advantage is that refinement can be stopped and restarted at any point. By connecting the formal refinement process with software equivalents, high assurance prototypes or demonstrators can be produced, with details left to be implemented at a later date.

Lesson 4: Ensure Consistency. A fourth lesson relates to testing and verification. By using a formal approach, it is easy to demonstrate consistency between the design and the implementation. Formal properties can be derived, either manually or directly from a specification, that can then be used as part of a methodical property-based testing approach, e.g. QuickCheck [CH00] or Hedgehog (https://hackage.haskell.org/package/hedgehog). At IOHK, we manually translated the required formal properties into property-based tests. The same properties can be used to support formal proofs, to drive a model checker or some other formal verification technique. It is not necessary to use multiple techniques to verify the same property, but this can give higher assurance. For example, a property can be manually proved to be sound, an automated proof can be produced based on this, and assertions can be introduced into the code. Since properties are derived systematically from the specification, effort can be focused on the most important issues.

Lesson 5: Maintain Progress. A final lesson relates to diversion of effort. By maintaining focus on the end goal of the software development process, as required by good agile development methodologies, we can avoid diverting effort to short-term fixes that have no long-term benefit. For example, by prioritising the properties that need to be proved or tested, we can avoid wasting effort and so maintain progress towards the most important goals.

5.3   Flexible Formal Software Engineering

Our flexible software engineering methodology is made of up the following essential activities which together comprise a full development cycle. These may apply at different levels of the classical software lifecycle (requirements, design, implementation, testing, deployment etc.).

Gather Informal Requirements. Start with a good understanding of the problem, and describe the solution in an informal but unambiguous way. Note however, that it is not always the case that *all* requirements can be captured beforehand. It is permissible to add requirements iteratively (see *Iterate* and *Redesign* below).

Isolate and Abstract. Consider how the functionality can be made modular. Divide the problem into non-overlapping but interacting parts, figure out what is required from each of them.

Generate Semi-Formal Specification. For each component, develop the informal requirements into a semi-formal specification with an appropriate choice of denotational or operational semantics.

Identify Properties. Identify important properties that the software should have. State these precisely and formally. Prove the most important properties. Other properties can be used either as the basis for formal verification, for property-based testing, or for normal unit testing etc.

Build the Executable Specification. Produce an executable specification. By writing our implementation in Haskell, it was possible to maintain a high degree of consistency between the design and implementation.

Iterate. Work iteratively. Refine the system design to add more detail, verifying that these details do not violate the required properties. By using an executable specification approach, it is possible to ensure that a working prototype is always available.

Redesign. Maintain design flexibility. Use suitable levels of abstraction (e.g. in Haskell, type classes or polymorphic types), so that alternative implementations can be produced. Feed new or changing requirements into the design and implementation process.

Prove, Test and Verify. Apply the right technology (manual and automated proof, automated testing, etc.) to obtain the required assurances in the correct operation of the software.

Communicate. Hold regular meetings to discuss progress, focus design and implementation effort, discuss technical issues, and ensure that the team is aware of each other's activities. Encourage all team members to express concerns, suggest ideas, or to ask for technical help. Hold regular detailed technical seminars to discuss new techniques or to investigate specific issues in detail. Make sure that results are communicated throughout the organisation (it may be necessary to use different techniques for this – senior management is unlikely to read detailed soundness proofs, for example) and that input is taken.

By combining the best features of both agile and formal software development, we can obtain significant advantages over either approach used independently. Functional programming technology is, of course, critical to achieving this. Functional programming naturally supports many lightweight formal methods, including advanced type mechanisms such as dependent types, session types etc. Higher-order functions provide excellent abstraction mechanisms, and enable flexible design and implementation. Formal proofs are much easier to relate to implementations in a functional style. High levels of abstraction mean that it is easy to maintain consistency between the design and implementation. Properties are easy to relate to software, and there are good property-based testing systems. Software is concise, can often be executed interactively, prototypes can easily be produced and demonstrated. Effects can be isolated and contained using well-understood structuring mechanisms. The semantic gap between specification and implementation languages is typically much smaller when using functional languages.

Issue	Agile	Formal	Flexible
Identify the requirements for the software	Y?	Y	**Y**
Ensure that the software meets these requirements	Y?	Y	**Y**
Provide usable prototypes rapidly	Y	Y?	**Y**
Minimise the costs of development	Y?	N?	**Y**
Ensure that code is high quality	N	Y	**Y**
Ensure that software is easy to use	N	N	**N**
Ensure that changes can be made easily	Y	N	**Y**
Be easily applied without extensive training	N	N	**?**

In short, we have found that we can obtain major practical benefits from our approach in terms of both the speed of development and the quality of code that is produced.

6   Related Work

There is a vast literature on software development, and an equally vast literature on formal methods. The potential for interaction between the two has not gone unnoticed: the annual *Formal Methods for Software Engineering* conference publishes a regular collection of the latest formal methods techniques and suggests how they might be deployed in practice. Software engineering has moved away from classical "Waterfall" development towards "Agile" development. This means a move away from a rigid specification-design-implement-test-debug-deploy cycle towards a more flexible approach where phases are intermingled and a software development team can work in a less hierarchical way.

In many ways, combining the best of both approaches is more of a philosophy. It reflects how actual software engineering has always been practiced, but encourages better internal and external communication, earlier product release, and ideally responsiveness. *Continuous testing* [AD14] using automated frameworks is a key part of the corpus: no software should be committed without being tested against the recognised test suite. *Continuous integration*, where changes are continually applied to a master version, is also key to the success of an agile approach, ensuring that fixes and improvements can quickly be made available to end-users. In the most ambitious projects, this can result in daily, or even more frequent, software releases.

"Lean" software development [PP03] is one of the more extreme forms of agile development. Here, the focus is on strong product design and minimising wasted effort. The goal is to produce a "Minimal Viable Product" as quickly as possible. This requires very high levels of discipline: it is necessary to avoid deviating from the most important goals, to avoid adding unnecessary features, to test adequately but not excessively, and to quickly adapt to changing goals.

A noteworthy body of research is the work on *Cleanroom Software Engineering* [HLT94] from the 80–90s, an incremental engineering approach, which makes use of specifications and refinements, and a sophisticated statistical model-based testing approach.

What is less common is the recognition that *functional programming* techniques can play a key part in agile software engineering. They are the glue that holds together the *flexible* software engineering methodology that we have described above, and that enables us to quickly incorporate appropriate lightweight formal methods, while maintaining high levels of flexibility. By building on well-understood, malleable and abstract functional components, we can quickly and easily refine designs, use existing components as part of a new design, and the discipline that is imposed by strong type systems means that we can have a high degree of confidence in the correctness of any software that is released.

Safety critical systems are the more traditional application area of formal methods, as errors in software for these systems can have grave impact, potentially causing accidents and hurting or even killing people. At the same time there is a strong pressure to realize more and more functionality in software which makes agile development approaches attractive for critical systems.

One research project in critical systems was the openETCS[9] project from the rail domain. The project developed a toolchain for ETCS (European train control system) which supports agile development combined with formal methods [openetcs-miv07]. Another research project which investigated this was the Open-DO[10] project from the avionics domain. In the hi-lite[11] subproject, there was considerable tool development for making the use of formal methods easier [hilite-L5.3], in particular by automating large parts of the formal proof effort. Increased automation allows for more frequent changes by reducing the required work on the formal model and proof part.

Even for interactive theorem provers, this now allows for proof-replay, automated proof-finding [CK18] and counterexample detection [BN10]. There have also been considerable formal verification efforts at the operating system level [KEH+09]. The microkernel seL4 is both high-performance and extremely thorough in the depth of its formal verification, which includes the compiler, assembly code, and hardware. Moreover, it follows a similar iterative cycle of prototyping, formal specification, verification, requirements adjustment, all the while reflecting the changes in the actual implementation. The actual implementation, however, is manually derived from the prototype and specifications. This is potentially a source of incongruety between the specification and implementation, which is different from our approach of the specification and implementation being one in the same. These examples of formal specification approaches are quite specific to their application domains.

Within the last few years, there have been calls to action to devise a methodology that combines agile and formal methods approaches in a general way (see [Ghe18]), but the specifics of the methodology of producing such a piece of software are not well-documented. The approach we present is universal. As there is currently no standard or regulation for development of cryptocurrencies, there is more freedom in our domain. Regardless, the approaches do share automation as a common topic.

7   Conclusions

This paper has described the approach to complex software engineering that has been successfully deployed at IOHK for the construction of a new distributed blockchain. The Cardano system is designed to support large-scale, verifiable transactions in a decentralised way, without requiring the inefficient PoW consensus mechanism that is used by e.g. BitCoin. The flexible formal software development approach that we describe in this paper combines the speed and visibility advantages of agile software development with the correctness advantages of formal methods development, while also delivering additional new advantages in terms of the ease of design change. This approach codifies our own experience,

---

[9] www.openetcs.org.

[10] www.open-do.org.

[11] http://www.open-do.org/projects/hi-lite/.

as well as that of others at the many companies that are using functional programming and formal methods as part of an integrated software development approach.

The key take-aways from our experience honing a software development methodology that fuses formal and agile approaches in a flexible way are:

(i) it is imperative to maintain a disciplined and structured approach to prototyping, implementation, verification, and testing, as the foundation of the development (no ad-hoc solutions!)

(ii) maintaining transparecy (e.g. decision tracking), explainability (both external and internal), clarity of requirements, and good communication during the development process as well as the deployment cycle are key to the success of our approach

(iii) if we faithfully adhere to these principles, we will be rewarded with the benefits of both formal methods and the agile approach to engineering, which means high-assurance software that is fast to deliver and amenable to changing requirements

7.1   Possible Improvements

We will continue to evolve our methodology, based on our experience in developing Cardano and future projects. Below, we list some concrete improvements we will be pursuing. Firstly, in certain places, we failed to use the right abstractions in our code. Refactoring the code to change properties on Haskell type classes was time-consuming, for example. In hindsight, greater abstraction would have allowed more flexibility and saved overall development time. Secondly, we could and should have produced more prototypes and demonstrators. There was a tendency for the team to hold back until software was correct rather than when it was working, which could be perceived as a lack of progress. We could also have achieved better visibility of our results both internally and externally (for example, some documents could be hard to find, more blog posts could have been written, more interviews given, etc.).

Thirdly, we produced our executable specification and tests manually from the formal specification. It would have been more efficient and provided greater confidence in their consistency if we had instead produced the executable specification and property-based tests directly from the formal specification. We are not aware of suitably robust tooling that would allow us to do this, unfortunately, but we would welcome any suggestions and future developments.

Acknowledgements. We like to thank to Charles Hoskinson for his commitment to using a formal approach for the flagship product of IOHK. This is a bold step in a young and fast moving industry, and we are grateful for his confidence. We would also like to thank our friends and colleagues at IOHK and elsewhere who have contributed ideas and suggestions for this paper but who are not listed as authors. This includes several software developers from other organisations, who have commented on their own experiences, but who wish to remain anonymous.

References

[AD14] Ariola, W., Dunlop, C.: Continuous Testing. CreateSpace Independent Publishing Platform, North Charleston (2014)

[BBvB+01] Beck, K., et al.: Manifesto for agile software development (2001). http://www.agilemanifesto.org/

[Bec00] Beck, K.: Extreme Programming Explained: Embrace Change. Addison-Wesley Longman Publishing Co. Inc., Boston (2000)

[BGK+18] Badertscher, C., Gazi, P., Kiayias, A., Russell, A., Zikas, V.: Ouroboros genesis: composable proof-of-stake blockchains with dynamic availability. Cryptology ePrint Archive, Report 2018/378 (2018). https://eprint.iacr.org/2018/378

[BKKS18] Bruenjes, L., Kiayias, A., Koutsoupias, E., Stouka, A.-P.: Reward sharing schemes for stake pools. Computer Science and Game Theory (cs.GT). arXiv:1807.11218 (2018)

[BN10] Blanchette, J.C., Nipkow, T.: Nitpick: a counterexample generator for higher-order logic based on a relational model finder. In: Kaufmann, M., Paulson, L.C. (eds.) ITP 2010. LNCS, vol. 6172, pp. 131–146. Springer, Heidelberg (2010). https://doi.org/10.1007/978-3-642-14052-5_11

[Bra16] Brad, E.: Type-driven Development With Idris. Manning (2016). http://www.worldcat.org/isbn/9781617293023

[Bre15] Brechner, E.: Agile Project Management with Kanban, 1st edn. Microsoft Press, Redmond (2015)

[CC77] Cousot, P., Cousot, R.: Abstract interpretation: a unified lattice model for static analysis of programs by construction or approximation of fixpoints. In: Proceedings of the 4th ACM SIGACT-SIGPLAN Symposium on Principles of Programming Languages, POPL 1977, pp. 238–252. ACM, New York (1977) . https://doi.org/10.1145/512950.512973

[CGP99] Clarke Jr., E.M., Grumberg, O., Peled, D.A.: Model Checking. MIT Press, Cambridge (1999)

[CH00] Claessen, K., Hughes, J.: QuickCheck: a lightweight tool for random testing of Haskell programs. In: Proceedings of the Fifth ACM SIGPLAN International Conference on Functional Programming, ICFP 2000, pp. 268–279. ACM, New York (2000). https://doi.org/10.1145/351240.351266

[CK18] Czajka, Ł., Kaliszyk, C.: Hammer for Coq: automation for dependent type theory. J. Autom. Reason. **61**(1), 423–453 (2018). https://doi.org/10.1007/s10817-018-9458-4

[CKNW19] Chapman, J., Kireev, R., Nester, C., Wadler, P.: System F in Agda, for fun and profit. In: Hutton, G. (ed.) Mathematics of Program Construction. Lecture Notes in Computer Science, vol. 11825, pp. 255–297. Springer, Cham (2019). https://doi.org/10.1007/978-3-030-33636-3_10

[DGKR17] David, B.M., Gazi, P., Kiayias, A., Russell, A.: Ouroboros Praos: an adaptively-secure, semi-synchronous proof-of-stake protocol. IACR Cryptology ePrint Archive 2017, 573 (2017)

[DHST99] Davies, N., Holyer, J., Stephens, A., Thompson, P.: Generating service level agreements from user requirements. In: The Management and Design of ATM Networks, vol. 5, pp. 4/1–4/9, December 1999

[DHT99a] Davies, N., Holyer, J., Thompson, P.: End-to-end management of mixed applications across networks. In: IEEE Workshop on Internet Applications, pp. 12–19. IEEE, September 1999

[DHT99b] Davies, N., Holyer, J., Thompson, P.: An operational model to control loss and delay of traffic at a network switch. In: The Management and Design of ATM Networks, vol. 5, pp. 20/1–20/14, December 1999

[DMB08] de Moura, L., Bjørner, N.: Z3: an efficient SMT solver. In: Ramakrishnan, C.R., Rehof, J. (eds.) TACAS 2008. LNCS, vol. 4963, pp. 337–340. Springer, Heidelberg (2008). https://doi.org/10.1007/978-3-540-78800-3_24

[Dou02] Douceur, J.R.: The Sybil attack. In: Druschel, P., Kaashoek, F., Rowstron, A. (eds.) IPTPS 2002. LNCS, vol. 2429, pp. 251–260. Springer, Heidelberg (2002). https://doi.org/10.1007/3-540-45748-8_24

[FM-TR-2018-01] IOHK Formal Methods Team: Small step semantics for Cardano. IOHK Technical report FM-TR-2018-01 (2018). https://github.com/input-output-hk/cardano-ledger-specs

[Ghe18] Ghezzi, C.: Formal methods and agile development: towards a happy marriage. The Essence of Software Engineering, pp. 25–36. Springer, Cham (2018). https://doi.org/10.1007/978-3-319-73897-0_2

[hilite-L5.3] Hi-Lite Team: Hi-Lite - Simplifying the use of formal methods (2013). http://www.open-do.org/wp-content/uploads/2013/05/hilite-L5.3.pdf

[HLT94] Hausler, P.A., Linger, R.C., Trammell, C.J.: Adopting cleanroom software engineering with a phased approach. IBM Syst. J. **33**, 89–109 (1994)

[IOH] IOHK Marlowe Team. https://testnet.iohkdev.io/en/marlowe/tools/marlowe-playground/

[Jel19] Jeltsch, W.: A process calculus for formally verifying blockchain consensus protocols. To appear, November 2019. https://github.com/jeltsch/wflp-2019/tree/master/Paper

[KEH+09] Klein, G., et al.: Sel4: formal verification of an OS kernel. In: Proceedings of the ACM SIGOPS 22nd Symposium on Operating Systems Principles, SOSP 2009, pp. 207–220. Association for Computing Machinery, New York (2009). https://doi.org/10.1145/1629575.1629596

[KKL18] Karakostas, D., Kiayias, A., Larangeira, M.: Account management and stake pools in proof of stake ledgers (2018)

[KRDO17] Kiayias, A., Russell, A., David, B., Oliynykov, R.: Ouroboros: a provably secure proof-of-stake blockchain protocol. In: Katz, J., Shacham, H. (eds.) CRYPTO 2017. LNCS, vol. 10401, pp. 357–388. Springer, Cham (2017). https://doi.org/10.1007/978-3-319-63688-7_12

[LGPC+16] Leon Gaixas, S., et al.: Assuring QoS guarantees for heterogeneous services in RINA networks with ΔQ. In: IEEE International Conference on Cloud Computing Technology and Science (CloudCom), pp. 584–589. IEEE, December 2016

[LST18] Lamela Seijas, P., Thompson, S.: Marlowe: financial contracts on blockchain. In: Margaria, T., Steffen, B. (eds.) ISoLA 2018. LNCS, vol. 11247, pp. 356–375. Springer, Cham (2018). https://doi.org/10.1007/978-3-030-03427-6_27

[MOG+14] Mulligan, D., Owens, S., Gray, K., Ridge, T., Sewell, P.: Lem: reusable engineering of real-world semantics. ACM SIGPLAN Not. **49**, 08 (2014)

[Nak09] Nakamoto, S.: Bitcoin: a peer-to-peer electronic cash system. Cryptography Mailing list, March 2009. https://metzdowd.com

[OBZNS11] Owens, S., Böhm, P., Zappa Nardelli, F., Sewell, P.: Lem: a lightweight tool for heavyweight semantics. In: van Eekelen, M., Geuvers, H., Schmaltz, J., Wiedijk, F. (eds.) ITP 2011. LNCS, vol. 6898, pp. 363–369. Springer, Heidelberg (2011). https://doi.org/10.1007/978-3-642-22863-6_27

[openetcs-miv07] Hase, K.-R.: openETCS: model-based, agile and open-source (2016). http://www.schienenfahrzeugtagung.at/download/PDF2016/MiV07_Hase.pdf

[PF01] Palmer, S.R., Felsing, M.: A Practical Guide to Feature-Driven Development. Pearson Education, London (2001)

[PJGK+19] Peyton Jones, M., Gkoumas, V., Kireev, R., MacKenzie, K., Nester, C., Wadler, P.: Unraveling recursion: compiling an IR with recursion to system F. In: Hutton, G. (ed.) MPC 2019. LNCS, vol. 11825, pp. 414–443. Springer, Cham (2019). https://doi.org/10.1007/978-3-030-33636-3_15

[PP03] Poppendieck, M., Poppendieck, T.: Lean Software Development: An Agile Toolkit. Addison-Wesley Longman Publishing Co. Inc., Boston (2003)

[Ree03] Reeve, D.C.: A new blueprint for network QoS. Ph.D. thesis, Computing Laboratory, University of Kent, Canterbury, Kent, UK, August 2003. http://www.cs.kent.ac.uk/pubs/2003/1892

[SB01] Schwaber, K., Beedle, M.: Agile Software Development with Scrum, 1st edn. Prentice Hall PTR, Upper Saddle River (2001)

[SL-D1] IOHK Formal Methods Team: Design Specification for Delegation and Incentives in Cardano, IOHK Deliverable SL-D1 (2018). https://github.com/input-output-hk/cardano-ledger-specs

[SZNO+10] Sewell, P., et al.: Ott: effective tool support for the working semanticist. J. Funct. Program. **20**, 71–122 (2010)

White-Box Path Generation in Recursive Programs

Ricardo Peña$^{(\boxtimes)}$ and Jaime Sánchez-Hernández

Computer Science School, Complutense University of Madrid, Madrid, Spain
{ricardo,jaime}@sip.ucm.es

Abstract. We present an algorithm for generating paths through a set of mutually recursive functions. The algorithm is part of a tool for white-box test-case generation. While in imperative programs there is a well established notion of path depth, this is not the case in recursive programs. We define what we mean by path and path depth in these programs and propose an algorithm which generates all the static paths up to a given depth. When the algorithm is applied to transformed iterative programs, giving as a result tail-recursive functions, the defined depth corresponds to the maximum number of times the loop condition is evaluated. When applied to non-tail recursive functions, the meaning is their maximum unfolding depth along the path, for each initial call to the function. It can also be applied to hybrid programs where both iteration and recursion are present.

Keywords: White-box testing · Static path · Recursion depth

1 Introduction

Testing is very important for increasing program reliability. Thorough testing ideally exercises all the different situations described in the specification, and all the instructions and conditions of the program under test, so that it would have a high probability of finding bugs, if they are present in the code. There is a general agreement that automatic tools can alleviate most of the tedious and error prone activities related to testing. One of them is test-case generation (TCG). Traditionally (see, for instance [1]), there are two TCG variants: black-box TCG and white-box TCG. In the first one, test-cases are solely based on the program specification, and in the second one, they are additionally based on a particular reference implementation. Each one complements each other, so both are needed if we aim at performing thorough testing.

White-box TCG is concerned with first defining a coverage criterion for the Unit Under Test (UUT), and then generating a set of test-cases which, when executed, will implement this criterion. A usual criterion is to require the test

Research paper. Partially funded by the Spanish Ministry of Science, Innovation and Universities, under the grant TIN2017-86217-R.

A. Byrski and J. Hughes (Eds.): TFP 2020, LNCS 12222, pp. 121–135, 2020.
https://doi.org/10.1007/978-3-030-57761-2_6

suite to exercise all the statements or all the condition outcomes of the UUT. A more complete criterion is to exercise all the execution paths through the UUT. When there exist loops in the code, the number of paths is potentially infinite, so a limit on the number of allowed iterations executed in each loop must be established. This limit is usually referred to as the path *depth*. For instance, depth-1 paths will be those that never execute the loop bodies; depth-2 paths will execute each loop body at most once; and so on. Once the paths are generated, each one is defined by the sequence of decisions that the UUT takes when executing that path. By collecting the conditions involved, and the expected outcome of evaluating each one, a test-case for the path can be synthesised by using for instance symbolic execution [2].

Functional programs do not contain loops, but use recursion instead. There is no established criterion on what a path and its path depth mean in a recursive program. Intuitively, a path should require a complete execution of the UUT main function and it would involve a sequence of decisions taken by the UUT along the execution. In a path, the UUT functions may be recursively invoked a number of times, either directly or indirectly. So, multiple and mutual recursion should be taken into account when defining the meaning of a path. By analogy to the iterative case, in recursive programs the path depth should be related to the number of invocations the UUT, or any of its auxiliary functions, undergo in the path.

In this work, we define a UUT to be a collection of (potentially) mutually recursive functions with a main, or top, visible one, which may invoke any of the other ones. Then, we define a notion of path and of path depth for that UUT, and present an algorithm for generating an exhaustive set of paths up to a given depth.

This work has been developed in the context of our computer assisted validation platform CAVI-ART [5,6]. The platform uses a functional language as its Intermediate Representation (IR) to which both imperative and functional programs are translated. Imperative loops are translated into a set of mutually tail recursive functions and, if recursion is present in the input program, it is preserved by the translation. In the end, only recursion remains in the IR. Given a UUT, the platform automatically generates white-box paths, and synthesises a test-case for each one, by using an SMT solver [7] which checks the satisfiability of the conditions required by the path, and assigns appropriate values to the involved variables.

In Fig. 1 we show a picture of the complete testing system. As the platform is also intended for formal verification, the UUT visible function is endowed with a formal precondition and postcondition. These are translated by the tool into SMT constraints. In this way, the test cases generated by the tool, not only satisfy the path constraints, but also the precondition ones. By requiring to only satisfy the precondition constraints, the tool can also generate black-box test cases. In our approach, the user fixes some sizes for the data types of the UUT arguments (for instance, the range of the integers, the length of an array, the cardinal of a tree, etc.), and the tool generates an exhaustive set of cases up to the

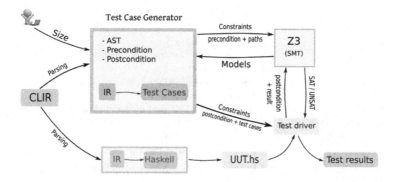

Fig. 1. CAVI-ART testing tool

given size. The reason for fixing these sizes is that we seek for exhaustiveness but also for getting a finite number of cases. Additionally, the validity of the test cases is automatically checked by the tool, just by checking whether the result returned by the UUT satisfies the postcondition constraints. So, the user responsibilities are only to provide a precondition and a postcondition, to fix sizes for the arguments and to choose a maximum depth for the white-box paths. After that, the whole testing process—test case generation, test execution and test validation—is automatically performed by the tool.

In principle, the IR language is not executable. In order to actually run the tests, the tool provides a translation from the IR to Haskell (see the bottom part of Fig. 1). The generic test driver is also written in this language. The translation is straightforward since, as we have already said, the IR is in fact a functional language.

2   Functional Intermediate Representation

Our intermediate representation is a first-order eager core functional language which supports mutually recursive function definitions. In Fig. 2 we show its abstract syntax. Notice that all expressions are flattened in the sense that all the arguments in function and constructor applications, and also the **case** discriminants, are atoms. An additional feature is that IR programs are in **let** A-normal form [4], and also in SSA[1] form, i.e. all **let** bound variables in a nested sequence of **let** expressions are distinct, and also different to the function arguments.

In Fig. 3 we show a Java version of the *quicksort* algorithm. This algorithm is translated by the platform into the IR code shown in Fig. 4. As there is no mutable state in the IR, the array updates of the Java version are simulated by passing an array as an argument, both to the *partition* and *qsort* functions,

---

[1] Static Single Assignment.

a	$::= c$	{ constant }
	$\mid x$	{ variable }
be	$::= a$	{ atomic expression }
	$\mid f\ \overline{a_i}$	{ function/primitive operator application }
	$\mid \langle \overline{a_i} \rangle$	{ tuple construction }
	$\mid C\ \overline{a_i}$	{ constructor application }
e	$::= be$	{ binding expression }
	$\mid \mathbf{let}\ \langle \overline{x_i :: \tau_i} \rangle = be\ \mathbf{in}\ e$	{ sequential let. Left part of the binding can be a tuple }
	$\mid \mathbf{letfun}\ \overline{def_i}\ \mathbf{in}\ e$	{ let for mutually recursive function definitions }
	$\mid \mathbf{case}\ a\ \mathbf{of}\ \overline{alt_i}[;\ \_ \rightarrow e]$	{ case distinction with optional default branch }
$tldef$	$::= \mathbf{define}\ \{\psi_1\}\ def\ \{\psi_2\}$	{ top level function definition with pre- and post-conditions }
def	$::= f\ (\overline{x_i :: \tau_i}) :: (\overline{y_j :: \tau_j}) = e$	{ function definition. Output results are named }
alt	$::= C\ \overline{x_i :: \tau_i} \rightarrow e$	{ case branch }
τ	$::= \alpha$	{ type variable }
	$\mid T\ \overline{\tau_i}$	{ type constructor application }

Fig. 2. CAVI-ART IR abstract syntax

```java
public class Quick {
  public static void quicksort (int [] v) {
     int n = v.length;
     qsort (v, 0, n-1);
  }
  public static int partition (int [] v, int a, int b) {
     int i = a+1; int j = b; int piv = v[a];
     while (i <= j) {
       if (v[i] <= piv) {
          i = i+1;
       } else if (v[j] >= piv) {
          j = j-1;
       } else { // v[i] > piv && v[j] < piv
          int temp = v[i]; v[i] = v[j]; v[j] = temp;
          i = i+1; j = j-1;
       }
     }
     int temp = v[a]; v[a] = v[j]; v[j] = temp;
     return j;
  }
  public static void qsort (int [] v, int a, int b)  {
     if (a < b) {
       int p = partition(v, a, b);
       qsort(v, a, p-1);
       qsort(v, p+1, b);
     }
  }
}
```

Fig. 3. A Java version of *quicksort*

```
define quicksort (v::Array Int)::(res::Array Int) =
  letfun
    qsort (v::Array Int, a::Int, b::Int)::(res::Array Int) =
      let b::Bool = a < b in
      case b of
        True  -> f1 v a b
        False -> v
    f1 (v::Array Int, a::Int, b::Int)::(res::Array Int) =
      let (p::Int, v1::Array Int) = partition v a b in
      let p1::Int = p - 1 in
      let v2::Array Int = qsort v1 a p1 in
      let p2::Int = p + 1 in
        qsort v2 p2 b
    partition (v::Array Int, a::Int, b::Int)::(p::Int, res::Array Int) =
      let i::Int = a + 1 in
      let j::Int = b in
      let piv::Int = get-array v a in
        f2 v a piv i j
    f2 (v::Array Int, a::Int, piv::Int, i::Int, j::Int)::(res::Array Int) =
      let b::Bool = i <= j in
      case b of
        True  -> let ei::Int = get-array v i in
                 let b2::Bool = ei <= piv in
                 case b2 of
                   True  -> let i2::Int = i + 1 in
                            f2 v a piv i2 j
                   False -> let ej::Int = get-array v j in
                            let b3::Bool = ej >= piv in
                            case b3 of
                              True  -> let j2::Int = j - 1 in
                                       f2 v a piv i j2
                              False -> let temp::Int = get-array v i in
                                       let ej::Int = get-array v j in
                                       let v1::Array Int = set-array v i ej in
                                       let v2::Array Int = set-array v1 j temp in
                                       let i2::Int = i + 1 in
                                       let j2::Int = j - 1 in
                                       f2 v2 a piv i2 j2
        False -> let temp::Int = get-array v a in
                 let ej::Int = get-array v j in
                 let v1::Array Int = set-array v a ej in
                 let v2::Array Int = set-array v1 j temp in
                 (j, v2)
  in let n::Int  = length v in
     let n1::Int = n - 1    in
        qsort v 0 n1
```

Fig. 4. CAVI-ART IR for function *quicksort*

and returning a different one as a result. The predefined function **set-array**[2] simulates the assignments of the form $v[i] = exp$. Notice also that the **while** loop has been translated into the tail-recursive function *f2*, and that the conditional **if** statements are translated into **case** expressions. In the IR program, there is also mutual recursion between the functions *qsort* and *f1*, being *qsort* non-tail recursive and showing double recursion. The four mentioned functions are

---

[2] **set-array** v i e builds a new array identical to v, except the i-th component which is replaced by the value e. An assignment of the form v[i]=e in the source program is translated to **set-array** v i e. This translation may have an impact on the execution time of the (translated to Haskell) IR version with respect to the Java one, but not on the correctness of the algorithm.

defined in a **letfun** expression within the top level visible function *quicksort*. We will use this IR program as a running example of UUT along the paper, since it illustrates some features we are interested in: mutual recursion, non-tail recursion, and dealing with arrays.

We define a *static path* through a set of mutually recursive functions declared together in a UUT, as a potential execution path starting at the top level function, and ending when this function produces a result. Not all the static paths correspond to actual execution paths, since some static paths may be infeasible. The detection of infeasible paths will be done in a subsequent phase by checking the satisfiability of the set of boolean conditions defining the path.

We define the *depth* of a static path, as the maximum unfolding depth of the UUT recursive functions when performing the actions implied by the path. When all the UUT functions are tail recursive, this definition corresponds to the number of times the loop condition is evaluated in imperative loops. When there is at least one non-tail recursive function in the UUT, the depth path is the depth of the call tree deployed during the path execution, considering only the calls to the non-tail recursive function. A depth-1 path is one in which each non-tail recursive function executes one of its base cases, i.e. an invocation to them immediately returns without triggering further recursive invocations; depth-2 ones correspond to executions in which at least one recursive function has executed a recursive case, by generating one or more recursive calls, and then these recursive calls have executed a base case; and so on.

For instance, there is one depth-1 path in function *f2* of Fig. 4, namely the one in which the condition of the first **case** expression is evaluated to *false*, i.e. the condition $i > j$ holds. This corresponds to an execution of the *partition* function in the Java program of Fig. 3 in which the **while** body is not entered. There are also three depth-2 paths in function *f2*, each one ending in a tail recursive call to itself. These recursive calls then execute the depth-1 path.

In the mutually recursive set formed by *qsort* and *f1*, there is one depth-1 path, namely the one in which the **case** condition of *qsort* is evaluated to *false*. There are also four depth-2 paths. In all of them, the **case** condition of *qsort* is evaluated to *true*, and the path continues by calling to *partition*, then to *qsort*, and then to *qsort* a second time. The two latter calls execute the only *qsort* depth-1 path, and the call to *partition* may execute either its depth-1 path, or one of its three depth-2 paths. However, only the *qsort* depth-1 path, and the *qsort* depth-2 path in which *f2* executes any of its depth-2 paths, are feasible. The first one corresponds to an empty array segment as input, and the other three correspond to an array segment having 2 or 3 elements. The infeasible path (the depth-2 path in *qsort* combined with the depth-1 path in *f2*) forces the array segment to have at least two elements in *qsort* (i.e. $a < b$), and to have at most one element in *partition* (i.e. $i = a + 1$, $j = b$, $i > j$), which is contradictory.

Given a UUT written in the IR language, and a maximum depth fixed by the user, our tool generates all the static paths having a depth smaller than or equal to this maximum depth.

3   Two-Level Representation and Assumed Properties

Generating paths in recursive programs cannot be regarded as just a graph problem, as it is the case in iterative programs. In the latter, the control flow graph (CFG) can be depicted as a directed planar graph. Loops become the strongly connected components (SCC) of those graphs. Computing paths is then a combination of computing the graph SCCs, then collapsing them into single nodes, and then computing paths in the resulting DAG (directed acyclic graph), which is an easy problem. The path depth corresponds to the number of iterations the path undergoes in each SCC.

Recursive programs cannot be depicted as planar graphs, unless recursive calls are represented as non-expanded nodes in those graphs. But, as soon as recursive calls are unfolded and replaced by their bodies, the graph representation is not possible anymore. A different number of unfoldings would result in different graphs. When iterative programs are translated into recursive ones, all the resulting functions are tail recursive, as we have seen in the *partition* example above. But, as long as there are non-tail recursive functions in the source program, analyzing the CFG in order to extract the paths is not enough. One may wonder why not to translate non-tail recursive programs into tail-recursive ones by using the well-known continuation passing style translation of functional programs (see, for example [4]). By doing that, the non-tail recursive functions are somehow 'hidden' in the continuation and will be unfolded when the continuation is applied. So, it seems rather difficult to extract the paths from a static code which may undergo a variable number of unfoldings. Also, the resulting program is higher-order, which makes the approach more difficult.

We follow here a different strategy: to propose a graph representation of recursive programs at two different levels:

- One level consists of the CFG of each function body. These are DAGs in which the internal calls are represented as non-expanded nodes.
- The other level is the call-graph (CG) of the whole function collection. An edge (f, g) here represents one or more calls from function f to function g. An SCC in this graph represents a loop of functions calling each other in a mutually recursive way.

These two kinds of representations are not arbitrary directed graphs. By knowing that they come from code written in a programming language, we can assume them to satisfy the following properties:

1. Each SCC in the CG has at least one entry node. This is because we assume each function in the CG to be reachable from the top one. Otherwise, it would represent dead code. When the UUT is the result of transforming an iterative program, each SCC has a unique entry node. This holds because iterative loops in conventional programming languages have a unique entry point.

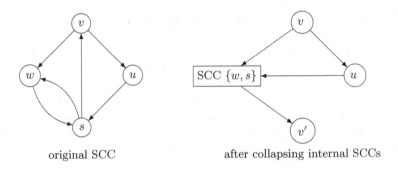

original SCC   after collapsing internal SCCs

Fig. 5. Illustration of Proposition 1.

2. On the other hand, a SCC in the CG may have more than one exit to nodes
   external to it. This is because a loop or a function may abruptly terminate by
   sentences such as **break, continue, return**, or an exception, which interrupt
   the normal flow. Also, a function belonging to an SCC may issue a call to a
   function external to it.
3. In a SCC, all paths starting at an entry node, not exiting the SCC, and not
   infinitely iterating inside a nested SCC, must eventually reach again that
   entry node. We justify this statement by Propositon 1 below.
4. Each function CFG has a single source node and a single sink node. Each
   internal node is reachable from the source and the sink is reachable from
   each internal node. This is because we assume no dead code, (statically)
   terminating loops, and also that recursive functions have at least a base case.

A SCC may contain nested SCCs. Our path generation algorithm will not
infinitely loop inside any SCC. In order to control the number of iterations inside
a SCC, we will count the number of visits the path pays to a single node per
SCC. This will be one of its entry nodes. So, it is important to prove that, after
visiting all the internal SCCs, a path will reach again the entry node of the
external SCC.

Proposition 1. *Given a SCC $G = (V, E)$, subgraph of a directed graph, and
an entry vertex $v \in V$, all paths starting at v, not exiting V, and not infinitely
looping inside any nested SCC, must go again through v.*

Proof. By definition of SCC, V is a maximal set of vertices such that $\forall v, w \in V$
there exist paths $v \rightsquigarrow w$ and $w \rightsquigarrow v$ not leaving V. G may contain proper
subgraphs which are themselves SCCs. Let us assume that we remove v from
V and all its incoming and outgoing edges. In the resulting graph, we compute
its internal SCCs, and collapse them to single vertices. Let $G' = (V', E')$ be the
resulting DAG. Then, we build the following graph $G'' = (V'', E'')$, as follows:

– $V'' = V \cup \{v'\}$, where v' is a fresh vertex aiming at being a duplicate of v.

– E'' is built from E', by adding all the outgoing edges $(v, u) \in E$ from v to vertices $u \in V'$ but, for each incoming edge $(u, v) \in E$, we add instead an edge (u, v') to the duplicate v' of v.

It is clear the G'' is a DAG. Moreover, all paths in G'' starting at v can be extended to paths ending up in v'. This is because G is a SCC and so there exist paths from every vertex of V' to v. The only paths not reaching v' are those exiting G'' or iterating infinitely often in one internal SCC of G. In Fig 5, we illustrate the above construction with an example.   □

4   Path Generation Algorithm

As said above, a UUT consists of a top function—we will call it *top*—and a set of internal functions defined in a **letfun** expression within it. Function *top* may call any of them, but not the other way around. The path generation algorithm consists of the following phases:

1. Generating the CFG of each function.
2. Generating the *template paths* (TP) of each function. These are all the paths from its source to its sink.
3. Generating the UUT CG.
4. Computing the CG SCCs.
5. Computing the paths by expanding the TP.

The essential idea of phase 5 is to continuously replace nodes representing calls to functions by all the paths across the bodies of those functions. In order to guarantee termination, an additional control is needed on the unfolding level of some particular functions.

4.1   Generating the CFGs and the TP

We assume a fresh name supplier so that every node of any graph is given an identifying key which is unique in the whole set of graphs. The CFG of each function is a DAG having five types of nodes:

Source. This is the unique entry point of the function. It may have some code associated to it.
Block. This is either a basic block node—having associated sequential code consisting of a sequence of **let** bindings not containing calls, and ending in an edge to another node—, or it is a conditional block node having as associated code a **case** expression. In this case, the node has outgoing edges to more than one node.
Call g. Node exactly containing a call to a function, where g is the key of the called function source node.

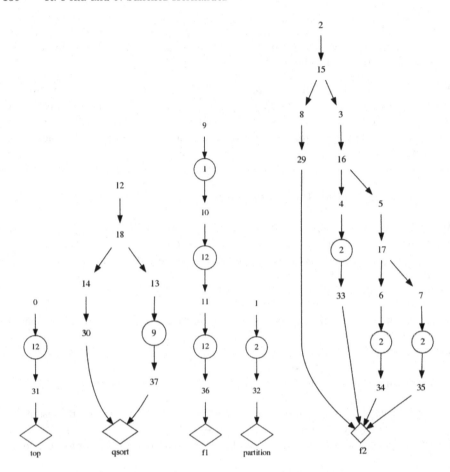

Fig. 6. Control flow graphs for functions top, qsort, f1, partition, and f2.

Return. In our tool, there is one such a node at the end of each execution path. Their next node is always the sink. We associate some code to these nodes related to returning to the caller the result of the function. For the purpose of this paper, it will be dealt with as a block node.

Sink. Node with no associated code representing the unique sink of the function.

From the UUT IR, the algorithm computes the CFG of each function by using conventional techniques such as those one can find in compilers. The resulting graphs are DAGs. In Fig. 6 we show the CFGs computed for all the functions of the *quicksort* UUT. Uncircled nodes are source, block or return nodes; circled nodes are calls; and the diamond node is the sink. For convenience, we only show the keys associated to the nodes.

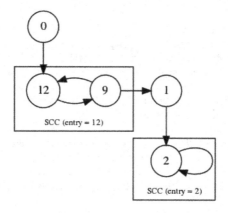

Fig. 7. Call graph and SCCs for function *quicksort*.

Then, a simple recursive algorithm computes all the paths from the source to the sink in each DAG. By convention, the sink node is not included in any path. These are called *template paths* (TP). The algorithm will return a list of TP associated to each function. We call them *template* because they may contain call nodes which should be later expanded in order to compute the final paths. A final path does contain neither call nodes, nor sink ones. It just consists of a sequence of source, block and return nodes.

4.2   Generating the CG and Computing the SCCs

From the TP, the next phase of the algorithm generates the CG. This one consists only of call nodes. An edge (f, g) represents one or more calls from function f to function g. We include in the graph a node with an initial call to the *top* function. In Fig. 7 we show the CG computed by this algorithm for our running example.

Now, all the SCCs of the CG are computed, included the nested ones. This phase uses standard algorithms. Thanks to the restrictions assumed in Sect. 3, each SCC has at least an entry point. Moreover, by Proposition 1, all the paths not exiting the SCC must pass again through that entry point. So, these entry points provide us a convenient way for controlling the depth of the paths: each time we unfold an entry point corresponding to a call to a function f, the subsequent calls to f in the unfolded path represent a depth one unit smaller than the depth of the unfolded f.

Consequently, our algorithm computes an entry point for each SCC and returns the set of them. In Fig. 7 we show the SCCs computed for *quicksort* and the entry points computed.

```
expand ds tp []                        = [[]]
expand ds tp ((Source,k): pth)         = map ((Source,k):)  $ expand ds tp pth
expand ds tp ((Block,k): pth)          = map ((Block,k):)   $ expand ds tp pth
expand ds tp ((RetNode,k): pth)        = map ((RetNode,k):) $ expand ds tp pth
expand ds tp ((CallNode k,_):pth)      = concatMap (expand ds tp)
                                                    [p1 ++ pth | p1 <- kPaths]
     where kPaths = map (map $ annotate ds) (tp ! k)
expand ds tp ((EntryCall k d,_):pth)
     | d == 0    = []                              -- remove this path
     | otherwise = [p1 ++ p2 | p1 <- concatMap (expand ds' tp) kPaths,
                               p2 <- expand ds tp pth]
     where kPaths = map (map $ annotate ds') (tp ! k)
           ds'    = insert k (d - 1) ds            -- decrease k's recursion depth

annotate :: Map Key Int -> (Node,Key) -> (Node,Key)
annotate ds (CallNode f,i)
          | member f ds = (EntryCall f (ds ! f),i)
annotate ds other       = other
```

Fig. 8. The *expand* algorithm.

4.3 Computing the Paths

The algorithm starts by creating a map from the SCC's entry points to their initial depth. This is the maximum depth established by the user for the intended white-box paths. Then, the recursive algorithm *expand* is invoked. It is written in Haskell, and its signature is the following:

```
expand :: Map Key Int -> TemplatePaths -> [(Node,Key)] -> [[(Node,Key)]]
```

It receives as arguments the depth map, the template paths, and a single path to be expanded. It traverses the path from left to right and *expands* it by systematically replacing call nodes by their template paths. So, in general, the expansion of a path produces a list of paths as a result. Initially, *expand* is invoked with a path consisting of a single call node *Call top*. It processes a path node at a time and invokes itself recursively on the rest of the path.

Its complete code is shown in Fig. 8. Nodes of type *Source*, *Block*, and *Return* are simply bypassed, and the expansion continues on the remaining path. Call nodes are replaced by their template paths but, prior to that, the possible calls to the SCC's entry points are annotated with their current remaining depth registered in the depth map. When a node corresponding to an entry node calling to function f is expanded, the expansion of its template paths is done with a depth for f one unit smaller than the current depth for that entry. However, the expansion of the remaining path is done with the original path depth, as they may occur new calls to f in that path, and these should be expanded by starting at the initial path depth. If an entry node is found with its current depth being zero, then the complete path is removed.

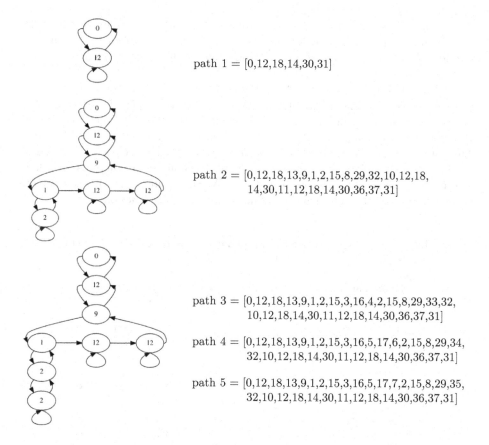

path 1 = [0,12,18,14,30,31]

path 2 = [0,12,18,13,9,1,2,15,8,29,32,10,12,18,
14,30,11,12,18,14,30,36,37,31]

path 3 = [0,12,18,13,9,1,2,15,3,16,4,2,15,8,29,33,32,
10,12,18,14,30,11,12,18,14,30,36,37,31]

path 4 = [0,12,18,13,9,1,2,15,3,16,5,17,6,2,15,8,29,34,
32,10,12,18,14,30,11,12,18,14,30,36,37,31]

path 5 = [0,12,18,13,9,1,2,15,3,16,5,17,7,2,15,8,29,35,
32,10,12,18,14,30,11,12,18,14,30,36,37,31]

Fig. 9. The 5 paths of *quicksort* up to depth 2.

In Fig. 9 we show the 5 paths generated by the algorithm for the *quicksort* UUT when the initial depth is set to 2. We have depicted them graphically on the left part of the figure as the call tree deployed by each path. Notice that, by setting the depth to 2, also the paths of depth 1 are generated (in this example, there is only one such path). Moreover, all the combinatorics arising when varying the depths of the different SCCs from 1 to the maximum depth, and building the cartesian product of the corresponding paths, are also achieved by our expansion algorithm. For that reason, setting the maximum depth to 3 in this example results in a combinatorial explosion and produces 2 549 paths (see Fig. 10).

5   Experiments

We have applied the above algorithm to a collection of UUTs including purely functional algorithms such as the insertion of a key in an AVL tree, or computing the union of two leftist heaps; purely iterative ones, such as inserting and searching a value in a sorted array, or the Dutch National Flag problem [3]; and to hybrid ones, such as our *quicksort* running example, which includes an iterative version of *partition*.

In Fig. 10 we show the results of these experiments. The number of static white box paths computed by our algorithm at several depths is shown in the first three columns. The column T/NT specifies whether all functions in the UUT are tail-recursive (T), or there exists some non-tail recursive (NT) ones. The column S/D tells us whether all functions are simple recursive or at least one is double recursive. The last column shows the number of functions included in the UUT, excluding the top visible one. We make note that the number of paths grows very quickly for units having more than one function.

UUT	depth=1	depth=2	depth=3	T/NT	S/D	#f
quicksort	1	5	2 549	NT	D	4
binSearch	1	3	7	T	S	1
DutchNationalFlag	1	4	13	T	S	1
linearSearchArray	2	4	6	T	S	1
insertArray	2	4	6	T	S	1
insertList	2	4	6	NT	S	1
deleteList	3	6	9	NT	S	1
searchBST	2	6	14	T	S	1
insertBST	2	6	14	NT	S	1
searchAVL	2	6	14	T	S	1
insertAVL	2	10 306	(*)	NT	S	6
searchRedBlack	2	6	14	T	S	1
unionLeftist	2	34	20 202	NT	D	3
insertLeftist	2	34	20 202	NT	D	4

(*) It runs out of memory after 40 minutes running.

Fig. 10. White-box paths in a suit of UUTs

We have confirmed in the experiments that the notion of path depth defined here coincides both with the number of iterations in loops incremented by 1, and with the unfolding depth of the call tree in recursive functions. A single algorithm suffices, then, to generate exhaustive white-box paths in iterative, recursive, and hybrid programs.

6   Conclusions

We have not found papers in the literature on the specific subject of white-box path generation in recursive programs. In a comprehensive study conducted in 2014 [8] on white-box and black-box test-case generation, and surveying 85 papers published in journals between 2004 and 2013, there is no mention to this problem. The papers on white-box paths are mainly devoted to how to generate concrete values satisfying a particular path, or to compare the path coverage of a suit of test-cases generated by using a variety of techniques. But, consistently, all of them assume that paths are directly obtained from the program control flow graph. That is, they assume an iterative unit under test.

We believe that the approach presented here is simple enough to be implemented in a practical tool and it can deal with all kinds of recursive programs: simple and multiple recursive, tail and non-tail recursive, and directly and mutually recursive. It is appropriate for unit white-box testing, and could be easily adapted to bottom-up integration testing. For that purpose, the UUT must distinguish between the externally called functions and the ones belonging to the UUT (for instance, by declaring the former in an import clause). Then, the external functions would simply not be expanded by the algorithm.

References

1. Anand, S., et al.: An orchestrated survey of methodologies for automated software test case generation. J. Syst. Softw. **86**(8), 1978–2001 (2013). https://doi.org/10.1016/j.jss.2013.02.061
2. Cadar, C., Sen, K.: Symbolic execution for software testing: three decades later. Commun. ACM **56**(2), 82–90 (2013). https://doi.org/10.1145/2408776.2408795
3. Dijkstra, E.W.: A Discipline of Programming. Prentice-Hall, Upper Saddle River (1976)
4. Flanagan, C., Sabry, A., Duba, B.F., Felleisen, M.: The essence of compiling with continuations. In: Cartwright, R. (ed.) Proceedings of the Conference on Programming Language Design and Implementation (PLDI 1993), pp. 237–247. ACM (1993). https://doi.org/10.1145/155090.155113
5. Montenegro, M., Nieva, S., Peña, R., Segura, C.: Liquid types for array invariant synthesis. In: D'Souza, D., Narayan Kumar, K. (eds.) ATVA 2017. LNCS, vol. 10482, pp. 289–306. Springer, Cham (2017). https://doi.org/10.1007/978-3-319-68167-2_20
6. Montenegro, M., Peña, R., Sánchez-Hernández, J.: A generic intermediate representation for verification condition generation. In: Falaschi, M. (ed.) LOPSTR 2015. LNCS, vol. 9527, pp. 227–243. Springer, Cham (2015). https://doi.org/10.1007/978-3-319-27436-2_14
7. de Moura, Leonardo, Bjørner, Nikolaj: Z3: an efficient SMT solver. In: Ramakrishnan, C.R., Rehof, Jakob (eds.) TACAS 2008. LNCS, vol. 4963, pp. 337–340. Springer, Heidelberg (2008). https://doi.org/10.1007/978-3-540-78800-3_24
8. Mustafa, S., Deris, S., Mohamad, R.: Systematic Mapping Study in Automatic Test Case Generation, pp. 703–720. IOS Press, Amsterdam (2014)

Reasoning and Effects

A Proof Assistant Based Formalisation of a Subset of Sequential Core Erlang

Péter Bereczky[1]([✉])[iD], Dániel Horpácsi[1][iD], and Simon Thompson[1,2][iD]

[1] Eötvös Loránd University, Budapest, Hungary
berpeti@inf.elte.hu, daniel-h@elte.hu
[2] University of Kent, Canterbury, UK
S.J.Thompson@kent.ac.uk

Abstract. We present a proof-assistant-based formalisation of a subset of Erlang, intended to serve as a base for proving refactorings correct. After discussing how we reused concepts from related work, we show the syntax and semantics of our formal description, including the abstractions involved (e.g. the concept of a closure). We also present essential properties of the formalisation (e.g. determinism) along with the summary of their machine-checked proofs. Finally, we prove expression pattern equivalences which can be interpreted as simple local refactorings.

Keywords: Erlang formalisation · Formal semantics · Machine-checked formalisation · Operational semantics · Term rewrite system · Coq

1 Introduction

There are a number of language processors, development and refactoring tools for mainstream languages, but most of these tools are not theoretically well-founded: they lack a mathematically precise description of what they do to the source code. In particular, refactoring tools are expected to change programs without affecting their behaviour, but in practice, this property is typically verified by regression testing alone. Higher assurance can be achieved by making a formal argument – a proof – about this property, but neither programming languages nor program transformations are easily formalised.

When arguing about behaviour-preservation of program refactoring, we argue about program semantics. To be able to do this in a precise manner, we need a formal, mathematical definition of the semantics in question, on which to base formal verification. Unfortunately, most programming languages lack fully formal definitions, which makes it challenging to deal with them in formal ways.

Erlang, similarly to its younger siblings like Elixir and LFE, is having its renaissance in implementing instant messaging, e-commerce and fintech. Extensive code bases therefore need to be developed and maintained in these languages, which in turn requires refactoring support. Our work aims to improve trustworthiness of Erlang refactorings via formal verification, and in particular

© Springer Nature Switzerland AG 2020
A. Byrski and J. Hughes (Eds.): TFP 2020, LNCS 12222, pp. 139–158, 2020.
https://doi.org/10.1007/978-3-030-57761-2_7

we formalise Core Erlang, which is not only a subset of Erlang, but also the target for translation of Erlang and Elixir in the compiler front-end. The formalisation of Core Erlang can also be seen as a stepping stone toward a definition for the entire Erlang language.

This paper presents the Coq [19] formalisation of a big-step semantics for a subset of sequential Core Erlang. In building this we rely not only on the language specification and the reference implementation, but also on some earlier work on semantics. Using this we made a definition of a semantics that can be properly embedded in Coq, and, on the basis of this, we also proved some basic properties of the semantics and some simple program equivalences. The main contributions of this paper are:

1. The definition of a formal semantics for a sequential subset of Erlang (Core Erlang), based partly on existing formalisations.
2. An implementation for this semantics in the Coq Proof Assistant.
3. Theorems that formalise a number of properties of this formalisation, e.g. determinism, with their machine-checked proofs.
4. Results on program evaluation and equivalence verification using the semantics definition, all formalised in Coq.

The rest of the paper is structured as follows. In Sect. 2 we review the existing formalisations of Core Erlang and Erlang, and compare them in order to help understand the construction of our formal semantics. In Sect. 3 we describe the proposed formal description, including abstractions, syntax, and semantics, while in Sect. 4 we describe a number of applications of the semantics. Section 5 discusses future work and concludes.

2   Related Work

Although there have already been a number of attempts to build a fully-featured formal definition of the Erlang programming language, the existing definitions show varying language coverage, and only some of them, covering mostly the concurrent part of Core Erlang or Erlang, are implemented in a machine-checked proof system. This alone would provide a solid motivation for the work presented in this paper, but our ultimate goal is to prove refactoring-related theorems, such as program equivalences, in the Coq Proof Assistant, based on this semantics.

We have reviewed the extensive related work on formalisations of both Erlang [6,7,9,18] and Core Erlang [5,8,11–13,15,16], incorporating ideas from these sources as appropriate.

The vast majority of related work on Erlang formalisations presents small-step operational semantics. In particular, one of our former project members has already defined most elements of sequential Erlang in the K specification language [9]. We could reformalise this small-step semantics in Coq, but for the proofs to be carried out in the proof assistant, it is too fine-grained. As Owens and others point out, (functional) big-step semantics is a good compromise in terms of amount of detail and ease of use [17]; furthermore, our definition of equivalence does not rely on intermediate execution steps. Thus, our current approach is to define an inductive relational big-step semantics for the language, and down the road we may derive its computable function.

Most papers addressing the formal definition of Erlang focus on the concurrent part of the language, including process management and communication primitives, which is not relevant to our current formalisation goals. Harrison's formalisation of CoErl [8] concentrates on how communication works, and in particular how mailboxes are processed.

Although the papers dealing with the sequential parts tend to present different approaches to defining the semantics, the elements of the language covered and the syntax used to describe them are very similar; there are, however, some minor differences. Some definitions model the language very closely, whilst others abstract away particular aspects; for instance, unlike the work of Neuhäußer et al. [15], the semantics of Lanese et al. [11] describes function applications only for named functions. There is another notable difference in the existing formalisations from the syntactic point of view: some define values as a subclass of expressions by representing them as a distinct syntactic category [6,7,15,18], while others define values as "ground patterns" [11–13,16], that is as a subset of patterns. Both approaches have their advantages and disadvantages, and we discuss this question in more detail in Sect. 3.

We principally used the work by Lanese et al. on defining reversible semantics for Erlang [11–13,16], by defining a language "basically equivalent to a subset of Core Erlang" [16]. Although they do not take Core Erlang functions and their closures into consideration (except for top-level functions), which we needed to define from scratch, their work proved to be a good starting point for defining a big-step operational semantics. In addition, we took the Core Erlang language specification [4] and the Erlang/OTP compiler for Core Erlang as reference points for understanding the basic abstractions of the language in more detail. When defining function applications, we took some ideas from a paper embedding Core Erlang into Prolog [5], and when tackling match expressions, the big-step semantics for FMON [3] proved to be useful. Fredlund's fundamental work [6] was very influential, but his treatment of Erlang formal semantics mainly discusses concurrency.

There were some abstractions missing in almost all papers (e.g. the `let` binding with multiple variables, `letrec`, *map* expressions), for which we had to rely on the informal definitions described in the language specification [4] and the Erlang/OTP compiler. Also, in most of the papers, the global environment is modified at step of the execution; in contrast, our semantics is less fine-grained as side-effects have not been implemented yet. Unfortunately, the official language specification document was written in 2004, and there were some new features (e.g. the *map* data type) introduced to Core Erlang since then. These features do not have an informal description either; however, we took the Erlang/OTP compiler as the reference implementation and build the formalisation on that.

There is a considerable body of work on formalisations of other sequential languages, both functional, as is the case of CakeML [10], and imperative, as in CompCert [14], and indeed the trend to formalising programming language metatheory has been systematised in the POPLmark challenge [2].

3   Formal Semantics of Core Erlang

Here we present our formal definition of Core Erlang formalised in Coq. Throughout this section, we will frequently quote the Coq definition; in some cases, we use the Coq syntax and quote literally, but in case of the semantic rules, we turned the consecutive implications into inference rule notation for better readability. The Coq formalisation is available on Github [1].

3.1   Syntax

This section gives a brief overview of the syntax in our formalisation.

```
Inductive Literal : Type :=
| Atom (s: string)
| Integer (x : Z)
| EmptyList
| EmptyTuple
| EmptyMap.
```

```
Inductive Pattern : Type :=
| PVar (v : Var)
| PLiteral (l : Literal)
| PList (hd tl : Pattern)
| PTuple (t : list Tuple)
```

Fig. 1. Syntax of literals

Fig. 2. Syntax of patterns

The syntax of literals and patterns (Figs. 1 and 2) is based on the papers mentioned in Sect. 2.

For the definition of the syntax of expressions, we need an auxiliary type, which represents function identifiers. In Core Erlang these are pairs of function names and arities (number of arguments). Note that the language allows the overloading of function names as long as it is done with different arities.

$$\text{Definition } \textit{FunctionIdentifier} : \text{Type} := string \times nat.$$

With the help of this type alias and the previous definitions, we can describe the syntax of expressions (Fig. 3).

As it can be seen, we only include atoms and integers as base type literals in the formalisation. These are representatives of built in data types in the language, and other types (such as floats and binaries) can be added in the future. As mentioned in Sect. 2, our expression syntax is very similar to the existing definitions found in the related work. The main abstractions are based on Fredlund and Vidal's work [6,7,18] and the additional expressions (e.g. let, letrec, apply, call) on the Core Erlang specification [4] as well as work by Lanese, Neäuhußer, Nishida and their co-authors [11–13,15,16].

Moreover, in our formalisation, we included the *map* type, primitive operations and function calls are handled alike, and in addition, the *ELet* and *ELetrec* statements handle multiple simultaneous bindings.

```
Inductive Expression : Type :=
| ELiteral (l : Literal)
| EVar (v : Var)
| EFunSig (f : FunctionIdentifier)
| EFun (vl : list Var) (e : Expression)
| EList (hd tl : Expression)
| ETuple (l : list Expression)
| ECall (f: string) (l : list Expression)
| EApply (exp: Expression) (l : list Expression)
| ECase (e : Expression) (l : list Clause)
| ELet (s : list Var) (el : list Expression) (e : Expression)
| ELetrec (fnames : list FunctionIdentifier) (fsᵃ : list ((list Var) × Expression)) (e :
Expression)
| EMap (kl vl : list Expression)
with Clause : Type :=
| CCons (p : Pattern) (guard e : Expression).
```

ᵃ This is the list of the defined functions (list of variable lists and body expressions)

Fig. 3. Syntax of expressions

Values. In Core Erlang, literals, lists, tuples, maps, and closures can be values, i.e. results of the evaluation of other expressions. We define values as a separate syntactic category and also include function closures in the definition. Values should be seen as a semantic domain, to which expressions are evaluated (see Fig. 4). This distinction of values allows the semantics to be defined as a big-step relation with a codomain of semantic objects. This approach creates duplication in the syntax, since expression syntax is not reused, but it substantially simplifies building proofs of theorems about values.

```
Inductive Value : Type :=
| VLiteral (l : Literal)
| VClosureᵃ (ref : Environment + FunctionIdentifier) (vl : list Var) (e : Expression)
| VList (vhd vtl : Value)
| VTuple (vl : list Value)
| VMap (kl vl : list Value).
```

ᵃ A closure represents a function definition together with an environment representing the context in which the function was defined: *ref* will be the environment or a reference to it, *vl* will be the function parameter list and *e* will be the body expression. *Environment* is defined in Section 3.2 below.

Fig. 4. Syntax of values

In the upcoming sections, we will use the following syntax abbreviations:

$$tt := VLiteral\,(Atom\ "true")$$
$$ff := VLiteral\,(Atom\ "false")$$

We now discuss why we this particular approach. As noted in Sect. 2, other approaches are possible: either they are related to patterns (in the work of Lanese et al. [11–13,16]) or to expressions, as in the Erlang formalisations and in the work of Neuhäußer et al. [6,7,15,18]. Moreover, there are two main approach to define the aforementioned relation of values and expressions or patterns:

- Values are not a distinct syntactic category, so they are defined with an explicit subset relation;
- Values are syntactically distinct, and there is no explicit subset relation between values and expressions or patterns [6,7,15,18].

When values are not defined as a distinct syntactic set (or as a semantic domain), a subset relation has to be defined that tells whether an expression represents a value. In Coq, this subset relation is defined by a judgment on expressions, but this would require a proof every time an expression is handled as a value: the elements of a subset are defined by a pair, i.e. the expression itself and a proof that the expression is a value. While this is a feasible approach, it generates lots of unnecessary trivial statements to prove in the dynamic semantics: instead of using a list of values, a list of expressions has to be used, for which proofs must be given about the head and tail being values (see the example in Sect. 3.2 for more details about list evaluation). In addition, the main issue with these approaches is that values do not always form a proper subset of either patterns or expressions [4]: when lambda functions and function identifiers (signatures) are considered, values must include closures (i.e. the normal form of function expressions), which are not included in the expression syntax.

We chose to relate values to expressions, because semantically expressions are evaluated to values and not patterns. In particular, we reused the constructs in the expression syntax in our value definition, and we also included closures, rather than functions as in the work of Neuhäußer et al. [15].

3.2 Semantics

We define a big-step operational semantics for the Core Erlang syntax described in the previous section. In order to do so, we need to define environment types to be included in the evaluation configuration. In particular, we define *environments* which hold values of variable symbols and function identifiers, and separately we define *closure environments* to store closure-local context.

Environment. The variable environment stores the bindings made with pattern matching in parameter passing as well as in `let`, `letrec`, `case` (and `try`) expressions. Note that the bindings may include both variable names and function identifiers, with the latter being associated with function expressions in normal form (closures). In addition, there are top-level functions in the language, and they too are stored in this environment, similarly to those defined with the `letrec` statement.

Top-level, global definitions could be stored in a separate environment in a separate configuration cell, but we decided to handle all bindings in one environment, because this separation would cause a lot of duplication in the semantic rules and in the actual Coq implementation. Therefore, there is one union type to construct a single environment for function identifiers and variables, both local and global. It is worth mentioning that in our case the environment always stores values since Core Erlang evaluation is strict, i.e. an expression first evaluates to some value, then a variable can be bound to this value.

We define the environment in the following way:

`Definition` *Environment* : `Type` := *list* ((*Var* + *FunctionIdentifier*) × *Value*).

We denote this mapping by Γ in what follows, whilst $\varnothing$ is used to denote the empty environment. We also define a number of helper functions to manage environments, which will be used in formal proofs below. For the sake of simplicity, we omit the actual Coq definitions of these operations and rather provide a short summary of their effect.

- *get_value* Γ *key*: Returns the value associated with *key* in Γ. In the following sections it will be denoted by $\Gamma(key)$.
- *insert_value* Γ *key value*: Inserts the (*key,value*) pair into Γ. If this *key* is already included, it will replace the original binding with the new one (according to the Core Erlang specification [4], Sect. 6). The next three function is implemented with this replacing insertion.
- *add_bindings bindings* Γ: Appends to Γ the variable-value pairs given in *bindings*.
- *append_vars_to_env varlist valuelist* Γ: It is used for `let` statements and adds the bindings (variables in *varlist* to values in *valuelist*) to Γ.
- *append_funs_to_env funsiglist param-bodylist* Γ: Appends function identifier-closure pairs to Γ. These closure values are assembled from *param-bodylist* which contains the parameter lists and body expressions.

Closure Environment. In Core Erlang, function expressions evaluate to closures. Closures have to be modeled in the semantics carefully in order to capture the bindings in the context of the closure properly. The following Core Erlang program shows an example where we need to explicitly store a binding context to closures:

```
let X = 42 in
  let Y = fun() -> X in
    let X = 5 in
      apply Y()
```

The semantics needs to make sure that we apply static binding here: the function Y has to return 42 rather than 5. This requires the Y's context to be stored along with its body, which is done by coupling them into a *function closure*.

When evaluating a function expression a closure is created. This value is a copy of the current environment, an expression (the function body), and a variable list (the parameters of the function). The mentioned environment could be encoded with the *VClosure* constructor in the *Value* inductive type using the actual environment (see Fig. 4), however, this cannot be used when the function is recursive. Here is an example:

```
letrec 'x'/0 = fun() -> apply 'x'/0() in apply 'x'/0()
```

In Core Erlang, `letrec` allows definition of recursive functions, so the body of the $'x'/0$ must be evaluated in an environment which stores $'x'/0$ mapped to a closure. But this closure contains the environment in which the body expression must be evaluated and that is the same environment we are trying to define. So the this is a recursively defined structure in embedded closures in the environment where the recursion has no base case. Here is the problem visualized (we denote `apply` $'x'/0()$ with *body*):

$$\{'x'/0 : VClosure \{'x'/0 : VClosure \{'x'/0 : ...\} \; [] \; body\} \; [] \; body\}$$

In Coq such constructs or functions cannot be computed without using a clock or fuel [17] which ensures termination. Instead of this we can use the step-by-step unfolding of the environment. This means that, while using the big-step semantics, the environment of the next proving step will be constructed by the current step.

We could use a simple additional attribute in the closure values which marks that the closure is recursive, then it is enough to store the non-recursive part of the environment in the closure. However, if multiple functions are defined at a time and they can potentially apply one another, they do not store information (parameter lists and body expressions) about the other functions. Therefore, we need another approach.

We do not make any syntactic changes to the function body, but we solve this issue by introducing the concept of closure environments. The idea is that the name of the function (variable name or function identifier) is mapped to the application environment (this way, it can be used as a reference). It is enough to encode the function's name with the *VClosure* constructor. This closure environment can only be used together with the use of the environment and items cannot be deleted from it.

`Definition` *Closures* : `Type` := *list* (*FunctionIdentifier* × *Environment*).

All in all, closures will ensure that the functions will be evaluated in the right environments. We also describe the formal evaluation proofs of the examples above in Sect. 4.2. There are two ways of using their evaluation environment (*ref* attribute of *Environment* + *FunctionIdentifier* type):

- Either using the concrete environment from the closure value directly if *ref* is from the type *Environment*;
- Or using the reference and the closure environment to get the evaluation environment when the type of *ref* is *FunctionIdentifier*.

In the next sections, we denote this function-environment mapping with Δ, and $\varnothing$ denotes the empty closure environment. Similarly to ordinary environments, closure environments are managed with a number of simple helper functions; like before, we omit the formal definition of these and provide an informative summary instead.

- *get_env key* Δ: Returns the environment associated with *key* in Δ if *key* is a *FunctionIdentifier*. If *key* is an *Environment*, the function simply returns it. This function is implemented with the help of the next function.
- *get_env_from_closure key* Δ: Returns the environment associated with *key*. If the *key* is not present in the Δ, it returns $\varnothing$.
- *set_closure* Δ *key* Γ: Adds (*key*, Γ) pair to Δ. If *key* exists in Δ, its value will be replaced. Used in the next function.
- *append_funs_to_closure fnames* Δ Γ: Inserts a (*funid$_i$*, Γ) binding into Δ for every *funid$_i$* function identifier in *fnames*.

Dynamic Semantics. The presented semantics, theorems, tests and proofs are available in Coq on the project's Github repository [1].

With the language syntax and the execution environment defined, we are ready to define a big-step semantics for Core Erlang. The operational semantics is denoted by

$$|\Gamma, \Delta, e| \xrightarrow{e} v ::= eval\_expr\ \Gamma\ \Delta\ e\ v$$

where *eval_expr* is the semantic relation in Fig. 5. This means that *e Expression* evaluates to *v Value* in the environment Γ and closure environment Δ. We reused *length, combine, nth* and *In* from Coq's built-ins [19] in the following definitions.

Prior to presenting the rules of the operational semantics, we define a helper for pointwise evaluation of multiple independent expressions: *eval_all* states that a list of expressions evaluates to a list of values.

$$eval\_all\ \Gamma\ \Delta\ exps\ vals :=$$
$$length\ exps = length\ vals \Longrightarrow$$
$$(\forall\ (exp : Expression), (val : Value),$$
$$In\ (exp, val)\ (combine\ exps\ vals) \Longrightarrow$$
$$|\Gamma, \Delta, exp| \xrightarrow{e} val)$$

With the help of this proposition, we will be able to define the semantics of function calls, tuples, and expressions of other kinds in a more readable way.

There are two other auxiliary definition which will simplify the main definition:

– *match_clause* (*v* : *Value*) (*cs* : *list Clause*) (*i* : *nat*) tries to match the *i*th pattern given in the list of clauses (*cs*) with the value *v*. The result is optional; if the *i*th clause does not match the value, it returns Coq's built-in *None* value while the matching has been successful, it returns the guard and body expressions with the pattern variable-value bindings from the *i*th clause.

– The *no_previous_match* property states that the clause selection cannot be successful up to the *i*th clause:

$$no\_previous\_match \ i \ \Delta \ \Gamma \ cs \ v :=$$
$$\forall j : nat, \ j < i \Longrightarrow (\forall \ (gg, ee : Expression), \ (bb : list \ (Var \times Value)),$$
$$match\_clause \ v \ cs \ j = Some \ (gg, \ ee, \ bb) \Longrightarrow$$
$$(|\, add\_bindings \ bb \ \Gamma, \Delta, gg \ |\, \overset{e}{\rightarrow} f\!f))$$

The formal definition of the proposed operational semantics for Core Erlang is presented in Fig. 5. This figure presents the actual Coq definition, but the inductive cases are formatted as inference rules. In the next paragraphs, we provide short explanations of the less trivial rules.

– Rule 3.7: At first, the case expression *e* must be evaluated to some *v* value. Then this *v* must match to the pattern (*match_clause* function) of the specified *i*th clause. This match provides the guard, the body expressions of the clause and also the pattern variable binding list. The guard must be evaluated to *tt* in the extended environment with the result of the pattern matching (the binding list mentioned before). The *no_previous_match* states, that for every clause before the *i*th one the pattern matching cannot succeed or the guard expression evaluates in the extended environment to *ff*. Thereafter the evaluation of the body expression can continue in the above mentioned extended environment.

– Rule 3.8: At first, the parameters must be evaluated to values. Then these values are passed to the auxiliary *eval* function which simulates the behaviour of inter-module function calls (e.g. the addition inter-module call is represented in Coq with the addition of numbers). This results in a value which will be the result of the *ECall* evaluation.

– Rule 3.9: This rule works in similar way that given by de Angelis and co-authors in [5] with the addition of closures. To use this rule, first *exp* has to be evaluated to a closure. Moreover, every parameter must be evaluated to a value. Finally, the closure's body expression evaluates to the result in an extended environment which is constructed from the parameter variable-value bindings and the evaluation environment of the closure. This environment can be acquired from the closure environment indirectly or it is present in the closure value itself (Sect. 3.2).

– Rule 3.10: At first, every expression given must be evaluated to a value. Then the body of the `let` expression must be evaluated in the original environment extended with the variable-value bindings.

– Rule 3.11: From the functions described (a list of variable list and body expressions), closures will be created and appended to the environment and

Inductive *eval_expr : Environment → Closures → Expression → Value →* **Prop** :=

$$\overline{|\Gamma, \Delta, ELiteral\ l\ | \xrightarrow{e} VLiteral\ l} \quad (3.1) \qquad \overline{|\Gamma, \Delta, EFunSig\ fsig| \xrightarrow{e} \Gamma(inr\ fsig)} \quad (3.2)$$

$$\overline{|\Gamma, \Delta, EVar\ s| \xrightarrow{e} \Gamma(inl\ s)} \quad (3.3) \qquad \overline{|\Gamma, \Delta, EFun\ vl\ e| \xrightarrow{e} VClosure\ (inl\ \Gamma)\ vl\ e} \quad (3.4)$$

$$\frac{eval\_all\ \Gamma\ \Delta\ exps\ vals}{|\Gamma, \Delta, ETuple\ exps| \xrightarrow{e} VTuple\ vals} \quad (3.5) \qquad \frac{|\Gamma, \Delta, hd| \xrightarrow{e} hdv \quad |\Gamma, \Delta, tl| \xrightarrow{e} tlv}{|\Gamma, \Delta, EList\ hd\ tl| \xrightarrow{e} VList\ hdv\ tlv} \quad (3.6)$$

$$\frac{\begin{array}{c} match\_clause\ v\ cs\ i = Some\ (guard, exp, bindings) \\ |add\_bindings\ bindings\ \Gamma, \Delta, guard| \xrightarrow{e} tt \\ |add\_bindings\ bindings\ \Gamma, \Delta, exp| \xrightarrow{e} v' \\ |\Gamma, \Delta, e| \xrightarrow{e} v \\ no\_previous\_match\ i\ \Delta\ \Gamma\ cs\ v \end{array}}{|\Gamma, \Delta, ECase\ e\ cs| \xrightarrow{e} v'} \quad (3.7)$$

$$\frac{eval\_all\ \Gamma\ \Delta\ params\ vals \quad eval\ fname\ vals = v}{|\Gamma, \Delta, ECall\ fname\ params| \xrightarrow{e} v} \quad (3.8)$$

$$\frac{eval\_all\ \Gamma\ \Delta\ params\ vals \quad |\Gamma, \Delta, exp| \xrightarrow{e} VClosure\ ref\ var\_list\ body}{|\Gamma, \Delta, EApply\ exp\ params| \xrightarrow{e} v} \quad (3.9)$$

$$\frac{eval\_all\ \Gamma\ \Delta\ exps\ vals \quad |append\_vars\_to\_env\ vars\ vals\ \Gamma, \Delta, e| \xrightarrow{e} v}{|\Gamma, \Delta, ELet\ vars\ exps\ e| \xrightarrow{e} v} \quad (3.10)$$

For the following rule we introduce $\Gamma' ::= append\_funs\_to\_env\ fnames\ funs\ \Gamma$

$$\frac{length\ funs = length\ fnames \quad |\Gamma', append\_funs\_to\_closure\ fnames\ \Delta\ \Gamma', e| \xrightarrow{e} v}{|\Gamma, \Delta, ELetrec\ fnames\ funs\ e| \xrightarrow{e} v} \quad (3.11)$$

$$\frac{eval\_all\ \Gamma\ \Delta\ kl\ kvals \quad eval\_all\ \Gamma\ \Delta\ vl\ vvals \quad length\ kl = length\ vl}{|\Gamma, \Delta, EMap\ kl\ vl| \xrightarrow{e} VMap\ kvals\ vvals} \quad (3.12)$$

Fig. 5. The big-step operational semantics of Core Erlang

closure environment associated with the given function identifiers (*fnames*). In these modified contexts the evaluation continues.

– Rule 3.12: Introduces the evaluation for maps. This rule states that every key in the map's key list and value list must be evaluated to values resulting in two lists of values (for the map keys and their associated values) from which the value map is constructed[1].

We also note that this big-step definition has been partly based on the small-step definition introduced by Lanese [11,13], Nishida [16], and Neuhasser[15] and in some aspects on the big-step semantics in Focaltest [3] and de Angelis' symbolic evaluation [5]. In addition, for most of the language elements discussed, an informal definition is available in the language specification [4].

After discussing these rules, we show an example where the approach in which values are defined as a subset of expressions is more difficult to work with. Let us consider a unary operator (*val*) on expressions which marks the values of the expressions. With the help of this operator, the type of values can be defined:

$$Value ::= \{e : Expression \mid e \; val\}.$$

Let us consider the key ways in which this would modify our semantics.

- *Environment* → *Closures* → *Expression* → *Expression* → Prop would be the type of *eval_expr*. This way we need an additional proposition which states that values are expressions in normal form, *i.e.* they cannot be used on the left side of the rewriting rules.
- The expressions which are in normal form could not be rewritten.
- Function definitions have to be handled as values
- Because of the strictness of Core Erlang, the derivation rules change, additional checks are needed in the preconditions, e.g. in the Rule 3.6:

$$\frac{\begin{array}{ll} tlv\; val & |\Gamma, \Delta, hd| \xrightarrow{e} hdv \lor hd = hdv \\ hdv\; val & |\Gamma, \Delta, tl| \xrightarrow{e} tlv \lor tl = tlv \end{array}}{|\Gamma, \Delta, EList\; hd\; tl| \xrightarrow{e} EList\; hdv\; tlv}$$

This approach has the same expressive power as the presented one, but it has more preconditions to prove while using it. For reason, argue that our formalisation is easier to use.

Proofs of Properties of the Semantics. We have formalised and proved theorems about the attributes of the operations, auxiliary functions and the semantics. We present two examples here, together with sketches of their proofs.

Theorem 1 (Determinism)
$\forall \; (\Gamma : Environment), (\Delta : Closures), (e : Expression), (v_1 : Value),$
$|\Gamma, \Delta, e| \xrightarrow{e} v_1 \implies (\forall v_2 : Value, |\Gamma, \Delta, e| \xrightarrow{e} v_2 \implies v_1 = v_2).$

Proof. Induction by the construction of the semantics.

---

[1] In the future, this evaluation has to be modified, because the normal form of maps cannot contain duplicate keys, moreover it is ordered based on these keys.

- Rules 3.1, 3.2, 3.3 and 3.4 are trivial: e.g. a value literal can only be derivated from its expression counterpart.
- Rules 3.5 and 3.12 are similar, a map is basically a double tuple in the current semantics. According to the induction hypothesis each element in the expression tuple can be evaluated to a single value, so the tuple itself evaluates to the tuple which contains these values. The proof for maps is similar.
- Rule 3.6 The head and the tail expression of the list can be evaluated to a single head and tail value according to the induction hypotheses. So the list constructed from the head and tail expressions can only be evaluated to the value list constructed from the head and tail values.
- Rule 3.7 The induction hypothesis states that the base and the clause body and guard expressions evaluate deterministically. The clause selector functions are also deterministic, so there is only one possible way to select a body expression to evaluate.
- The other cases are similar to those presented above.

□

Theorem 2 (Commutativity). $\forall$ *(v, v' : Value)*,
eval "plus"[v; v'] = eval "plus"[v'; v].

Proof. First we separate cases based on the all possible construction of values (5 constructors, v and v' values, that is 25 cases). In every case where either of the values is not an integer literal, the *eval* function results in the same error value (in this version we can not distinguish errors) on both side of the equality.

One case is remaining, when both v and v' are integer literals. In this case the definition of *eval* is the addition of these numbers, and the commutativity of this addition has already been proven in the Coq standard library [19].   □

It is important to note that if exceptions are included in the formalisation, then this theorem probably would not be correct as it stands, and would need to be adjusted.

4   Application and Testing the Semantics

In this section we present some use cases. First, we elaborate on the verification of the semantics definition by testing it against the Erlang/OTP compiler, then we show some examples on how we used the formalisation for deriving program behaviour and for proving program equivalence.

4.1   Testing the Semantics

Due to a lack of an up-to-date language specification, we validated the correctness of our semantics definition by comparing it to the behaviour of the code emitted by the Erlang/OTP compiler.

To test our formal semantics, we first used equivalence partitioning. We have written tests both in Coq (v 8.11.0) and in Core Erlang (OTP 22.0) for every type of expression defined in our formalisation (i.e. for every possible inference rule application). There are also some special complex expressions that require separate test cases (e.g. using bound variables in `let` expressions, application of recursive functions, returned functions etc.). In the future, we plan to automate the evaluation of both Coq and Core Erlang code and comparison of the results.

Apart from the formal expression evaluation examples, the proofs about the properties of the semantics (e.g. determinism) and the expression equivalences also provided an additional layer of assurance about complying to the behaviour of the Erlang/OTP compiler.

4.2 Formal Expression Evaluation

Here we demonstrate how Core Erlang expressions are evaluated in the formal semantics. For readability, we use concrete Core Erlang syntax in the proofs, and trivial statements (e.g. the use of Rule 3.9) are omitted from the proof tree. The first example shows how to evaluate a simple expression with binding:

$$\cfrac{\cfrac{\overline{\{X:5\}(X)=5}}{|\{X:5\},\varnothing,X|\overset{e}{\to}5}\ 3.3}{|\varnothing,\varnothing,\texttt{let }X=5\texttt{ in }X|\overset{e}{\to}5}\ 3.10$$

The next example is the first one mentioned in Sect. 3.2 and intends to demonstrate the purpose of the closure values. Here at the application of 3.9 it is shown that the body of the application is evaluated in the environment given by the closure. For readability, we denote the inner `let` $X = 5$ in `apply` $Y()$ expression with *exp*.

$$\cfrac{\cfrac{\cfrac{\cfrac{\overline{\{X:42\}(X)=42}}{|\{X:42\},\varnothing,X|\overset{e}{\to}42}\ 3.3}{|\{X:5,Y:VClosure\ (inl\ \{X:42\})\ []\ X\},\varnothing,\texttt{apply }Y()|\overset{e}{\to}42}\ 3.9}{|\{X:42,Y:VClosure\ (inl\ \{X:42\})\ []\ X\},\varnothing,exp|\overset{e}{\to}42}\ 3.10}{|\{X:42\},\varnothing,\texttt{let }Y=\texttt{fun}()\to X\texttt{ in }exp|\overset{e}{\to}42}\ 3.10}{|\varnothing,\varnothing,\texttt{let }X=42\texttt{ in let }Y=\texttt{fun}()\to X\texttt{ in }exp|\overset{e}{\to}42}\ 3.10$$

Next we show the previous example, but now using a recursive function between the two `let` expressions in order to demonstrate the use of the closure environment. For readability we denote $VClosure\ (inr\ 'f'/0)\ []\ X$ with *clos* and the inner `let` $X = 5$ in `apply` $'f'/0()$ with *exp*, just like before.

$$\cfrac{\cfrac{\cfrac{\cfrac{\cfrac{\{X:42,'f'/0:clos\}(X)=42}{|\{X:42,'f'/0:clos\},\{'f'/0:\{X:42,'f'/0:clos\}\},X|\overset{e}{\rightarrow}42}3.3}{|\{X:5,'f'/0:clos\},\{'f'/0:\{X:42,'f'/0:clos\}\},\mathtt{apply}\ Y()|\overset{e}{\rightarrow}42}3.9}{|\{X:42,'f'/0:clos\},\{'f'/0:\{X:42,'f'/0:clos\}\},exp|\overset{e}{\rightarrow}42}3.10}{|\{X:42\},\varnothing,\mathtt{letrec}\ 'f'/0=\mathtt{fun}()\rightarrow X\ \mathtt{in}\ exp|\overset{e}{\rightarrow}42}3.11}{|\varnothing,\varnothing,\mathtt{let}\ X=42\ \mathtt{in}\ \mathtt{letrec}\ 'f'/0=\mathtt{fun}()\rightarrow X\ \mathtt{in}\ exp|\overset{e}{\rightarrow}42}3.10$$

At the point of the use of Rule 3.11 we save in the closure environment the current local environment extended with the closure value of the function bound to this function's identifier. This way, later in the evaluation, this environment can be used (e.g. when using Rule 3.3).

The last example is the second one mentioned in Sect. 3.2 and cannot be evaluated in our formalisation, because of divergence. For readability we introduce $\Gamma := \{'x'/0 : VClosure\ (inr\ 'x'/0)\ [\![\ (\mathtt{apply}\ 'x'/0())\}$ (the environment after the binding is added).

$$\cfrac{\cfrac{\cfrac{...}{|\Gamma,\{'x'/0:\Gamma\},\mathtt{apply}\ 'x'/0()|\overset{e}{\rightarrow}??}3.9}{|\Gamma,\{'x'/0:\Gamma\},\mathtt{apply}\ 'x'/0()|\overset{e}{\rightarrow}??}3.9}{|\varnothing,\varnothing,\mathtt{letrec}\ 'x'/0=\mathtt{fun}()\rightarrow\mathtt{apply}\ 'x'/0()\ \mathtt{in}\ \mathtt{apply}\ 'x'/0()|\overset{e}{\rightarrow}??}3.11$$

4.3 Expression Equivalence Proofs

Last but not least, let us present some expression equivalence proofs demonstrating the usability of this semantics definition implemented in Coq. This is a significant result of the paper since our ultimate goal with the formalisation is to prove refactorings correct.

For the simplicity, we use + to refer to the *append_vars_to_env* function and also for the addition inter-module call (i.e. $e_1 + e_2$ will denote the expression *ECall "plus"* $[e_1, e_2]$ in the following proofs) both in proofs and quoted code.

First, we present a rather simple example of expression equivalence.

Example 1 (Swapping variable values).

```
let X = 5 in let Y = 6 in X + Y
```

is equivalent to

```
let X = 6 in let Y = 5 in X + Y
```

Proof. This example can be proved by specialising Example 2 with concrete values.   □

Also a more abstract local refactoring also can be proved correct in our system.

Example 2 (Swapping variable expressions). If we make the following assumptions:

$$|\Gamma, \Delta, e_1| \xrightarrow{e} v_1 \qquad\qquad |\Gamma + \{A : v_2\}, \Delta, e_1| \xrightarrow{e} v_1$$
$$|\Gamma, \Delta, e_2| \xrightarrow{e} v_2 \qquad\qquad |\Gamma + \{A : v_1\}, \Delta, e_2| \xrightarrow{e} v_2$$
$$A \neq B$$

then

    let A = e1 **in let** B = e2 **in** A + B

is equivalent to

    let A = e2 **in let** B = e1 **in** A + B

Proof. First, we present the problem formalised.

$$\forall\,(\Gamma : Environment), (\Delta : Closures), (t : Value), (A, B : Var)$$
$$|\Gamma, \Delta, e_1| \xrightarrow{e} v_1 \implies |\Gamma + \{A : v_2\}, \Delta, e_1| \xrightarrow{e} v_1 \implies$$
$$|\Gamma, \Delta, e_2| \xrightarrow{e} v_2 \implies |\Gamma + \{A : v_1\}, \Delta, e_2| \xrightarrow{e} v_2 \implies A \neq B \implies$$
$$|\Gamma, \Delta, ELet\ [A]\ [e_1]\ (ELet\ [B]\ [e_2]$$
$$\qquad (ECall\ "plus"\ [EVar\ A; EVar\ B]))| \xrightarrow{e} t \iff$$
$$|\Gamma, \Delta, ELet\ [A]\ [e_2]\ (ELet\ [B]\ [e_1]$$
$$\qquad (ECall\ "plus"\ [EVar\ A; EVar\ B]))| \xrightarrow{e} t$$

The two directions of this equivalence are proved in exactly the same way, so only the forward ($\implies$) direction is presented here.

Now the main hypothesis has two let statements in itself. These statements could have only been evaluated with Rule 3.10, i.e. there are two values (v_1 and v_2 because of the determinism and the assumptions) to which e_1 and e_2 evaluates:

$$|\Gamma, \Delta, e_1| \xrightarrow{e} v_1 \text{ and } |\Gamma + \{A : v_1\}, \Delta, e_2| \xrightarrow{e} v_2$$

It is important to note, that during the evaluation of the inner let, A has already been bound to v_1. Moreover a new hypothesis also appeared:

$$|\Gamma + \{A : v_1, B : v_2\}, \Delta, A + B| \xrightarrow{e} t$$

This hypothesis implies that $t = eval\ "plus"\ [v_1, v_2]$ because of the evaluation with Rule 3.8 and 3.3, also when we add variables to the environment, the existing binding will be replaced.

Now, the goal can be solved with the construction of a derivation tree. We denote $\Gamma + \{A : v_2, B : v_1\}$ with Γ_v.

$$
\cfrac{
\cfrac{}{|\Gamma, \Delta, e_2| \xrightarrow{e} v_2}
\quad
\cfrac{
|\Gamma_v, \Delta, A + B| \xrightarrow{e} t
\quad
|\Gamma + \{A : v_2\}, \Delta, e_1| \xrightarrow{e} v_1
}{
|\Gamma + \{A : v_2\}, \Delta, \mathtt{let}\ B = e_1\ \mathtt{in}\ A + B| \xrightarrow{e} t
}\ 3.10
}{
|\Gamma, \Delta, \mathtt{let}\ A = e_2\ \mathtt{in}\ \mathtt{let}\ B = e_1\ \mathtt{in}\ A + B| \xrightarrow{e} t
}\ 3.10
$$

According to our assumptions, e_1 and e_2 evaluates to v_1 and v_2 in Γ and also in its extensions which contains bindings to A. Now for the addition, the following derivation tree can be used.

$$
\cfrac{
\cfrac{\Gamma_v(B) = v_1}{|\Gamma_v, \Delta, B| \xrightarrow{e} v_1}\ 3.3
\quad
\cfrac{\Gamma_v(A) = v_2}{|\Gamma_v, \Delta, A| \xrightarrow{e} v_2}\ 3.3
\quad
eval\ \text{``}plus\text{''}\ [v_2, v_1] = t
}{
|\Gamma_v, \Delta, A + B| \xrightarrow{e} t
}\ 3.8
$$

We can use the Rule 3.8 to evaluate the addition. The parameter variables will evaluate to v_2 and v_1 because of the replacing insertion mentioned before. With this knowledge, we get: $eval\ \text{``}plus\text{''}\ [v_2, v_1] = t$. As mentioned before $t = eval\ \text{``}plus\text{''}\ [v_1, v_2]$. So it is sufficient to prove, that:

$$
eval\ \text{``}plus\text{''}\ [v_2, v_1] = eval\ \text{``}plus\text{''}\ [v_1, v_2] \tag{4.1}
$$

The commutativity of $eval$ (Theorem 2) can be used to solve this equality.   □

Is it possible to replace the assumptions of Example 2 with statements about e_1 and e_2 not containing the variables A and B? Not directly; it it would require a theorem stating the evaluation of an expression that does not contain the variable A does not change in the extended environment which contains a binding of the variable A. This statement is not true for closure values, because they potentially save their evaluation environment which would differ in this case.

Now, we prove a similar simple local refactoring (this example is also generalised over the A, B variables).

Example 3 (Swapping variables in simultaneous let). If we assume that $A \neq B$ then

```
let <A, B> = <e1, e2> in A + B
```

is equivalent to

```
let <A, B> = <e2, e1> in A + B
```

Proof. The proof for this example is very similar to the proof for Example 2. The only difference is that one step is enough to evaluate the let expression. Inside it both e_1 and e_2 expressions evaluate in the same environment and that is the reason why no assumptions are needed.   □

Finally, we show another simple local refactoring about moving an expression to a function.

Example 4 (Moving an expression to a function).

    e

is equivalent to

```
let A = fun() -> e in
    apply A()
```

Proof. In this case, both directions should be proved. At first, we formalise the problem:

$$\forall \, (\Gamma : Environment), (\Delta : Closures), (t : Value), (A : Var)$$

$$|\Gamma, \Delta, e| \xrightarrow{e} t \Longleftrightarrow$$

$$|\Gamma, \Delta, ELet \, [A] \, [EFun \, [] \, e] \, (EApply \, (EVar \, A) \, [])| \xrightarrow{e} t$$

$\Longrightarrow$ direction:

This can be proved by the construction of a derivation tree. We denote $\Gamma + \{A : VClosure \, (inl \, \Gamma) \, [] \, e\}$ with Γ_A and the value $VClosure \, (inl \, \Gamma) \, [] \, e$ with cl in the tree.

$$\frac{\dfrac{}{|\Gamma, \Delta, \mathtt{fun}() \to e| \xrightarrow{e} cl} \; 3.3 \qquad \dfrac{\dfrac{}{|\Gamma_A, \Delta, A| \xrightarrow{e} cl} \; 3.4 \quad \dfrac{}{|\Gamma, \Delta, e| \xrightarrow{e} t} \; \text{Hypo.}}{|\Gamma_A, \Delta, \mathtt{apply} \; A()| \xrightarrow{e} t} \; 3.9 \;\; 3.10}{|\Gamma, \Delta, \mathtt{let} \; A = \mathtt{fun}() \to e \; \mathtt{in} \; \mathtt{apply} \; A()| \xrightarrow{e} t}$$

$\Longleftarrow$ direction:

This can be proved by the deconstruction of the hypothesis for the `let` expression. First only the 3.10 could have been used for the evaluation. This means that the function evaluates to some value, i.e. to the closure $VClosure \, (inl \, \Gamma) \, [] \, e$, because of Rule 3.4. We get a new hypothesis:

$$|\Gamma + \{A : VClosure \, (inl \, \Gamma) \, [] \, e\}, \Delta, \mathtt{apply} \; A()| \xrightarrow{e} t$$

Then the evaluation continued with the application of Rule 3.9. This means, that the A variable evaluates to the above mentioned closure (because Rule 3.3 and the replacing insertion into the environment) and the body of this closure evaluates to t in the closure's stored environment extended with the parameter-value bindings (in this case there is none). This means we get the following hypothesis: $|\Gamma, \Delta, e| \xrightarrow{e} t$ which is exactly what we want to prove.   □

To prove these examples in Coq, a significant number of lemmas were needed, such as the expansion of lists, the commutativity of *eval*, and so forth. However, the proofs mostly consist of the combination of hypotheses similar to the proofs in this paper. Although sometimes additional case analyses were needed, resulting in lots of sub-goals, these were solved similarly. In the future, these proofs should be simplified with the introduction of smart tactics and additional lemmas.

5   Future Work and Conclusion

Using Coq we have formalised a substantial subset of (Core) Erlang together with its semantics, and proved results on the formalisation itself as well as establishing a number of program equivalences in that semantics. Use of this formalisation is demanding in practice, partly because the Coq Proof Assistant makes its users write down proofs explicitly step by step. Of course this is a necessity of the correctness, however, this property results in lengthy proofs. This work is a first step in our project to establish a platform on which we can build and prove correct a range of refactorings for an existing programming language: Erlang.

There are several ways to enhance our formalisation. We intend to focus first on extending the semantics with additional expressions (e.g. binaries); formalising exceptions and exception handling, so that we can distinguish between different errors and also divergence; and handling and logging side-effects. To improve the formalisation we will create new lemmas, theorems and tactics to shorten the Coq implementation of the proofs; formalise and prove more refactoring strategies; and move to automate the testing process, running and comparing the results of the Core Erlang code and the theorems automatically.

Our longer-term goals include extending the work to Erlang (semantics and syntax), including concurrency, and distinguishing primitive operations and inter-module calls. The ultimate goal of the project is to change the core of a scheme-based refactoring system to a formally verified core.

Acknowledgements. The project has been supported by the European Union, co-financed by the European Social Fund (EFOP-3.6.2-16-2017-00013, "Thematic Fundamental Research Collaborations Grounding Innovation in Informatics and Infocommunications (3IN)").

Project no. ED_18-1-2019-0030 (Application domain specific highly reliable IT solutions subprogramme) has been implemented with the support provided from the National Research, Development and Innovation Fund of Hungary, financed under the Thematic Excellence Programme funding scheme.

References

1. Core Erlang Formalization. https://github.com/harp-project/Core-Erlang-Formalization/tree/general-proofs-with-clos-env. Accessed 11 Jun 2020
2. Aydemir, B.E., et al.: Mechanized metatheory for the masses: the POPLMARK challenge. In: Hurd, J., Melham, T. (eds.) TPHOLs 2005. LNCS, vol. 3603, pp. 50–65. Springer, Heidelberg (2005). https://doi.org/10.1007/11541868_4
3. Carlier, M., Dubois, C., Gotlieb, A.: A first step in the design of a formally verified constraint-based testing tool: FocalTest. In: Brucker, A.D., Julliand, J. (eds.) TAP 2012. LNCS, vol. 7305, pp. 35–50. Springer, Heidelberg (2012). https://doi.org/10.1007/978-3-642-30473-6_5
4. Carlsson, R., et al.: Core Erlang 1.0 language specification (2004)
5. De Angelis, E., et al.: Bounded symbolic execution for runtime error detection of Erlang programs. In: Kahsai, T., Vidal, G. (eds.) Proceedings 5th Workshop on Horn Clauses for Verification and Synthesis, HCVS 2018. EPTCS, vol. 278 (2018). https://doi.org/10.4204/EPTCS.278.4

6. Fredlund, L.Å.: A framework for reasoning about Erlang code. Ph.D. thesis, Royal Institute of Technology, Stockholm (2001)
7. Fredlund, L.Å., Gurov, D., Noll, T., Dam, M., Arts, T., Chugunov, G.: A verification tool for ERLANG. Int. J. Softw. Tools Technol. Transf. **4**(4), 405–420 (2002). https://doi.org/10.1007/s100090100071
8. Harrison, J.R.: Towards an Isabelle/HOL formalisation of core Erlang. In: Proceedings of the 16th ACM SIGPLAN International Workshop on Erlang, Erlang 2017. ACM (2017). https://doi.org/10.1145/3123569.3123576
9. Kőszegi, J.: KErl: Executable semantics for Erlang. In: CEUR Workshop Proceedings, vol. 2046, pp. 144–160 (2018)
10. Kumar, R., Myreen, M.O., Norrish, M., Owens, S.: CakeML: a verified implementation of ML. In: Principles of Programming Languages (POPL), January 2014. ACM Press (2014). https://doi.org/10.1145/2535838.2535841
11. Lanese, I., Nishida, N., Palacios, A., Vidal, G.: A theory of reversibility for Erlang. J. Log. Algebr. Methods Program. **100** (2018). https://doi.org/10.1016/j.jlamp.2018.06.004
12. Lanese, I., Nishida, N., Palacios, A., Vidal, G.: CauDEr: a causal-consistent reversible debugger for Erlang. In: Gallagher, J.P., Sulzmann, M. (eds.) FLOPS 2018. LNCS, vol. 10818, pp. 247–263. Springer, Cham (2018). https://doi.org/10.1007/978-3-319-90686-7_16
13. Lanese, I., Sangiorgi, D., Zavattaro, G.: Playing with bisimulation in Erlang. In: Boreale, M., Corradini, F., Loreti, M., Pugliese, R. (eds.) Models, Languages, and Tools for Concurrent and Distributed Programming. LNCS, vol. 11665, pp. 71–91. Springer, Cham (2019). https://doi.org/10.1007/978-3-030-21485-2_6
14. Leroy, X.: Formal verification of a realistic compiler. Commun. ACM **52** (2009). https://doi.org/10.1145/1538788.1538814
15. Neuhäußer, M.R., Noll, T.: Abstraction and model checking of core erlang programs in Maude. In: Denker, G., Talcott, C.L. (eds.) 6th International Workshop on Rewriting Logic and its Applications, WRLA 2006. ENTCS, vol. 174. Elsevier (2007). https://doi.org/10.1016/j.entcs.2007.06.013
16. Nishida, N., Palacios, A., Vidal, G.: A reversible semantics for Erlang. In: Hermenegildo, M.V., Lopez-Garcia, P. (eds.) LOPSTR 2016. LNCS, vol. 10184, pp. 259–274. Springer, Cham (2017). https://doi.org/10.1007/978-3-319-63139-4_15
17. Owens, S., Myreen, M.O., Kumar, R., Tan, Y.K.: Functional big-step semantics. In: Thiemann, P. (ed.) ESOP 2016. LNCS, vol. 9632, pp. 589–615. Springer, Heidelberg (2016). https://doi.org/10.1007/978-3-662-49498-1_23
18. Vidal, G.: Towards symbolic execution in Erlang. In: Voronkov, A., Virbitskaite, I. (eds.) PSI 2014. LNCS, vol. 8974, pp. 351–360. Springer, Heidelberg (2015). https://doi.org/10.1007/978-3-662-46823-4_28
19. The Coq Proof Assistant Documentation. https://coq.inria.fr/documentation. Accessed 21 Feb 2020

One-Shot Algebraic Effects as Coroutines

Satoru Kawahara and Yukiyoshi Kameyama$^{(\boxtimes)}$

Department of Computer Science, University of Tsukuba, Tsukuba, Japan
`sat@logic.cs.tsukuba.ac.jp`, `kameyama@acm.org`

Abstract. This paper presents a translation from algebraic effects and handlers to asymmetric coroutines, which provides a simple, efficient and widely applicable implementation for the former. Algebraic effects and handlers are emerging as main-stream language technology to model effectful computations and attract attention not only from researchers but also from programmers. They are implemented in various ways as part of compilers, interpreters, or as libraries. We present a direct embedding of one-shot algebraic effects and handlers in a language which has asymmetric coroutines. The key observation is that, by restricting the use of continuations to be *one-shot*, we obtain a simple and sufficiently general implementation via coroutines, which are available in many modern programming languages. Our translation is a macro-expressible translation, and we have implemented its embedding as a library in Lua and Ruby, which allows one to write effectful programs in a modular way using algebraic effects and handlers.

Keywords: Algebraic effect and handler · Coroutine · Continuation · Control operator · Macro expressibility

1 Introduction

Algebraic effects [21] and handlers [22] (AEH for short) are emerging as main-stream language technology to model effectful computations in a modular way. They are gaining more and more attention not only from researchers but also from practitioners. There are a few dedicated programming languages such as Eff [1], Multicore OCaml [7] and Koka [17] which have AEH as language primitives, and several main-stream programming languages such as Haskell, OCaml, Scala, JVM bytecode and C have library implementations for AEH. However, AEH is not yet available in many other main-stream programming languages, which is a big obstacle to utilize theoretical results on AEH in real-world software. We, therefore, think that it is an important and timely issue to develop a systematic and efficient implementation method for AEH which is available in many existing programming languages.

AEH have been so far implemented in several ways such as the one based on stack manipulation, delimited-control operators [6], or free monad. Unfortunately, none of them are fully satisfactory; The implementation method based on stack manipulation is used for JVM bytecode and C [4,18], however, an

© Springer Nature Switzerland AG 2020
A. Byrski and J. Hughes (Eds.): TFP 2020, LNCS 12222, pp. 159–179, 2020.
https://doi.org/10.1007/978-3-030-57761-2_8

implementer needs deep insight on the internal structure of run-time systems. It then follows that the implementation cost is rather high, which prevents the feature from being implemented in various language systems. The implementation method via delimited-control operators is used for OCaml and Scala [3,16]. It is a systematic way to implement AEH, since it needs no knowledge on low-level features, however, only few languages have delimited-control operators as built-in primitives. The implementation method based on free monads is yet another systematic way, and used in Haskell and Scala [14,15]. While elegant, it enforces a programmer to use the monadic style, and it is often inefficient.

This paper presents a new systematic method of implementing algebraic effects and handlers which is simple, efficient, and available in many languages. compared to the existing implementations based on free monads. The key of our method is to use coroutines to embed them in programming languages. Today we see a number of programming languages which have coroutines as a built-in feature.[1] which makes it possible to apply our implementation method in various languages with no or little cost. While coroutines are less expressive than general delimited-control operators, they are as expressive as *one-shot* delimited control-operators, a restricted control operator that is allowed to invoke a delimited continuation at most once [20]. One-shot delimited-control operators are known to be implemented more efficiently than general, multi-shot ones, thanks to the fact that no copying of continuations is necessary [5]. Hence, we face the trade-off between expressiveness and efficiency. This paper studies the one-shot variant which gives less expressive, but more performant primitives for AEH. In fact, various control effects are expressible by the one-shot variant.

We translate one-shot AEH to asymmetric coroutines. The salient feature of our translation is that it is a *macro-expressible translation* in the sense of Felleisen [8]. Thanks to this property, we can implement AEH as a simple library, and we have built AEH libraries for Lua and Ruby which have been published via GitHub[2,3]. Our libraries have been used by several users, and interested users have ported our libraries to other languages such as JavaScript and Rust using generators[4,5].

Our main contributions in this paper are the following.

- We show an embedding of one-shot algebraic effects and handlers. We use standard asymmetric coroutines only, and no special control features are needed. Hence our embedding is applicable to various languages as long as they have asymmetric coroutines.
- Comparing to the embedding based on free monads, our method does not force programmers to use monadic style, and our embedding is more performant in many cases than the one based on free monads.

---

[1] The Wikipedia article on coroutine (access date: June 1, 2020) lists fifty programming languages which have native support for coroutines.

[2] https://github.com/nymphium/eff.lua.

[3] https://github.com/nymphium/ruff.

[4] https://github.com/MakeNowJust/eff.js.

[5] https://github.com/pandaman64/effective-rust.

– Our embedding is defined as a local and compositional translation from algebraic effects and handlers. Thanks to this property, we can implement the embedding as a library, and in fact we have done it for Lua and Ruby, which is available on GitHub. Implementing AEH is a complicated task which is often error prone, and our simplistic approach based on a formal translation is desirable.

This paper is organized as follows. Section 2 shows typical examples using AEH and demonstrates our algebraic-effect library for Lua. Section 3 describes the embedding method by defining the translation from λ_{eff}, a language with algebraic effect handlers, to λ_{ac}, a language with asymmetric coroutines. We also show that our translation is macro expressible in the sense of Felleisen. Section 4 discusses the extension of our model definitions for implementing our libraries in Lua and Ruby, and problems in actual use. Section 5 shows the performance evaluation of our embedding by comparing ours with the embedding based on free monads. Section 6 describes related work, and Sect. 7 concludes.

2 Examples of *One-Shot* Algebraic Effects

This section illustrates programming with AEH by examples. To express them, we use the programming language Lua extended with our library, which is implemented using our embedding explained in the subsequent sections.

2.1 Exception

In our view, AEH is a generalization of exceptions, which is justified by the following examples.

The function `inst` provided by our library creates, when called with zero argument, a new label for an algebraic effect, and returns it.

```
1  local DivideByZero = inst()
```

We can invoke the labeled effect by calling the function `perform` in our library.

```
1  local div = function(x, y)
2    if y == 0 then
3      return perform(DivideByZero, nil)
4    else
5      return x / y
6    end
7  end
```

This code snippet is Lua's definition for the function `div`, which takes two arguments `x` and `y`. It returns the result of dividing `x` by `y` unless `y` is 0. If `y` is 0, it performs the effect labeled by `DivideByZero`, which means that an effect is raised and the control of the program is brought to the nearest effect handler (which is not shown in the above code) similarly to exception handling.

Our library has the function `handler` which creates a new effect handler.

```
1  local with_nil = handler {
2    val = function(_) return nil end,
3    [DivideByZero] = function(_, _)
4      return nil
5    end
6  }
```

The function `handler` receives a `table`, Lua's data structure for an associative array[6], as its sole argument. On Line 2, e1 = e2 represents the key-value pair `["e1"] = e2`, which has the key `val` and whose value is a value handler which is used when no effect occurs. The second key-value pair (Lines 3 and 4) defines how the effect `DivideByZero` is processed. The value part of the key-value pair is a function in both cases. While the value handler receives one argument (which corresponds to the result of the handled expression), the effect handler receives two arguments, the first of which is the argument of the effect invocation and the second is a delimited continuation when the effect has been invoked (up to the handler invocation). In the above snippet, the arguments are ignored, and the whole computation returns `nil` in both cases, representing simple exception capturing. By evaluating `with_nil(function() return div(3, 0) end)`, we get `nil` as the result.

We can turn the above simple exception to a *resumable* exception by changing the effect handler as follows.

```
1  local with_default_zero = handler {
2    val = function(v) return v end,
3    [DivideByZero] = function(_, k)
4      return k(0)
5    end
6  }
```

Here we changed the second case of the handler (Lines 3 and 4) so that a parameter `k` is bound to the second argument (a delimited continuation), which is invoked with the argument 0, and its value becomes the final result.

We can test the handler `with_default_zero` as follows.

```
1  with_default_zero(function()
2    local v = div(3, 0)
3    return v + 20
4  end)
```

---

[6] https://www.lua.org/manual/5.3/manual.html#3.4.9.

When we execute Line 2 of this code, the effect `DivideByZero` is performed (raised) as before. Then the handler `with_default_zero` catches it, and captures the delimited continuation `local v = □; return v + 20`, to which the variable `k` is bound. (Strictly speaking, the delimited continuation should be surrounded by the handler `with_default_zero`, but we omit it here since there is no effect in the continuation and its value handler is the identity function.) Then we execute `k(0)`, which is equivalent to `local v = 0; return v + 20`. The net effect is the same as the case when `div(3,0)` returns 0, and the entire computation results in `0 + 20 = 20`.

2.2 State

AEH can express not only exceptions, but also many other effects. Here, we show how state can be expressed in terms of these operations using the state-passing technique.

We first create two effect labels.

```
1  local Get = inst()
2  local Put = inst()
```

We then define the function `run` which executes stateful computations.

```
1  local run = function(init, task)
2    local step = handler {
3      val = function(_) return function() end end,
4      [Get] = function(_, k)
5        return function(s)
6          return k(s)(s)
7        end
8      end,
9      [Put] = function(s, k)
10       return function(_)
11         return k()(s)
12       end
13     end
14   }
15
16   return step(task)(init)
17  end
```

The function takes two arguments `init` for the initial state and a thunk `task` for the stateful computation. It first defines the handler `step`, which manipulates the normal-return case and the two effects labeled by `Get` and `Put`. Following the state-passing scheme, the value handler returns a function which ignores its argument (for state). In the stateful computation, when the effect `Get` is invoked, then the handler returns the function that retrieves the current state s and supplies it to the current continuation (k(s) on Line 6) with the same state s. When the effect Put with an parameter s is invoked, the handler returns a thunk in which a meaningless value () is passed to the continuation, but a new state s is installed (Line 11). After defining the handler, the function run executes the computation task with the initial state init (Line 16).

It is important to note that the captured continuation is surrounded by the same handler step. In fact, the algebraic effects and handler are similar to the control operators shift0 and reset0 [19]; when an effect invoked by shift0 is captured by reset0, the captured delimited continuation is surrounded by the delimiter reset0.

2.3 Expressing Other Computational Effects

We can express other control effects using one-shot algebraic effects and handlers. Examples include generators and iterators, let-insertion in partial evaluation, and Go language's defer[7], We have already implemented by our library more advanced examples such as async/await, shift/reset, fetching the current time (a sort of dependency injection) and measuring the execution time. See our GitHub repository (see Footnote 2 and 3).

3 Embedding Algebraic Effects into Coroutines

This section explains our translation from one-shot algebraic effects and handlers to asymmetric coroutines. For this purpose, we define λ_{eff}, a language which has *one-shot* AEH, and λ_{ac}, a language which has asymmetric coroutines [20]. We then translate λ_{eff} to λ_{ac}, and show that it is a macro-expressible translation.

3.1 λ_{eff}

λ_{eff} is an untyped language with one-shot AEH based on Effy [23]. For simplicity, we omit dynamic creation of effect lablels.

Figure 1 defines the syntax of λ_{eff}. The set *Effects* is a finite set of effect lables, and we use *eff* as a meta variable for it. The syntactic categories v, e, and h, resp. represent values, expressions and handler expressions, resp. The expression perform *eff* v invokes the effect *eff* with the argument v, and with v handle e evaluates e under the handler. A let binding is written as let $x = c_1$ in c_2.

The handler expression handler *eff* (val $x \to e_1$)(($y, k) \to e_2$) creates a handler which catches the effect *eff* and returns the value of e_2 where y is bound to the argument of the effect-performing operation, and k is bound to the delimited continuation when the effect is invoked. The expression val $x \to e_1$ gives a value handler, namely, a handler which is used when the body of a handler returns normally (no invocation of effects). For simplicity, λ_{eff} can handle only

---

[7] https://golang.org/ref/spec#Defer_statements.

$$x \ \in Variables$$
$$\textit{eff} \ \in Effects$$
$$v ::= x \mid h \mid \lambda x.\ e$$
$$e ::= v \mid v\ v \mid \mathtt{let}\ x = e\ \mathtt{in}\ e$$
$$\mid \mathtt{perform}\ \textit{eff}\ v \mid \mathtt{with}\ v\ \mathtt{handle}\ e$$
$$h ::= \mathtt{handler}\ \textit{eff}\ (\mathtt{val}\ \ x \to e)\ ((x, x) \to e)$$

$$w ::= \mathtt{clos}\,(\lambda x.e, E) \mid \mathtt{closh}\,(h, E)$$
$$F ::= (\square\ e, E) \mid w\ \square$$
$$\mid (\mathtt{let}\ x = \square\ \mathtt{in}\ e, E)$$
$$\mid (\mathtt{with}\ w\ \mathtt{handle}\ \square)^{\textit{eff}}$$
$$\mid (\mathtt{with}\ \square\ \mathtt{handle}\ e, E)$$
$$C ::= e \mid w$$
$$E ::= [] \mid (x = w) :: E$$
$$K ::= [] \mid F :: K$$

Fig. 1. Syntax and runtime representation of $\lambda_{\textit{eff}}$

one effect per handler, whereas handlers in Effy can cope with multiple effects. But the latter can be simulated by our single-effect handlers, and our library actually provides the multi-effect variant; see Sect. 4.

The syntactic category w and the subsequent lines are used to define the semantics of $\lambda_{\textit{eff}}$. The class w represents runtime values for function closures ($\mathtt{clos}\,(\lambda x.e, E)$) and handlers ($\mathtt{closh}\,(h, E)$) where E is a runtime environment, and F represents a *frame*, or a singular context, which means a 'one-step' fragment of a continuation. A (delimited) continuation K is a list of frames.

The call-by-value operational semantics of $\lambda_{\textit{eff}}$ is defined in the CEK-machine style [9]. Here we informally explain the semantics of effect primitives. Its details can be found in the full version of this paper; see our GitHub repository.

The handler expression $\mathtt{handler}\ \textit{eff}\ (\mathtt{val}\ x \to e_v)\,((x, k) \to e_{ef})$ creates a handler which consists of a value handler and an effect handler, and associates the effect label $\textit{eff}$ to it. The expression $\mathtt{with}\ h\ \mathtt{handle}\ e$ (called a handling expression) evaluates the expression e under the handler h. The expression $\mathtt{perform}\ \textit{eff}\ v$ invokes the effect $\textit{eff}$ with an argument v. Note that handling expressions may be nested, and an effect invocation is handled by the nearest (innermost) handler which can handle the effect. When the handled expression is evaluated to a value, the value handler is used.

3.2 λ_{ac}

The seminal work by de Moura and Ierusalimschy [20] classified various forms of coroutines found in programming languages, and formalized calculi for symmetric coroutines and asymmetric coroutines. The former represents classic coroutines which can call (resume) other coroutines, but coroutines cannot return to their callers. The latter represents modern coroutines where the caller-callee relation exists, hence, coroutines may return to their callers.

The language λ_{ac} is based on asymmetric coroutines[8]. For the purpose of translation and practical programming, we have added to this language several constructs such as data constructors, let with recursion, pattern matching, and comparison operators.

Figure 2 defines the syntax of λ_{ac}. The syntactic categories K and l, resp., represent data constructors and labels for coroutines, resp. The set *eff* corresponds to the set of effect labels in λ_{eff}, and we assume that its elements are constants in λ_{ac}. Values v are either constants, expressions formed by applying a data constructor to values $K\ \overrightarrow{v}^*$, labels, variables, or lambda expressions. Expressions e are those in lambda calculus extended with pattern matching and mutual recursion, plus those for asymmetric coroutines: $l : e$ for a labeled expression which represents the "return point" of resuming a coroutine, create e for creating a coroutine and returning its label, resume $e_1\ e_2$ for resuming a coroutine, and yield e for yielding a value and returning to the caller of the current coroutine. $f\ \overrightarrow{x}$ is an abbreviation of $f\ x_1\ \cdots\ x_n$ and and $g\ \overrightarrow{y} = e$ is of and $g_1\ \overrightarrow{y} = e_1\ \cdots$ and $g_n\ \overrightarrow{y} = e_n$. Similar abbreviation is used for constructors and pattern matching. The expression match e with *cases* is for pattern matching. We allow (restricted) guards in pattern matching so that *cases* $\overrightarrow{pat \to e}$ may have a guard when $x = x$.

The call-by-value operational semantics of λ_{ac} is defined in the same way as de Moura and Ierusalimschy, which is given in the full version of this paper. Here we briefly explain the semantics of the primitives for coroutines. create e creates a fresh label and a coroutine with its body being the value of e, and returns the label. The expression resume $l\ v$ resumes the coroutine labeled with l with the argument v. It is an error if a coroutine whose label is l does not exist, or has already been called. A resumed coroutine must return to the caller, so we create an expression $l : e'$ where e' is the body of the resumed coroutine. When an expression yield v is called during the evaluation of a coroutine, the coroutine is suspended and stored for future use, and v is returned to the caller of the current coroutine. It is an error if there is no caller of the current coroutine when yield is invoked.

3.3   Translation from λ_{eff} to λ_{ac}.

This section presents a program translation from λ_{eff} to λ_{ac}, which is syntax-directed and compositional. The translation essentially does two things: to emu-

---

[8] Strictly speaking, our calculus is the one for *stackful* asymmetric coroutines according to de Moura and Ierusalimschy's classification.

$$
\begin{aligned}
x &\in \textit{Variables} \\
K &\in \{\textit{Eff}, \textit{Resend}, \textit{True}, \textit{False}\} \\
l &\in \textit{Labels} \\
\textit{eff} &\in \textit{Effects} \\
v &::= \texttt{nil} \mid \textit{eff} \mid K\ \overrightarrow{v} \mid l \mid x \mid \lambda x.e \\
e &::= v \mid K\ \overrightarrow{e} \mid l : e \mid e\ e \mid \texttt{let}\ x = e\ \texttt{in}\ e \\
&\quad \mid \texttt{match}\ e\ \texttt{with}\ \textit{cases} \\
&\quad \mid \texttt{create}\ e \mid \texttt{resume}\ e\ e \mid \texttt{yield}\ e \\
\textit{letrec} &::= \texttt{let rec}\ x\ \overrightarrow{x} = e\ \left[\overrightarrow{\texttt{and}\ x\ \overrightarrow{x} = e}\right]\ \texttt{in}\ e \\
\textit{cases} &::= \overrightarrow{\textit{pat}\ [\textit{guard}] \to e} \\
\textit{guard} &::= \texttt{when}\ x = x \\
\textit{pat} &::= K\ \overrightarrow{\textit{pat}} \mid x
\end{aligned}
$$

Fig. 2. Syntax of λ_{ac}

late multiple-effects AEH by a single-effect AEH, and then to emulate a single-effect AEH by an asymmetric coroutine. The first one is done by adding tags to distinguish different effects and by forwarding (resending) the raised effect if its tag does not match the tag of the handler. The second one is done by emulating a (one-shot) delimited continuation by an asymmetric coroutine. To save space, we give the whole translation as a single translation.

The whole translation is defined in Fig. 3 where a $\lambda_{\textit{eff}}$-term e is translated to a λ_{ac}-term $[\![e]\!]$. The translation is homomorphic for a variable, a λ-abstraction, an application, and the **let** expression. An effect label $\textit{eff}$ is translated to a constant with the same name.

We translate **perform** to **yield** based on the following observation. In the calculus for AEH, when an effect is invoked, the control is transferred to a handler corresponding to the effect, while in the calculus for coroutines, when a **yield** is called, the control is transferred to its parent coroutine. Hence we can emulate the behavior of **perform** by **yield**. The translation wraps the arguments of **perform** with the tag $\textit{Eff}$. This tag is used to determine whether the effect has been *yield*ed from the handled expression itself, or it has been resent by the handler. The handling expression **with** h **handle** e is translated to a simple application as the handler is translated to a function.

The translation for a handler (the last case in Fig. 3) is intricate, and we shall explain it by an example.

Consider the program M with the effects C_1, C_2, and C_3 in Fig. 4. Here we assume that our calculus is extended to have natural numbers arithmetic operations. Then M is translated to the program in Fig. 5 where some variables and **let**-bindings are renamed or inlined for readability.

$$\llbracket x \rrbracket = x$$
$$\llbracket \lambda x.e \rrbracket = \lambda x.\llbracket e \rrbracket$$
$$\llbracket v_1 \; v_2 \rrbracket = (\llbracket v_1 \rrbracket) \; (\llbracket v_2 \rrbracket)$$
$$\llbracket \mathtt{let} \; x = e \; \mathtt{in} \; e' \rrbracket = \mathtt{let} \; x = \llbracket e \rrbracket \; \mathtt{in} \; \llbracket e' \rrbracket$$
$$\llbracket \mathit{eff} \rrbracket = \mathit{eff}$$
$$\llbracket \mathtt{perform} \; \mathit{eff} \; v \rrbracket = \mathtt{yield} \; (\mathit{Eff} \; (\llbracket \mathit{eff} \rrbracket) \; (\llbracket v \rrbracket))$$
$$\llbracket \mathtt{with} \; h \; \mathtt{handle} \; e \rrbracket = \llbracket h \rrbracket \; (\lambda\_.\llbracket e \rrbracket)$$

$$\llbracket \mathtt{handler} \; \mathit{eff} \; (\mathtt{val} \; x \to e_v) \; ((x,k) \to e_{\mathit{eff}}) \rrbracket =$$

$$\mathtt{let} \; \mathit{eff} = \llbracket \mathit{eff} \rrbracket \; \mathtt{in}$$
$$\mathtt{let} \; vh = \lambda x.\llbracket e_v \rrbracket \; \mathtt{in}$$
$$\mathtt{let} \; \mathit{effh} = \lambda x \; k.\llbracket e_{\mathit{eff}} \rrbracket \; \mathtt{in}$$
$$\mathit{handler} \; \mathit{eff} \; vh \; \mathit{effh}$$

where $\mathit{handler} =$

```
let rec handler eff vh effh th =
  let co = create th in
  let rec continue arg = handle (resume co arg)
  and rehandle k arg = handler eff continue effh (λ_.k arg)
  and handle r =
    match r with
```

$\mid$ *Eff eff′ v*	**when** $\mathit{eff}' = \mathit{eff} \to$	$\mathit{effh} \; v \; \mathit{continue}$
$\mid$ *Eff* _ _	$\to$	$\mathtt{yield} \; (\mathit{Resend} \; r \; \mathit{continue})$
$\mid$ *Resend (Eff eff′ v) k*	**when** $\mathit{eff}' = \mathit{eff} \to$	$\mathit{effh} \; v \; (\mathit{rehandle} \; k)$
$\mid$ *Resend effv k*	$\to$	$\mathtt{yield} \; (\mathit{Resend} \; \mathit{effv} \; (\mathit{rehandle} \; k))$
$\mid$ _	$\to$	$vh \; r$

```
  in continue nil
in handler
```

Fig. 3. Translation from λ_{eff} to λ_{ac}

The term after translation $\llbracket M \rrbracket$ contains the function *handler* defined in Fig. 3, which works as follows: `handler` makes a coroutine from a thunk, defines three functions *continue*, *rehandle* and *handle*, and then evaluates *continue* `nil`. *continue* passes *arg* to *co*, `resumes` it, and passes the return value to *handle*. *handle* dispatches the process by the return value of `resume` according to the equivalence of tags and effect labels.

Let us evaluate $\llbracket M \rrbracket$. It first binds h_1, h_2, and h_3 to the values of applying *handler* to three arguments. Since the function *handler* needs four arguments (see Fig. 3), the values of h_i are still closures. After setting h_i, we evaluate $h_3(\lambda\_. \cdots)$, which triggers the actual computation of the body of *handler*. It then creates a new coroutine for the argument of h_3, defines several functions and

$M = \mathtt{let}\ h_1 = \mathtt{handler}\ C_1$
$\quad (\mathtt{val}\ v \rightarrow v)\,((x, k) \rightarrow k\ x)\ \mathtt{in}$
$\mathtt{let}\ h_2 = \mathtt{handler}\ C_2$
$\quad (\mathtt{val}\ v \rightarrow v)\,((x, k) \rightarrow k\ x)\ \mathtt{in}$
$\mathtt{let}\ h_3 = \mathtt{handler}\ C_3$
$\quad (\mathtt{val}\ v \rightarrow v)\,((x, k) \rightarrow k\ x)\ \mathtt{in}$
$\mathtt{with}\ h_3\ \mathtt{handle}$
$\mathtt{with}\ h_2\ \mathtt{handle}$
$\mathtt{with}\ h_1\ \mathtt{handle}$
$\quad \mathtt{let}\ a = \mathtt{perform}\ (C_1\ 10)\ \mathtt{in}$
$\quad \mathtt{let}\ b = \mathtt{perform}\ (C_3\ 17)\ \mathtt{in}$
$\quad a + b$

Fig. 4. Example program in $\lambda_{e\!f\!f}$

$[\![M]\!] = \mathtt{let}\ h_1 = \mathtt{let}\ vh_1 = \lambda v.\ v\ \mathtt{in}$
$\qquad \mathtt{let}\ e\!f\!f\!h_1 = \lambda x.\ \lambda k.\ k\ v\ \mathtt{in}$
$\qquad handler\ C_1\ vh_1\ e\!f\!f\!h_1\ \mathtt{in}$
$\quad \mathtt{let}\ h_2 = \mathtt{let}\ vh_2 = \lambda v.\ v\ \mathtt{in}$
$\qquad \mathtt{let}\ e\!f\!f\!h_2 = \lambda x.\ \lambda k.\ k\ v\ \mathtt{in}$
$\qquad handler\ C_2\ vh_2\ e\!f\!f\!h_2\ \mathtt{in}$
$\quad \mathtt{let}\ h_3 = \mathtt{let}\ vh_3 = \lambda v.\ v\ \mathtt{in}$
$\qquad \mathtt{let}\ e\!f\!f\!h_3 = \lambda x.\ \lambda k.\ k\ v\ \mathtt{in}$
$\qquad handler\ C_3\ vh_3\ e\!f\!f\!h_3\ \mathtt{in}$
$\quad h_3\ (\lambda_-.\ h_2\ (\lambda_-.\ h_1\ (\lambda_-.$
$\qquad \mathtt{let}\ a = \mathtt{yield}\ (E\!f\!f\ C_1\ 10)\ \mathtt{in}$
$\qquad \mathtt{let}\ b = \mathtt{yield}\ (E\!f\!f\ C_3\ 17)\ \mathtt{in}$
$\qquad a + b\ )))$

Fig. 5. Example after translation

evaluates *continue nil*, which in effect applies the argument of h_3 (the thunk $\lambda_-.\cdots$) to *nil*. Similarly, $h_2(\lambda_-.\cdots)$ and then $h_1(\lambda_-.\cdots)$ are evaluated, and finally the subterm yield ($E\!f\!f\ C_1\ 10$) is evaluated, and a value is yielded. It is caught by the innermost handler h_1. Since it has the tag $E\!f\!f$ and h_1 can handle C_1, the first out of five patterns in *handle* matches it, and *effh* 10 *continue* is evaluated. By passing *continue* as the continuation, the computation of a handled expression can be resumed, which is suspended at the yielded position. Since *continue* passes the return value of resume to *handle*, the effect can be handled by the same handler again. Hence a is bound to 10.

The above case uses only the first pattern in the function *handle* which corresponds to a single effect. The handler needs to treat more involved cases when AEH allows multiple effects, which we shall explain shortly.

Continuing the evaluation of $[\![M]\!]$, we encounter the term yield ($E\!f\!f\ C_3\ 17$). When it is executed, the handler h_1 catches it, but h_1 cannot handle C_3. Hence the second pattern of *handle* matches, and another *yield* term with the tag *Resend* is evaluated which is caught by the next outside handler, namely, h_2. Since it has the tag *Resend* and h_2 cannot handle C_3, the fourth pattern of *handle* matches, which again yields the value with the tag *Resend*. A difference from the previous case is that the function *rehandle* is applied to k, where *rehandle* creates a handler that handles the thunk of the application of two given arguments. By setting *continue* to the value handler, the computation of the current handling expression can be resumed when the computation of the *rehandle* passed as a continuation is finished. *rehandle* has another role which adjusts the layers of the coroutines. In the second clause of *handle*, *yield* is called, so the execution exits from the coroutine.

The resent effect is captured by h_3 again. Now it matches the third pattern of *handle*, and similarly to the above case, *rehandle k* is passed to *effh* as a continuation. Then it returns 17, to which b is bound, and the value of the handled expression is 27. Then h_1 receives it, and the fifth wildcard pattern of *handle* matches, and the value of the entire expression is 27.

Although our translation looks complicated, we emphasize that our translation is compositional and local, syntax-directed, and needs only basic functionality of asymmetric coroutines. We also note that it does not rely on higher-order stores or other fancy features unlike de Moura and Ierusalimschy's work.[9] With this simplicity, several programmers have already ported our translation to other languages than Ruby and Lua.

3.4   Macro-expressible Translation

We will claim that the translation from λ_{eff} to λ_{ac} in the previous section is simple and efficient. To support the former claim, this subsection shows that it is a macro-expressible translation in the sense of Felleisen. The latter claim will be discussed in the subsequent section.

Felleisen studied the notion of macro expressivity, which is a more fine-grained notion than most others to measure the expressive power of language primitives [8]. For instance, *call/cc* (call-with-current-continuation) can be translated away by a CPS translation to a pure lambda calculus, yet, it is not macro-expressible in pure lambda calculus since the translation is global and not macro expressible. On the other hand, a simple let expression let $x = e_1$ in e_2 can be locally translated by $(\lambda x.e_2)\ e_1$, therefore, it is macro-expressible in the pure lambda calculus.

While Felleisen defined the notion for the setting where a language L_1 is a proper extension of another language L_2, we want to compare the expressive power of two languages L_1 and L_2 where L_1 and L_2 are extensions of a common language L_0. To deal with this setting, we use Forster et al.'s definition for the macro-expressible translation [10], and we give its slightly simplified version here.

Definition 1 (Macro-expressible translation). *Let L_0 be a language, and L_1 and L_2, resp., be the language L_0 augmented with a set of primitives $X_1, \cdots, X_n$ and $Y_1, \cdots, Y_m$, resp. A translation ϕ from L_1 to L_2 is a macro-expressible translation if and only if all of the following conditions hold.*

- *ϕ is homomorphic for the primitives in L_0. For instance, if a binary infix operator $\oplus$ is in L_0, then $\phi(e_1 \oplus e_2)$ is $\phi(e_1) \oplus \phi(e_2)$.*
- *ϕ maps each X_i of arity n to a syntactic expression M_i in L_2 which has n free variables $x_1, \cdots, x_n$ such that the following holds:*

$$\phi(X_i(e_1, \cdots, e_n)) = M_i[\phi(e_1)/x_1, \cdots, \phi(e_n)/x_n]$$

The expression in the right-hand side represents simultaneous substitution for the variables $x_1, \cdots, x_n$ in M_i.

---

[9] See Sect. 5.3 in [20].

To state the above definition we have made two simplifications. First, the equality in this definition should be, in general, semantic equality where we assume that each language is equipped with a certain semantics, but in this paper, we can regard it as syntactic equality. Second, we do not consider the case when X_i works as a binder such as the let expression[10], but we do not need to consider such cases.

It is easy to show that our translation in the previous subsection conforms the conditions for a macro-expressible translation.

Theorem 1. *Our translation in Fig. 3 is a macro-expressible translation.*

Proof Sketch. It is easy to check that our translation $[\![\cdot]\!]$ is homomorphic for the variable, lambda abstraction, application, let, the effect expression.

For the primitives of algebraic effects and handlers, we need to check each case. For the primitive perform, let M be yield (*Eff* x_1 x_2), then we have $[\![\text{perform } e_1\ e_2]\!] = M[[\![e_1]\!]/x_1,\ [\![e_2]\!]/x_2]$, and we are done. Other cases are similar. □

As we wrote above, a macro-expressible translation is rather discriminating, or sensitive to small differences between language primitives. Only local translations are macro-expressible translation. Since global translations such as a CPS translation and a state-passing translation do not qualify as macro-expressible, state and first-class continuations are not macro-expressible in pure lambda calculus.

Put differently, if we have a macro-expressible translation for a primitive X in a language L_0, then we can implement X using the translation without changing any other primitives in L_0 This is a simple, but rather important property for our work, as it is a necessary condition to implement X as a simple library in L_0, unless we have an access to language's run-time, or reification is allowed.

4   Implementation

We have implemented AEH in Lua and Ruby based on the translation in Sect. 3. Since the translation is macro-expressible, we can realize our implementation as a simple library. Our implementations are compact. The Lua library is implemented in 160 lines and the core of the Ruby library is in 340 lines, even including comments for documentation generation. All our code is available via GitHub.

Several issues have arisen in the process of implementation which we will explain below.

Multiple Effect Handlers: Our calculus λ_{eff} has the restriction that a handler can catch only one effect. However, this restriction is only for the presentation purpose, and in our actual implementation, one handler may catch multiple effects, All examples including the examples in this paper that use multiple effects per handler run without problems using our library. We also note that there is no critical performance downgrade of having multiple effects per handler.

---

[10] Felleisen considers the case where each argument may be bound by the construct.

Dynamic Effect Creation: In the language λ_{eff}, we have no way to create new effect labels dynamically. Again this is due to simplicity, and we have eliminated this restriction in our implementation. The merit of allowing dynamic creation of effect instances is that a certain kind of effectful programs require effect instances to be mutually distinct, for instance, higher-order effects [16].

Conflict with Other Effects: An assumption on our translation is that all effects are written via AEH. If our source program uses other effects than AEH, it will cause a problem as they may interfere with the internally used coroutines. For instance, if we use our library in Lua, and simultaneously use Lua's native coroutine directly, yielding a value in the source program may be accidentally caught by an internal coroutine. As consequence, we must not use native coroutines with our library for AEH.

However, this problem can be solved in the following way, thanks to the expressivity of AEH. See the following code.

```
1  local Yield = inst()
2
3  local yield = function(v)
4    return perform(Yield, v)
5  end
6
7  local create = function(f)
8    return { it = f, handled = false }
9  end
10
11  local resume = function(co, v)
12    if co.handled then
13      return co.it(v)
14    else
15      co.handled = true
16      return handler({
17        val = function(x) return x end,
18        [Yield] = function(u, k)
19          co.it = k
20          return u
21        end
22      })(function() return co.it(v) end)
23    end
24  end
```

The code implements asymmetric coroutines by algebraic effects and handlers in Lua. The function `yield` should throw a value to `resume`, so `yield` should be an effect invocation and `resume` should be a handler. This correspondence is the inverse of the translation in Fig. 3. So we define the effect `Yield` (Line 1) and the function `yield` (Line 3) as a wrapper for the invocation of the effect.

The function `create` (Line 7) creates a reference cell by a table. We represent a coroutine as a reference cell, which is initialized to the function `f` and the flag `handled` explained later. The handler `resume` (Line 11) catches the effect `Yield` with an argument and a continuation. This continuation is the rest of computation of the coroutine, so the handler stores the continuation to the cell and returns the value `u` (Lines 19 and 20). Since we provide a deep handler, it is not necessary to set the handler multiple times. The flag `handled` asserts if the function is handled by the handler (Line 12). The function `resume` checks the flag; if the flag is not set, it turns on the flag and runs the function with the handler. Otherwise, it runs the function alone.

Although we believe that the above technique may be used for other computational effects, it is left for future work to combine them with algebraic effect and handlers to obtain an efficient implementation.

5   Evaluation

We have conducted experiments on microbenchmark using our library in Lua, and implementation in Lua based on free monads [23], and compared their performance. All the code for the benchmark is publicly available in the GitHub repository[11]. In the following figures, the symbol ▲ represents the result of our library, and ■ the free-monad based implementation. One of the benchmarks compares to native coroutines of Lua and indicates the result as the symbol ⋆ in a graph. The experiments have been conducted on the environment in Table 1.

Table 1. Environment for benchmark

OS	Arch Linux
CPU	Intel Core i7-8565U
Main memory	16 GB DDR4
Lua processor	LuaJIT 2.05

Figure 6 is the result of the benchmark for emulating a state monad. The benchmark uses the function `count`, cited from [14], adjusted for our library and free monad, which recursively runs a simple computation consisting of single-layer, single-effect handlers for the number of times as the input parameter. The result shows that our library is approx. 10 times faster than the free-monad based implementation for this simple case. The reason why free monads are rather slow is that the bind operator requires a continuation as the next action, but the cost for creating function closures is rather high for imperative languages such as Lua. Also, functional languages such as Haskell may offer optimization for free monads, while the benchmark uses naive implementation. Nevertheless, the results are encouraging for our embedding.

---

[11] https://github.com/nymphium/effs-benchmark.

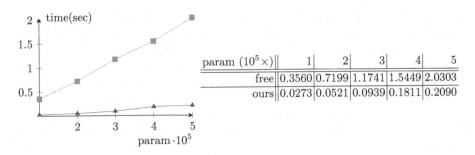

Fig. 6. Result of `onestate` benchmark

param ($10^5\times$)	1	2	3	4	5
free	0.3560	0.7199	1.1741	1.5449	2.0303
ours	0.0273	0.0521	0.0939	0.1811	0.2090

In the experiments in Fig. 7, the benchmark program runs the function `count` 3,000 times in deeply nested handlers. The parameter in the table corresponds to the number of nested handlers/coroutines, hence 50 (the right-most column) is an extreme case. As expected, our library runs three times slower than the free monad does for this case. The reason is that *rehandle* creates a new coroutine, which is called every time an effect is caught from the other handler shown in Fig. 3, so it degrades the performance.

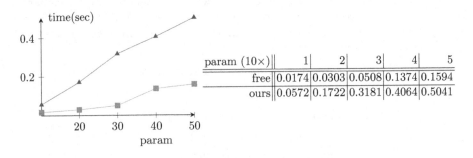

Fig. 7. Result of `multistate` benchmark

param ($10\times$)	1	2	3	4	5
free	0.0174	0.0303	0.0508	0.1374	0.1594
ours	0.0572	0.1722	0.3181	0.4064	0.5041

The next experiment executed a `for`-loop, where the number of iteration is given as a parameter in the table of Fig. 8. The benchmark program sets a handler outside of the loop, and invokes an effect in the `for`-loop. Our library runs 9 times as fast as the free-monad based implementation. Note that free monads need the `forM`-operator which has large overhead. Again an advanced compiler may reduce the overhead.

Figure 9 shows the result of the benchmark, which solves the same-fringe problem [11] by using algebraic effects and coroutines. The problem is to determine whether given two trees have the same "fringe", an enumeration of leaves of the tree in a certain order. The benchmark is given the number of leaves as a parameter. We implemented it by algebraic effects and handlers via free monad, and via our library, and the result is shown in Sect. 4. We also implemented the

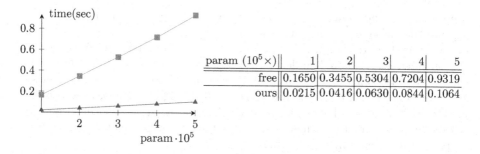

param $(10^5\times)$	1	2	3	4	5
free	0.1650	0.3455	0.5304	0.7204	0.9319
ours	0.0215	0.0416	0.0630	0.0844	0.1064

Fig. 8. Result of `looper` benchmark

solver with native coroutines of Lua. Our library yields 18 times performance gain compared to the free-monad method. Remarkably, our library is only 1.6 times slower than native coroutines, despite the overhead caused by the double translations.

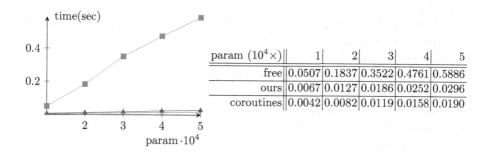

param $(10^4\times)$	1	2	3	4	5
free	0.0507	0.1837	0.3522	0.4761	0.5886
ours	0.0067	0.0127	0.0186	0.0252	0.0296
coroutines	0.0042	0.0082	0.0119	0.0158	0.0190

Fig. 9. Result of `same_fringe` benchmark

In summary, our way of implementing AEH is advantageous in several programming languages from the performance viewpoint. We also emphasize that writing effectful programs using coroutines is harder than writing the same programs using AEH, which provide high-level abstraction.

6   Related Work and Discussion

In this section, we discuss closely related work which has not been mentioned in this paper and picks up a few important issues for discussion.

Shallow Handler: We have shown the embedding with *deep handlers*, which inserts the handler to the topmost position of captured delimited continuations. In the literature, there has been discussion on the merits and demerits between deep handlers and *shallow handlers* [12], which do not insert the handler to captured delimited continuations, hence an effect invocation during the execution of a delimited continuation is not captured by the same handler. We have also implemented the shallow handler with coroutines shown in Fig. 10. The idea is simple; after a handler catches an effect, it resends any effects to an outer handler. We have already explained the role of *rehandle* in Fig. 3, namely, it adjusts the layer of coroutines, and handles the effect invocation in the continuation. For the shallow handlers, the former is necessary but the latter is not, hence we have prepared simplified functions $continue_0$ and $rehandle_0$.

$$[\![\text{handler}^\dagger \; eff \; (\text{val} \; x \to e_v) \; ((x, k) \to e_{eff})]\!] =$$

$$\text{let} \; eff = [\![eff]\!] \; \text{in}$$
$$\text{let} \; vh = \lambda x.[\![e_v]\!] \; \text{in}$$
$$\text{let} \; effh = \lambda x \; k.[\![e_{eff}]\!] \; \text{in}$$
$$handler^\dagger \; eff \; vh \; effh$$

where $handler^\dagger =$

  let rec $handler \; eff \; vh \; effh \; th =$

    let $co = \text{create} \; th$ in

    let rec $continue \; arg = handle \; (\text{resume} \; co \; arg)$

    and $rehandle \; k \; arg = handler \; eff \; continue \; effh \; (\lambda_\_.k \; arg)$

    and $continue_0 = \text{resume} \; co$

    and $rehandle_0 \; k = \text{resume} \; (\text{create} \; k)$

    and $handle \; r =$

      match r with

      | $Eff \; eff' \; v$ when $eff' = eff \to effh \; v \; continue_0$
      | $Eff \; \_ \; \_$ $\to \text{yield} \; (Resend \; r \; continue)$
      | $Resend \; (Eff \; eff' \; v) \; k$ when $eff' = eff \to effh \; v \; (rehandle \; k)$
      | $Resend \; effv \; k$ $\to \text{yield} \; (Resend \; effv \; (rehandle_0 \; k))$
      | $\_$ $\to vh \; r$

    in $continue \; \text{nil}$

  in $handler$

Fig. 10. Translation from shallow handlers to coroutines

One-Shot Continuations: We are not the first to study the one-shot variant of control operators. Bruggeman et al. gave a one-shot control operator *call/1cc* under the observation that most continuations are run at most once [5]. They showed that, by replacing *call/cc* by *call/1cc*, programs can be executed with less memory consumption and higher performance. Berdine et al. introduced a linear type system as static approximation of one-shotness, and showed that many control abstractions may be typed by their type system [2].

James and Sabry studied the *yield* operator for generators, and proved that it is as expressive as one-shot delimited continuations [13]. They also introduced a generalized *yield* operator for multi-shot continuations and showed the connection between it and delimited-control operators.

Multicore OCaml is a dialect of OCaml which natively supports algebraic effects by runtime stack manipulation. Its motivation is to write concurrent programming in direct style [7]. It provides one-shot continuations, and if multi-shot continuations are needed, they allow explicit copying of continuations.

Free Monad: We have already compared our work with free-monad based implementations of algebraic effects and handlers. On the positive side, it gives a systematic and elegant implementation for various effects. Its downside is significant overhead in performance. Note that our embedding-based implementation does not interfere with surface languages, while free-monad based implementations force a programmer to use the monadic style. With our implementation, the surface language with algebraic effects and handlers can be presented in direct style and monadic style.

7   Conclusion

We have presented a novel embedding technique for algebraic effects and handlers into asymmetric coroutines, and shown a translation from the former to the latter as a simple, direct, syntax-directed compositional translation. Compared with other implementation methods, our technique is applicable to many languages which have asymmetric coroutines. We have demonstrated the applicability of our embedding by implementing the libraries in Lua and Ruby. Our technique seems to be attractive for other researchers, and some of them have implemented our translation for other languages such as JavaScript and Rust. We expect that the simplicity of our implementation is advantageous to be used by more people, more languages, and more applications.

The key of our development is the one-shotness restriction of continuations. Our embedding relies on the fact that, many applications with computational effects use continuations at most once, and they allow more efficient implementation than the general, multi-shot continuations. One-shotness is a dynamic property, and its static approximation, linearly used (delimited) continuations, or linear continuation-passing style, are studied in the literature. We hope that the formal foundation of this paper's result is studied more deeply, and coroutines and their connection with other control operators find a solid theoretical foundation.

We briefly mention future work. There are many directions to extend our work. Of particular interest is to prove the semantics preservation of our translation. Introducing an appropriate type system is also an interesting next step. Another exciting issue is to relate and compare various control abstractions in the literature and in the practical programming languages. For instance, React, a popular web framework for JavaScript, has a utility software Hooks[12], which allows programmers to build components with side-effects modularly. Abramov pointed out the relevance between Hooks and algebraic effects in his blog post[13], and we think that investigating this relationship based on our work is promising. Finally embedding algebraic effects and handlers in modern languages such as Rust (via generators) may lead to a composable, efficient and safe implementation of controlful programs.

Acknowledgement. We are grateful for the reviewers of earlier versions of this paper for constructive comments and numerous suggestions. The second author is supported in part by JSPS Grants-in-Aid (B) 18H03218.

References

1. Bauer, A., Pretnar, M.: Programming with Algebraic Effects and Handlers. J. Log. Algebr. Methods Program. **84**, 108–123 (2012)
2. Berdine, J., O'Hearn, P., Reddy, U., Thielecke, H.: Linear continuation-passing. Higher-Order Symbolic Comput. **15**, 181–208 (2002). https://doi.org/10.1023/A:1020891112409
3. Brachthäuser, J., Schuster, P.: Effekt: extensible algebraic effects in Scala (short paper). In: Proceedings of the 8th ACM SIGPLAN Symposium on Scala, pp. 67–72 (2017)
4. Brachthäuser, J., Schuster, P., Ostermann, K.: Effect handlers for the masses. Proc. ACM Program. Lang. **2**, 1–27 (2018)
5. Bruggeman, C., Waddell, O., Dybvig, R.: Representing control in the presence of one-shot continuations, vol. 31, pp. 99–107 (1970)
6. Danvy, O., Filinski, A.: Abstracting control. In: Proceedings of the 1990 ACM Conference on LISP and Functional Programming, pp. 151–160 (1990)
7. Dolan, S., White, L., Madhavapeddy, A.: Multicore OCaml. In: OCaml Users and Developers Workshop (2014)
8. Felleisen, M.: On the Expressive Power of Programming Languages. In: Selected Papers from the Symposium on 3rd European Symposium on Programming, ESOP 1990, pp. 35–75. Elsevier North-Holland Inc., USA (1991)
9. Felleisen, M., Friedman, D.P.: Control operators, the SECD-machine, and the λ-calculus. In: Formal Description of Programming Concepts (1987)
10. Forster, Y., Kammar, O., Lindley, S., Pretnar, M.: On the expressive power of user-defined effects: Effect handlers, monadic reflection, delimited control. J. Funct. Program. **29**, e15 (2019). https://doi.org/10.1017/S0956796819000121
11. Gabriel, R.P.: The Design of Parallel Programming Languages, pp. 91–108. Academic Press Professional Inc., Cambridge (1991)
12. Hillerström, D., Lindley, S.: Shallow effect handlers. In: Ryu, S. (ed.) APLAS 2018. LNCS, vol. 11275, pp. 415–435. Springer, Cham (2018). https://doi.org/10.1007/978-3-030-02768-1_22

---

[12] https://reactjs.org/docs/hooks-reference.html.
[13] https://overreacted.io/algebraic-effects-for-the-rest-of-us/.

13. James, R., Sabry, A.: Yield: mainstream delimited continuations. In: Proceedings of Workshop on the Theory and Practice of Delimited Continuations, pp. 1–12 (2011)
14. Kammar, O., Lindley, S., Oury, N.: Handlers in action. In: ACM SIGPLAN International Conference on Functional Programming, pp. 145–158 (2013)
15. Kiselyov, O., Ishii, H.: Freer monads, more extensible effects. In: ACM SIGPLAN International Symposium on Haskell, pp. 94–105 (2015)
16. Kiselyov, O., Sivaramakrishnan, K.: Eff directly in OCaml. Electron. Proc. Theor. Comput. Sci. **285**, 23–58 (2018)
17. Leijen, D.: Algebraic effects for functional programming. Technical report, p. 15 (2016)
18. Leijen, D.: Implementing algebraic effects in C. In: Chang, B.-Y.E. (ed.) APLAS 2017. LNCS, vol. 10695, pp. 339–363. Springer, Cham (2017). https://doi.org/10.1007/978-3-319-71237-6_17
19. Materzok, M., Biernacki, D.: Subtyping delimited continuations. In: Chakravarty, M.M.T., Hu, Z., Danvy, O. (eds.) Proceeding of the 16th ACM SIGPLAN International Conference on Functional Programming, pp. 81–93. ACM (2011). https://doi.org/10.1145/2034773.2034786
20. Moura, A.D., Ierusalimschy, R.: Revisiting coroutines. ACM Trans. Program. Lang. Syst. **31**, 1–31 (2004)
21. Plotkin, G., Power, J.: Algebraic operations and generic effects. Appl. Categor. Struct. **11**, 69–94 (2003). https://doi.org/10.1023/A:1023064908962
22. Plotkin, G., Pretnar, M.: Handling algebraic effects. Log. Methods Comput. Sci. **9**, 1–36 (2013)
23. Pretnar, M., Saleh, A.H., Faes, A., Schrijvers, T.: Efficient compilation of algebraic effects and handlers. CW reports, volume CW708, Department of Computer Science, KU Leuven (2017)

An Equational Modeling of Asynchronous Concurrent Programming

David Janin$^{(\boxtimes)}$

Univ. Bordeaux, CNRS, Bordeaux INP, LaBRI, UMR 5800, Bordeaux, France
`janin@labri.fr`

Abstract. Asynchronous concurrent programing is a widely spread technique offering some simple concurrent primitives that are restricted in such a way that the resulting concurrent programs are deadlock free. In this paper, we develop, study and extend a formal model of the underlying application programmer interface. For such a purpose, we formally define the extension of a monad by some notion of monad references uniquely bound to running monad actions together with the associated asynchronous primitives fork and read. The expected semantics is specified via two series of equations relating the behavior of these extension primitives with the underlying monad primitives. Thanks to these equations, we recover a fairly general notion of promises and prove that they induce a monad isomorphic to the underlying monad. We also show how synchronous and asynchronous reactive data flow programming eventually derive from such a formalization of asynchronous concurrency, uniformly lifting fork and read primitives from monadic actions to monadic streams of actions. Our proposal is illustrated throughout by concrete extensions of Haskell IO monad that allows for proving the soundness of the proposed equations and the applicability of the resulting API.

1 Introduction

Asynchronous Programming with Promises. Asynchronous programming is quite a popular approach for programming lightly concurrent applications such as, for instance, web services or, as shown recently, realtime signal processing and control [5]. Based on *promises*, a notion introduced in the late 70s and eventually integrated into concurrent extension of functional programing languages such as Lisp [3] or ML [12], asynchronous concurrent programming is nowadays available in most modern programing languages, including modern typed functional languages such as OCaml [9] and Haskell [8].

One of the reasons of such a success is that asynchronous programing is both comfortable and safe. Comfort comes from asynchronism, safety comes from deadlock freedom. Most asynchronous libraries allow for forking programs while keeping promises of their returned values. Provided no other communication mechanisms are used, the dependency graph resulting from creating and reading promises is acyclic therefore deadlock free.

© Springer Nature Switzerland AG 2020
A. Byrski and J. Hughes (Eds.): TFP 2020, LNCS 12222, pp. 180–203, 2020.
https://doi.org/10.1007/978-3-030-57761-2_9

Monads of Promises vs Promises of Monads. Quite interestingly, in most libraries, promises are defined with some *flavor* of a monad. Discussions about the true monadic nature of promises are numerous on the web[1], with various and contradictory conclusions depending on the considered host languages and libraries. Most of the resulting APIs even seem incompatible one with the others.

For instance, in a language like OCaml, where there is only an *implicit* IO monad, the monadic flavor of promises is made *explicit*. In OCaml *async* libraries [9], binding the fullfillment of a promise with some callback function is offered via an explicit *bind* function, and simple promises can be created by an explicit *return* function. In other words, OCaml promises are presented as if they form a monad.

On the contrary, in Haskell, where there is an *explicit* IO monad, there is no specific monad of promises [8]. Instead, the *async* library *extends* the IO monad to asynchronous concurrency with function $async :: IO\ a \to IO\ (Async\ a)$ that allows for forking (in a non blocking way) a IO action together with function $wait :: Async\ a \to IO\ a$ that allows for waiting and reading (in a non destructive way) the value returned by a forked action. Elements of $Async\ a$ can be seen as promises: promises of a returned value. However, while $Async$ has a functor instance, it does not have any monad instance. Haskell promises, when simply derived from Haskell *async* library, are not monadic.

Instead, aiming at relating both Haskell and OCaml *async* APIs, one can define another kind of promises in Haskell: elements of type $IO\ (Async\ a)$. Such an idea makes a lot of sense. An adequate function *return* can simply be defined by:

$$returnAsync :: a \to IO\ (Async\ a)$$
$$returnAsync\ a = async\ (return\ a)$$

However, as we shall see, there is only one possible associated *bind* function, defined by:

$$bindAsync :: IO\ (Async\ a) \to (a \to IO\ (Async\ b)) \to IO\ (Async\ b)$$
$$bindAsync\ m\ f = m \ggg \lambda r \to async\ (wait\ r \ggg f \ggg wait)$$

that *almost* yields a valid monad instance. For such an instance to be valid, we need to *restrict* further to those elements of $Async\ (m\ a)$ that are, up to equivalence, of the form $async\ m$ for some monadic action m (see Theorem 4). Then, the resulting monad of promises is shown to be *isomorphic* to the IO monad itself (see Theorem 5).

In other words, the possibility of a specific monad of promises in Haskell is a bit lost in the surrounding IO monad even though it can eventually be recovered.

Main Results. In this paper we shall first prove the above claims by understanding the properties satisfied by these asynchronous concurrent primitives, not only as specific instances of the *async* Haskell library, but from some more

---

[1] See e.g. Why are promises monads on stack overflow.

general properties they satisfy as elements of an asynchronous concurrent programing interface. For such a purpose, we shall define a fairly general notion
of an asynchronous concurrent *extension* of an *arbitrary* monad, the current
Haskell *async* library providing such an extension instance for the IO Monad.

One type function generalizing *Async* and two primitives generalizing *async*
and *wait* are the key features of our proposal, defined as a Haskell type class. The
expected semantics of these primitives is then specified by means of equational
laws relating the behavior of the new primitives with the behavior of *return*
and *bind* in the underlying monad. One may wonder why bothering capturing
asynchronous concurrent semantics by means of equational laws. Elements of
an answer are numerous and essentially the same as when asking why defining
monad API semantics by means of monad laws.

These equations allow for defining unambiguously the semantics of the proposed asynchronous primitives which *properties* can therefore be examined in full
details. We also seek at finding a smallest possible set of such primitives therefore
increasing the *safety* of our proposal: only a small kernel of primitives needs to
be implemented and proved correct, other needed asynchronous functions uniformly deriving from these primitives. The *correctness* of any instance of these
primitives can also be checked against these equations, either by means of some
derived test suites [1] or by formal proofs. Last, many of the proposed equations
yield rewriting rules that can be used, at compile time, for *code optimization*,
reducing the number of forked processes.

Such a general approach also opens the way for the programmer to design
his or her own monad, a kind of a *domain specific monad*, with its specialized
and safe API, and a specific asynchronous concurrent extension attuned towards
the expected application. As an example, we have recently defined the notion of
timed monads which asynchronous extensions are specific to the timed setting [6].
Indeed, in a timed monad, a timed action not only returns an explicit value but
also an implicit duration. Promises associated to timed monad actions should
also handle these durations.

The proposed formal approach eventually provides a better understanding
of what *asynchronous concurrency* is, compared to *general concurrency*. Simply said, both are defined by means of some notions of *processes* that can be
forked and, some corresponding (shall we say derived) notion of communication
channels through which forked processes can communicate one with the other.
However, a major difference lays in the way these communication channel are
handled.

In asynchronous concurrency, communication channels are only created when
forking a process, as (one way) broadcast channels from that forked processes.
The resulting communication graphs are acyclic. On the contrary, in general
concurrency, (two way) communication channels are freely created and passed as
parameter of forked processes. The resulting communication graphs are arbitrary
ones. The safety of asynchronous concurrency compared to general concurrency
follows from this simple but crucial difference.

In this paper, such a difference is also be understood as a general guiding principle for developing asynchronous concurrency itself, beyond the simplest kind of processes one can define out of monad actions. As an example, we define (monadic) streams of values as inductively nested monad actions and we show that promises of such streams can simply be defined as streams of promises, that is, inductively nested monad promises. An associated artefact has been implemented in Haskell and available on the net[2]. It has been successfully applied to realtime synchronous processing and asynchronous control of audio streams [5] therefore illustrating the application scope of the proposed model.

Overview of Paper Content. Our presentation is organized as follows. After a short review of the basic features of functors and monads in Sect. 2, our abstraction of the *async* library is presented, in Sect. 3. There, a generic type class *MonadRef* specifies the asynchronous concurrent extension of a monad m, defined by an abstract type $Ref_m\ a$, whose elements, called *monad references* are created by $fork :: m\ a \to m\ (Ref_m\ a)$ and used by $read :: Ref_m\ a \to m\ a$. Simply said, every monad reference uniquely refers to a forked monad action which returned value can be read via that monad reference. The expected semantics of monad references is formalized by means of two series of equational laws describing the expected interplay between the monad primitives $return :: a \to m\ a$ and $bind :: m\ a \to (a \to m\ b) \to m\ b$ and the asynchronous primitives $fork$ and $read$.

In Sect. 3, a first series of laws aim at capturing the basic semantics of monad references: how monad references are indeed bound to forked actions. These laws essentially states that $fork$ and $read$ behave in a coherent way with respect to the underlying monad law. This allows for proving in Sect. 4 that the type function $m \circ Ref_m$ is a functor and, under some adequate restrictions, also a monad isomorphic to m itself.

In Sect. 5, a second series of laws is more concerned with the asynchronous and concurrent nature of monad references. One idempotency and two commutation rules are stated for ensuring that actions are indeed executed when forked and read actions essentially have no side effects but waiting for the referenced actions to terminate. As an illustration of this second series of laws, a number of instances of the *MonadRef* class, visibly not asynchronous nor concurrent but satisfying the first series of laws, are shown to be eventually ruled out by these additional rules.

In Sect. 6, we show how the notion of monad references can be lifted to more complex data types such as monadic streams. In some sense, monad streams can be forked into promises of monad streams that are simply encoded as streams of promises. Asynchronous concurrency is then further developed in Sect. 7. Defining a general notion of monad structure references, we eventually prove by examples that asynchronous concurrency is a fairly general programing paradigm that can be extended far beyond the existing libraries.

The general coherence and relevance of our proposal is illustrated throughout by defining a simple valid extension of Haskell IO monad, a self-contained simplified version of the existing Haskell *async* library.

---

[2] See https://github.com/djanin/TimedMonadStream.

Observational Equivalence in Haskell. Although aiming at achieving a formal modeling of asynchronous concurrency, throughout the paper most concepts are presented by means of Haskell type classes which instances are thus requested to satisfy some number of equational laws. Compared to a purely theoretical approach, such a presentation comes with some overhead. However, an immediate benefit is that it is directly applicable as demonstrated by associated libraries developed both in Haskell and, to a lesser extent, OCaml (see footnote 2).

Throughout the paper, we consider that two elements a_1 $a_2 :: a$ of a given type a are (observationally) *equal* when there are *indistinguishable* in any context of use. In other words, denoting by $\equiv$ such an observational equality, we have $a_1 \equiv a_2$ when for any function $f :: a \to IO$ (), there is no observable difference between running f a_1 and f a_2 in the (idealized) IO monad. For instance, when instance of the class Eq with a defined equality $==$, the observational equivalence $\equiv$ in a type a is generally finer than the defined equality. Whenever $a_1 \equiv a_2$ we have $a_1 == a_2$. Indeed, the context function $\lambda x \to return$ $(a_1 == x)$ distinguishes a_1 and a_2 in the case $a_1 == a_2$ is false[3]. In other words, observational equivalence in a given type depends on the primitives defined on that type.

2   Preliminaries on Monadic Functors and Monad Actions

For our presentation to be reasonably self-contained, we review below the definition and some properties of functors and monads, following the programmer's point of view offered by the pioneering works of Moggi [10] and Wadler [13].

2.1   Functors

A (type) functor is a type function $m :: * \to *$ equipped with an *fmap* function as specified by the following class type:

    class *Functor* m **where**
      $fmap :: (a \to b) \to m\ a \to m\ b$

such that the following laws are satisfied:

$$m \equiv fmap\ id\ m \tag{1}$$
$$fmap\ (g \circ f)\ m \equiv fmap\ g\ (fmap\ f\ m) \tag{2}$$

for every monad action $m :: m\ a$ and functions $f : a \to b$ and $g : b \to c$. In other words, the function *fmap* extends to typed functions the function m over types.

---

[3] This is a bit over simplified for one could also require such a distinguishing context to be itself definable in Haskell.

2.2   Monads

A monad is a (type) functor $m :: * \to *$ equipped with two additional primitives *return* and *bind* as specified by the class type:

class *Functor m* $\Rightarrow$ *Monad m* **where**
  $return :: a \to m\ a$
  $(\ggg) :: m\ a \to (a \to m\ b) \to m\ b$

The infix operator $(\ggg)$ is called *bind* when used as a function. Elements of type $(m\ a)$ are called *monad actions*.

Every instance of the *Monad* class shall satisfies the following laws:

$$return\ a \ggg f \equiv f\ a \tag{3}$$

$$m \ggg return \equiv m \tag{4}$$

$$(m \ggg f) \ggg g \equiv m \ggg (\lambda x \to f\ x \ggg g) \tag{5}$$

for every monad action $m :: m\ a$ and functions $f :: a \to m\ b$ and $g :: b \to m\ c$.

The first and second equations state that, in some sense, *return* acts as a *neutral element* for the bind, both on the left (3) and on the right (4). The third equation states that the bind operator is *associative* (5) in some sense.

2.3   Coherence Property

Under such a presentation of monads, every monad instance shall also satisfy the following *coherence property*:

$$fmap\ f\ m \equiv m \ggg (return \circ f) \tag{6}$$

for every monad action $m :: m\ a$ and function $f :: a \to b$. This equation states that the mapping function induced by the monad primitives equals the mapping function defined in the parent *Functor* class instance. Indeed, one can check that if m is a monad then the function $\lambda f\ m \to m \ggg (return \circ f)$ satisfies both functor laws, i.e. any monad is indeed a functor.

2.4   Alternative Syntax for Binds

Haskell *do-notation* allows writing simpler composition of monad actions. Indeed, we may write:

$$\mathbf{do}\ \{ x_1 \leftarrow m_1; x_2 \leftarrow m_2; ...; x_{n-1} \leftarrow m_{n-1}; m_n \}$$

the variables $x_1, x_2, \ldots, x_{n-1}$ possibly omitted when not used, in place for the bind series $m_1 \ggg \lambda x_1 \to m_2 \ggg \lambda x_2 \to ...m_{n-1} \ggg \lambda x_{n-1} \to m_n$ with m_1,

$m_2, \ldots, m_n$ some monadic actions possibly depending on variables with strictly lower indices.

Such a notation has a clear flavor of imperative programing. Moreover, since action m_i possibly depends on the values returned by all actions m_j with $j < i$, it even seems that such a composition of actions is necessarily evaluated from left to right. However, this is not true in general unless the considered monad is *strict* as the IO Monad reviewed below.

2.5   The IO Monad

For the reader not much familiar with monad programing, we review here some basic features of Haskell IO monad; a monad that allows pure functions to be used in communication with the real world.

The archetypal functions in the IO monad are *getChar* :: *IO Char* and *putChar* :: *Char* → *IO* () that respectively allows for getting the next character typed on the keyboard (*getChar*), or printing on the screen the character passed as argument (*putChar*). As a usage example, one can define the function:

$echo :: IO$ ()
$echo = getChar \gg\!\!= putChar \gg\!\!= echo$

that, when ran, repeatedly waits for a character to be typed on the standard input and prints it out on the standard output.

An important feature of monadic IO actions, as monad actions, is that they are *not* executed unless passed to the top level. This illustrates the fact that, especially in a concurrent setting, monads, with *return* and *bind* functions, can be used for dynamically *defining* actions that can later be *run* or even *forked*.

Another important aspect of the IO monad in Haskell is that it is a *strict* monad in the sense that, when executing *bind* m f, the monadic action m is executed for its argument to be given to function f *before* evaluating f. This contrasts significantly with Haskell principle of lazy evaluation but clearly allows a better control, or even any control at all, on IO scheduling.

In other words, asynchronous extension of the IO monad offers a way to reintroduce (controlled) laziness and, therefore, parallelism into such a strictness.

3   Elementary Monad References

We describe here the first half of our formalization of promises by defining the notion of monad references with a first series of equations that suffices for analyzing the monadic nature of (the derived notion of) promises in Sect. 4. Analyzing the concurrent nature of these monad references is postponed to Sect. 5.

3.1   Monad Reference

Simply said, a monad reference is a reference to a "running" monad action, created by forking such an action. Such a monad reference can then be read for accessing the value returned by that referenced action. In terms of Haskell type classes, this yields:

> **class** *Monad m* $\Rightarrow$ *MonadRef m* **where**
>   **type** *Ref$_m$* :: $* \rightarrow *$
>   *fork* :: $m\ a \rightarrow m\ (Ref_m\ a)$
>   *read* :: $Ref_m\ a \rightarrow m\ a$

where:

(a) *Ref$_m$ a* is a type of *monad references* bound to running actions of type $m\ a$,
(b) *fork m* is an action that *launches* the execution of the monadic action m and (immediately) return a *monad reference* bound to that action,
(c) *read r* is an action that (possibly) *waits for* and *returns* the *value* returned by the running action bound by the monad reference r,

respectively generalizing *Async a*, *async* and *wait* in the *async* library defined over Haskell IO monad.

3.2   Basic Semantics Laws

Every instance of the *MonadRef* class must first satisfy the following laws:

$$(fork\ m) \ggg read \equiv m \tag{7}$$

$$fork \circ read \equiv return \tag{8}$$

$$fork\ (m \ggg f) \equiv (fork\ m) \ggg \lambda r \rightarrow fork\ (read\ r \ggg f) \tag{9}$$

for every monad action $m :: m\ a$ and function $f :: a \rightarrow m\ b$.

   Intuitively, Law (7) states the basic semantics of forks and reads: reading a just forked action essentially behaves like that executing action, side effects included! Law (8) states that forking a read essentially amounts to returning an equivalent reference. In other words, reads followed by forks essentially behaves like kind of identities.

   Last, Law (9) states that forking a bind can be decomposed into two successive forks, provided the reference returned by the first fork is passed through as argument of the second one. To some extent, binds distribute over forks.

   In other words, these three laws essentially ensure that *fork* and *read* behave in a way compatible with the structure of the monad m. This will be formally stated in Sect. 4.

3.3 Default IO Monad References

The simplest and truly concurrent instance of IO references one can define, thanks to mutable variables *MVar* and the native thread provided by *forkIO* in concurrent Haskell [7], is described by the following instance:

> **newtype** *MRef a = MRef (MVar a)*
> **instance** *MonadRef (IO)* **where**
>   **type** *Ref$_{IO}$ = MRef*
>   *fork m =* **do** { *v ← newEmptyMVar; forkIO (m ⨟ putMVar v);*
>   *return (MRef v)* }
>   *read (MRef v) = readMVar v*

With this definition, one can review all expected rules and check to which extent they are satisfied. Law (7) is satisfied thanks to the fact that the side effects happening when executing *m* are the same as the side effects happening when executing *forkIO m*.

Law (8) is less obviously satisfied. Indeed, two *distinct* mutable variables are created and we need them to be observationally equivalent, at least when used as monad references therefore encapsulated under *MRef*. It occurs that, they refer to two forked monad actions that both return the same value, essentially at the same time. Since they can only be read in a non destructive way (via *readMVar*), these two encapsulated mutable variables can thus be replaced one with the other without observable differences.

Law (9) validity essentially follows from the same reason, *forkIO* being non blocking and *readMVar* returning, in a non destructive way, the expected value essentially as soon as it is available.

Again, encapsulating mutable variables with *MRef* is crucial for hiding all the other primitives usually defined over *MVars* such as, for instance, *takeMVar* that performs a destructive read on a mutable variable.

3.4 Comparison with *async* Library

Our definition of monad references is inspired and looks like a generalization of the *async* library of Haskell. As such, one could define instead another default IO instance of monad references by taking *Ref$_{IO}$ = Async*, *fork = async* and *read = wait*. Would such an instance be valid? It occurs that *Async a* just as *MVar a* is an instance of the class *Eq* therefore, as discussed in the introduction, this seems to prevent Laws (8) and (9) to be satisfied. However, encapsulating *Asyncs* just as done above for *MVars* also solves such an issue. Then, one could prefer such a *Async* based instance for it offers a better support for interruption handling [8].

3.5 Counter Examples for Other Possible Laws

We have stated some equational properties that should be satisfied by instances of monad references, and we shall even state some more. Still, one may wonder how to check that an equality *is not* satisfied. The above instance of IO references is our main source of counter-examples for examining other possible laws or bad instances. The reason for this is that the IO monad conveys an implicit but rather strong notion of time based on IO events.

More precisely, we have already mentioned that its bind is *strict* and some actions in the IO monad are blocking, such as *getChar*, while some others are not, such as *printChar c*. Two complex actions can thus be distinguished by the visible side effects they may performed before being eventually blocked.

For instance, with IO references, one can observe that *fork m* is non blocking, regardless of the forked action m. This provides the following provable example of inequality that we use several times in the text. With $m_0 :: m \; (Ref_{IO} \; Char)$ defined by $m_0 = getChar \ggg (fork \circ return)$, we have

$$fork \; (m_0 \ggg read) \not\equiv m_0$$

even though both actions essentially return equivalent monad references.

Indeed, the action m_0 returns a reference towards the next typed character. But its blocks until that character is typed. The action $fork \; (m_0 \ggg read)$ returns a similar reference since, by (7) and (4), it is equivalent to $fork \; (getChar)$. However, it is non blocking since *fork* is non blocking.

In other words, it is false that $fork \; (m \ggg read) \equiv m$ in general. However, in the next section, we shall use the fact that, provided $m = fork \; m'$ for some $m' :: m \; a$, then such an equation does hold.

4   Elementary Properties of Monad References

In this section, we study the properties deriving from our equational definition of elementary monad references. Readers more interested in using asynchronous extensions of a monad may directly jump to Sect. 5 for a discussion about the concurrent nature of monad references.

In this section, we assume a type function $m :: * \to *$ with its functor instance *Functor m*, its monad instance *Monad m*, and its extension with monad references as a *MonadRef m* instance. This means that we assume there are the function *fmap*, *return*, *bind*, *fork* and *read* typed as described above and satisfying (1)–(6) for monad primitives, and laws (7)–(9) for monad references primitives. As a matter of fact, the categorical property we examine here only depends on the above laws.

4.1   Induced Functor

Observe that, although $Ref_m :: * \to *$ is a type function, it cannot be a functor since there is no function that allows for creating or reading a monad reference without entering into the monad m. As well known by Haskell programmers, there is no general no way to go outside a monad. However, one can prove:

Theorem 1. *The type function $m \circ Ref_m$ equipped with fmapRef defined by*

$$fmapRef :: MonaRef\ m \Rightarrow (a \rightarrow b) \rightarrow m\ (Ref_m\ a) \rightarrow m\ (Ref_m\ b)$$
$$fmapRef\ f\ m = m \ggg \lambda r \rightarrow fork\ (read\ r \ggg (return \circ f))$$

yields a valid functor instance.

Proof (sketch of). The fact that *fmapRef* satisfies law (1) follows from (8) and standard monad laws. The fact that *fmapRef* satisfies law (2) follows from (9) and standard monad laws. □

In other words, we have proved that the composition $m \circ Ref_m$, that maps every type a to the type $m\ (Ref_m\ a)$ of monad actions returning monad references, is itself a functor. The reader may find surprising that law (7), though describing the basic semantics of forks and reads, is not mentioned here. It turns out that it has already been used in order to simplify the definition of function *fmapRef* given here as shown in Lemma 3.

Remark. We could have put $fmapRef\ f\ m = fork\ (m \ggg read \ggg return \circ f)$ instead. But then, we would have $fmapRef\ id\ m = fork\ (m \ggg read)$ which, as shown at the end of Sect. 3, is distinct from m in the IO monad as soon as m is blocking. In other words, such an alternative definition fails to satisfy law (1).

4.2 Induced Natural Transformations

Functors m and $m \circ Ref_m$ are tightly related. Indeed, slightly abusing Haskell notations, we define the *monad transformations*:

$$Fork :: m \overset{\cdot}{\rightarrow} m \circ Ref_m$$
$$Fork_a = fork :: m\ a \rightarrow m\ (Ref_m\ a)$$
$$Read :: m \circ Ref_m \overset{\cdot}{\rightarrow} m$$
$$Read_a = \lambda m \rightarrow m \ggg read :: m\ (Ref_m\ a) \rightarrow m\ a$$

defined for every type a, where $\overset{\cdot}{\rightarrow}$ denotes the (non Haskell) natural transformation type constructor, and we have:

Theorem 2. *Both Fork and Read are natural transformation, that is, for every function $f :: a \rightarrow b$ we have:*

$$fmapRef\ f\ (fork\ m) \equiv fork\ (fmap\ f\ m) \tag{10}$$

for every action $m :: m\ a$, and we have:

$$fmap\ f\ (m \ggg read) \equiv fmapRef\ f\ m \ggg read \tag{11}$$

for every action $m :: m\ (Ref_m\ a)$. Moreover, functor m turns out to be a retract of functor $m \circ Ref_m$, that is, Read $\circ$ Fork is the identity transformation.

Proof (sketch of). Equation (10) follows from Law (9), and Eq. (11) follows from Law (7). The fact $Read \circ Fork \equiv Id$ follows from Law (7). □

The reverse composition $Fork \circ Read$ is not the identity as shown in the IO monad by $fork\ (m \ggg read) \not\equiv m$ whenever m is a a blocking monad action. In other words, there may be more behaviors definable with monad references than behaviors definable without.

4.3   The Possibility of a Monad

We have shown that $m \circ Ref_m$ is a functor. Is this functor monadic? Strictly speaking, this is not true as we shall see here by enumerating all possible definitions for returns and binds.

First, up to equivalent definitions, the unique possibility of a function $return$ is defined by:

$$returnRef :: MonadRef\ a \Rightarrow a \to m\ (Ref_m\ a)$$
$$returnRef = fork \circ return$$

for it is the unique uniformly defined function inhabiting its type. For a function $bind$ there are four possible candidates:

$$bindRef :: m\ (Ref_m\ a) \to (a \to m\ (Ref_m\ b)) \to m\ (Ref_m\ b)$$
(a) $bindRef\ m\ f = fork\ (m \ggg read \ggg f \ggg read)$
(b) $bindRef\ m\ f = m \ggg \lambda r \to fork\ (read\ r \ggg f \ggg read)$
(c) $bindRef\ m\ f = m \ggg read \ggg \lambda a \to fork\ (f\ a \ggg read)$
(d) $bindRef\ m\ f = m \ggg read \ggg f$

Of course, the fact that such a list is, up to equivalence, complete necessitates a proof. One can observe that we have at least enumerated all possible insertions of a fork into the possible series of binds. In some sense, the IO monad instance forces to respect functional dependencies in sequence. Then it seems that adding additional forks and reads would essentially yield equivalent bind candidates thanks to rules (7)–(9).

Lemma 3. *Bind candidates (a), (c) and (d) fail to satisfy the right unit monad law (4) in the IO monad instance.*

In any instance, the bind candidate (b) satisfies the right monad unit law (4), the monad associativity law (5), as well as the coherence law (6) with respect to fmapRef, that is, with candidate (b), we have:

$$fmapRef\ f\ m \equiv bindRef\ m\ (returnRef \circ f) \tag{12}$$

for every $m :: m\ (Ref_m\ a)$ and $f :: a \to b$.

Moreover, while the bind candidate (b) fails to satisfy the left unit monad law (3) in the IO monad instance, if we restrict to functions of the form $fork \circ f$ some $f :: a \to m\ b$, then the bind candidate (b) also satisfies law (3) in arbitrary monad instances.

In other words, Lemma 3 states that the bind candidate (b) is a good candidate for us to prove that $m \circ Ref_m$ is our expected monad of promises *provided* we restrict ourselves to the subtype of $m\ (Ref_m\ a)$ defined by elements of the form $fork \circ m$ for some monad action $m :: m\ a$.

4.4   The Expected Monad of Promises

In Haskell, such an expected subset[4] of m $(Ref_m$ $a)$ is defined by the type:

> **newtype** $Promise$ m $a = Promise$ $\{thePromise :: m$ $(Ref_m$ $a)\}$

only equipped with the two primitives:

> $forkP :: MonadRef$ $m \Rightarrow m$ $a \rightarrow Promise$ m a
> $forkP = Promise \circ fork$
>
> $readP :: MonadRef$ $m \Rightarrow Promise$ m $a \rightarrow m$ a
> $readP$ $p = (thePromise$ $p) \ggg read$

Theorem 4. *The following definitions are valid instances of the Functor and Monad type classes:*

> **instance** $MonadRef$ $m \Rightarrow Functor$ $(Promise$ $m)$ **where**
> $fmap$ f $(Promise$ $m) = Promise$ $(fmapRef$ f $m)$

and

> **instance** $MonadRef$ $m \Rightarrow Monad$ $(Promise$ $m)$ **where**
> $return = Promise \circ returnRef$
> $(\ggg)$ $(Promise$ $m)$ f
> $= Promise$ $(bindRef$ m $(thePromise \circ f))$

with bind candidate (b) for bindRef.

Proof (sketch of). The fact $Promise$ m is a functor follows from Theorem 1. The fact it is also a monad follows from Lemma 3 proving additionally, by induction on the complexity of their definition, that every definable inhabitant of $Promise$ m a, that is, defined only with $ForkP$, $fmap$, $return$ and $bind$, is equivalent with an element of the form $Promise$ $(fork$ $m)$ for some $m :: m$ a. $\square$

Theorem 5. *Categorical functors m and $Promise$ m are isomorphic.*

Proof (sketch of). Follows from Theorem 2 and the proof argument of Theorem 4, since, restricted to monad action of the form $fork$ m with $m :: m$ a, we indeed have $fork$ $(fork$ $m \ggg read) \equiv fork$ m, by law (7), therefore $Promise \circ Fork$ is the inverse of $Read \circ thePromise$. $\square$

As a special case within the explicit Haskell IO monad, we thus have defined a monad of promises quite smilar to the one defined in the implicit IO monad of OCaml [9].

---

[4] We could call it a subtype for it has fewer inhabitants. However, since it also supports fewer operations, such a name for type $Promise$ m a would be confusing.

Of course, the purpose of such a definition of promises in Haskell is merely for stating and proving the above theorems. Programmers *are not* advised to use such a definition of promises for this would result in having to combine two distinct monads. Instead, from now on, we simply use monad references and the associated primitives, therefore staying within the underlying monad m, much in the same way one would use the *async* library staying within the IO monad.

5   Concurrent Monad References

We aim at capturing asynchronous concurrent behaviors by means of the notion of monad references. However, as we shall soon see, Laws (7)–(9) fail to achieve by themselves such a goal.

5.1   Pathological Instances

Each of the following instances, though satisfying Laws (7)–(9), violates (at least) one of the intuitive properties we expect asynchronous concurrent primitives to satisfy.

Read Effect-Freedom (A). As a first example, the following instance violates the intention that a monad reference should be freely readable, essentially with no side effects but waiting for the termination of the forked action.

```
instance MonadRef IO where
    type Ref_IO = IO
    fork = return :: IO a → IO (IO a)
    read = id :: IO a → IO a
```

Such an instance, that could be generalized to an arbitrary monad, is valid. Indeed, law (7) follows from (3), law (8) is immediate, and law (9) follows from (5). However, reading such a kind of reference just amounts to performing the referenced action. Read actions therefore have *arbitrary* side effects.

Non-blocking Fork (B). As another example, despite the fact we said *fork* should be instantaneous, or at least non blocking, the following valid instance provides a counter example to that claim.

```
instance MonadRef IO where
    type Ref_IO = MRef
    fork m = m ⋙ (MRef ∘ newMVar)
    read (MRef v) = readMVar v
```

where $newMVar :: a → m\ (MVar\ a)$ creates a new mutable variable filled with its argument. Compared to the instance of IO references given in Sect. 3, we just have changed the definition of *fork*. In this new instance, forking an action waits for that action to be completed before returning a reference. As a consequence, with $m = getChar$, the action *fork m* is now blocking.

Read Independence (C). With a bit more of coding, the following instance, although with non blocking forks, violates our requirement that forking an action amounts to executing it.

> **instance** *MonadRef IO* **where**
>   **type** Ref_{IO} $a = MRef$ $(Either$ $(IO$ $a)$ $a)$
> $fork$ $m = MRef$ $(newMVar$ $(Left$ $m))$
> $read$ $(MRef$ $v) =$ **do** $\{$ $c \leftarrow takeMVar$ $v;$
> $a \leftarrow$ **case** c **of** $\{$ $Left$ $m \rightarrow m;$ $Right$ $a \rightarrow return$ a $\};$
> $putMVar$ v $(Right$ $a);$ $return$ a $\}$

In this instance, a forked action is indeed executed only when its associated reference is read for the first time.

5.2   Concurrency Laws

We aim now at designing a second series of equational laws, called concurrency laws, that enforce the properties detailled above. From now on, these additional laws must also be satisfied by any monad instance of the class *MonadRef*.

Following a typical approach of concurrency theory, these additional laws simply state that certain idempotency and commutation propertics are satisfied:

$$read \; r \equiv read \; r \gg read \; r \tag{13}$$

$$fork \; m_1 \ggg \lambda r_1 \rightarrow (fork \; m_2 \ggg \lambda r_2 \rightarrow return \; (r_1, r_2))$$
$$\equiv fork \; m_2 \ggg \lambda r_2 \rightarrow (fork \; m_1 \ggg \lambda r_1 \rightarrow return \; (r_1, r_2)) \tag{14}$$

$$read \; r_1 \ggg \lambda x_1 \rightarrow (read \; r_2 \ggg \lambda x_2 \rightarrow return \; (x_1, x_2))$$
$$\equiv read \; r_2 \ggg \lambda x_2 \rightarrow (read \; r_1 \ggg \lambda x_1 \rightarrow return \; (x_1, x_2)) \tag{15}$$

for every monad reference r r_1 $r_2 :: Ref_m$ a and monad action m_1 $m_2 :: m$ a, with $m_1 \gg m_2$ denoting the composition $m_1 \ggg \lambda_- \rightarrow m_2$.

5.3   Discussion on Concurrency Laws

The intuitive meaning of these laws is detailed below.

By stating that reading actions are idempotent, Law (13) implies that values returned by read actions only depends on their parameter reference, i.e. reads are non destructive, and that side effects associated to readings a given reference occurs during the execution of the first (terminated) occurrence of such a read. After the return of a first read, any further reading of the its reference is side effect free and essentially instantaneous. The pathological instance (A) is ruled out by such a law. Indeed, there, monad references are arbitrary monad actions and reading amounts to executing them. Still, both pathological instances (B) and (C) satisfy such a law.

By stating that fork actions commute, Law (14) enforces the instantaneity of fork actions. This law rules out the pathological instance (B). Indeed, a blocking action such as *getChar* visibly does not commute with a non blocking but observable action such as *printChar c*. With instance (B) the forks of these two actions will surely not commute. However, the pathological instance (C) still satisfy such a law.

Last, by stating that read actions commute, Law (15) enforces the fact that the execution of a forked actions cannot depend on the associated readings. Monad references must truly refer to *running* monad actions, and read action cannot have other side effect but waiting for the these running action to terminate. Our last pathological instance (C) is eventually ruled out by such a rule as shown by forking both a blocking IO action and an observable non blocking one. The resulting reads do not commute.

In other words, these three additional rules have ruled out all pathological instances we could think of. This increase our confidence in the fact that they eventually form a complete axiomatization of asynchronous concurrent behaviors.

5.4   Validity in the Asynchronous Concurrent Extension of the IO Monad

In the IO instance of monad references defined in Sect. 3, law (13) follows from the fact that the action *readMVar* is non destructive.

Law (14) is perhaps the most debatable one. It may wrongly suggest that the side effects of action m_1 and m_2 commute. This is not true. In the concurrent framework of Haskell, these side effects are executed in parallel therefore, up to the possible non determinism induced by that parallelism, forking m_1 right before m_2 or forking m_2 right before m_1 essentially produces the same side effects.

Law (15) is easily accepted as valid since reads essentially wait for termination of (parallel) forked actions. Waiting for the termination of one action and then another just amounts to waiting for the termination of both.

5.5   Commutation Rules and Induced Non Determinism

Of course, concurrency yields non determinism as made explicit by the commutations of forks. An example of non determinism on outputs is given by any of the following equivalent programs:

fork (putChar 'a'*)* ≫ *fork (putChar* 'b'*)*
fork (putChar 'b'*)* ≫ *fork (putChar* 'a'*)*

that print non deterministically either "ab" or "ba". An example of non determinism on inputs is given by any of the following equivalent programs:

fork (getChar) ≫= λr_1 → *fork (getChar)* ≫= λr_2 → *read* r_1 ≫ *printChar*
fork (getChar) ≫= λr_2 → *fork (getChar)* ≫= λr_1 → *read* r_1 ≫ *printChar*

that both non deterministically print either 'a' or 'b' when reading the string "ab" from the standard input.

6   Asynchronous Concurrency and Data Flow Programing

So far, we have only defined references to running monad actions. We aim now at extending monad references to generalized monad actions, that is, structures of nested monad actions. Even though this can easily be generalized to more complex structure, we simply review here the case of monadic streams as they can be used for data flow programing in Haskell [5].

6.1   Monad Streams

Monad streams are defined by the following inductive data type:

data *Stream m a* = *Stream* { *next* :: *m* (*Maybe* (*a*, *Stream m a*)) }

In other words, a monad stream is essentially defined as a monad action that either returns nothing when the stream terminates, or just a value and the action defining the continuation of that stream otherwise. As an example of a monad stream, there is the standard input stream defined by:

stdinStream :: *Stream IO Char*
stdinStream = *Stream* $ **do** { *a* ← *getChar*; *return* $ *Just* (*a*, *stdinStream*) }

that, when executed, eventually returns all the characters typed from the standard input (*stdin*) one after the other.

A function printing a stream of characters to the standard output (*stdout*) can also be defined by:

streamStdout :: *Stream IO Char* → *IO* ()
streamStdout (*Stream m*) = **do** { *c* ← *m*; **case** *c* **of**
    { *Nothing* → *return* (); *Just* (*a*, *s*) → **do** { *putChar a*; *streamStdout s* } } }

Then, the function *echo* described above as an example of function in the IO monad can then be recoded by:

echo = *streamStdout stdinStream*

Such an example illustrates fairly well the power of monad streams for data flow programing, a kind of monad programing technique fairly popular among Haskell programmers.

6.2   Derived Functor Instance

As a typical example of monad stream programing, there is the following functor instance.

> **instance** *Monad m* $\Rightarrow$ *Functor* (*Stream m*) **where**
> *fmap f* (*Stream m*) = *Stream* \$ **do** { $c \leftarrow m$;
> **case** *c* **of** { *Nothing* $\rightarrow$ *return Nothing*;
> *Just* (*a, sc*) $\rightarrow$ *return* \$ *Just* (*f a, fmap f sc*)}}

Every function *fmap f* :: *Monad m* $\Rightarrow$ *Stream m a* $\rightarrow$ *Stream m b* is an archetypal example of a synchronous (or isochronous) function over monadic streams.

6.3   Horizontal Monoid Structure

There is the following monoid instance that essentially lifts to monadic stream the (free) monoid encoded by the list data type.

> **instance** *Monad m* $\Rightarrow$ *Monoid* (*Stream m a*) **where**
> *mempty* = *Stream* (*return Nothing*)
> ($\Diamond$) (*Stream m*) *s* = *Stream* \$ **do**
> { $c \leftarrow m$; **case** *c* **of** { *Nothing* $\rightarrow$ *next s*;
> *Just* (*a, sc*) $\rightarrow$ *return* \$ *Just* (*a, sc* $\Diamond$ *s*)}}

where the neutral element *mempty* is the (immediately) empty streams and ($\Diamond$) is function that concatenates two monad streams one after the other.

In a concurrent and reactive context, the horizontal concatenation is of little use unless its first argument is a constant and thus acts as a delay/buffering. We shall see below, in link with monad references, a much more interesting monoid instance for monad streams (called vertical) and the monad instance it induces.

6.4   Monad Stream References

Observe that *sharing* a monad stream such as *stdinStream* among several processes would result in *distributing* the standard inputs among these processes. The notion of monad references can be extended to monad streams and allows for *duplicating* monad streams. More precisely, there is a generalized notion of references applicable to monad streams defined by:

> **type** *StreamRef$_m$* = *Stream Ref$_m$*

i.e. a reference to a monad stream is simply a stream of nested monad references.

Then, forking a monad stream and reading the resulting monad stream reference can simply be defined by:

> *forkStream* :: *MonadRef m* $\Rightarrow$ *Stream m a* $\rightarrow$ *m* (*StreamRef$_m$ a*)
> *forkStream* = *fork* (*evalAndFork s*) $\ggg$ *return* $\circ$ *Stream*

where

$$evalAndFork\ (Stream\ m) = m \ggg mapM$$
$$(\lambda(a, sc) \rightarrow \mathbf{do}\ \{rc \leftarrow fork\ (evalAndFork\ sc); return\ (a, Stream\ rc)\})$$
$$readStream :: MonadRef\ m \Rightarrow StreamRef_m\ a \rightarrow m\ (Stream\ m\ a)$$
$$readStream\ (Stream\ r) = return \circ Stream\ \$\ read\ r \ggg$$
$$mapM\ (\lambda(a, rc) \rightarrow return\ (a, readStream\ rc))$$

A major application of *forkStream* and *readStream* is the possibility to share the content of a stream without duplicating its side effects. Such a possibility is especially useful in reactive on-the-fly data flow programming [5]. More formally, one can prove that:

Lemma 6. *For every* $s :: Stream\ m$ *we have:*

$$forkStream\ s \ggg readStream \equiv return\ s$$
$$forkStream \circ readStream \equiv return$$

In other words, with monadic stream references defined as above, the first two laws (7)–(8) lift to the case of monadic stream references. For Eq. (9) to be satisfied by streams and stream references, we eventually need to equip monad streams with an adequate monad structure.

7   More Asynchronous Concurrency

In order to equip monad streams with an adequate monad instance, we eventually define additional (asynchronous) concurrent primitives that cannot be derived from the *read* and *fork* primitives defined so far.

7.1   More Concurrent Primitives

These primitives are specified by the following type class refinement of the type class *MonadRef*:

class $MonadRef\ m \Rightarrow MonadRefPlus\ m$ **where**
$tryRead :: Ref_m\ a \rightarrow m\ (Maybe\ a)$
$parRead :: Ref_m\ a \rightarrow Ref_m\ b \rightarrow m\ (Either\ a\ b)$

where:

(a) *tryRead* r is the action that immediately returns nothing if the referenced action is not terminated or just its returned value otherwise,

(b) *parReadRef* $r_1\ r_2$ is the action that returns the value of the earliest terminated referenced actions or, in the case both actions are already terminated or are terminating at the same time, either of the returned values.

In the IO monad, such additional monad reference primitives can be defined by:

instance *MonadRefPlus IO* **where**
    tryRead (*MRef v*) = *tryReadMVar v*
    parRead r_1 r_2 = **do**
        $\{ v \leftarrow newEmptyMVar;$
        forkIO (*read* r_1 $\ggg$ (*tryPutMVar v*) $\circ$ *Left* $\gg$ *return* ());
        forkIO (*read* r_2 $\ggg$ (*tryPutMVar v*) $\circ$ *Right* $\gg$ *return* ());
        readMVar v$\}$

We may aim at axiomatizing the behavior of these newly introduced primitives. For instance, one may expect to have:

fork m $\ggg$ *tryRead* $\equiv$ *m* $\ggg$ *return* when *m* is instantaneous,
fork m $\ggg$ *tryRead* $\equiv$ *return Nothing* when *m* is not instantaneous.

However, these laws seem to be difficult to be enforced at runtime and, at compile time, they require some typing of action duration, a typing that is not (yet) available.

7.2   Vertical Monoid Structure

Thanks to *parRead* one can define the merge of two monadic streams by:

merge :: *MonadRefPlus m* $\Rightarrow$ *Stream m a* $\rightarrow$ *Stream m a* $\rightarrow$ *Stream m a*
merge s_1 s_2 = *Stream* $ do
    $\{ r_1 \leftarrow forkStream\ s_1; r_2 \leftarrow forkStream\ s_2; return\ (next\ \$\ mergeRef\ r_1\ r_2) \}$

with

mergeRef :: *MonadRefPlus m* $\Rightarrow$
    Stream Ref$_m$ a $\rightarrow$ *Stream Ref$_m$ a* $\rightarrow$ *Stream m a*
mergeRef (*Stream* r_1) (*Stream* r_2) = *Stream* $ **do**
    $\{ c \leftarrow parRead\ r_1\ r_2;$ **case** *c* **of** $\{$
    Left Nothing $\rightarrow$ *next* $ *readT* (*Stream* r_2);
    Right Nothing $\rightarrow$ *next* $ *readT* (*Stream* r_1);
    Left (*Just* (*a, src1*)) $\rightarrow$ *return* $ *Just* (*a, mergeRef src1 sr$_2$*);
    Right (*Just* (*a, src2*)) $\rightarrow$ *return* $ *Just* (*a, mergeRef sr$_1$ src2*) $\}\}$

Then, up to the possible non determinism yields by *parRead*, the type *stream m a* of monadic streams equipped with *merge* is essentially a commutative monoid with the empty stream *mempty* as neutral element.

7.3   Derived Stream Monad

Thanks to such a vertical monoid structure, we have the following valid monad instance:

instance *MonadRef m* $\Rightarrow$ *Monad* (*Stream m*) **where**
    return a = (*Stream* $\circ$ *return* $\circ$ *Just*) (*a, mempty*)
    ($\ggeq$) (*Stream m*) *f* = *Stream* \$ **do**
        { *c* $\leftarrow$ *m*; **case** *c* **of**
        { *Nothing* $\rightarrow$ *return Nothing*;
            Just (*a, mc*) $\rightarrow$ *next* \$ *merge* (*f a*) (*mc* $\ggeq$ *f*)}}

There, the flattening operation essentially amounts to merge monadic substreams from the moment they appear. This feature is especially useful when handling asynchronous control flows [5].

Lemma 7. *For every stream s* :: *Stream m a and function f* :: *a* $\rightarrow$ *Stream m b, we have:*

$$forkStream\ (s \ggeq f) \equiv forkStream\ s \ggeq \lambda r \rightarrow forkStream\ (readStream\ r \ggeq f)$$

In other words, the monad reference Law (9) also lifts to monad stream references.

7.4   Stream Monad as a Monad Extension

The above monad instance of *Stream m* is also an extension of the monad *m* in the sense that, with:

    liftStream :: *m a* $\rightarrow$ *Stream m a*
    liftStream m = *Stream* \$ **do** { *a* $\leftarrow$ *m*; *return* \$ *Just* (*a, emptyStream*)}

we have:

Lemma 8. *Function liftStream is a natural embedding of m into Stream m with:*

$$liftStream \circ return \equiv return$$
$$liftStream\ (m \ggeq f) \equiv liftStream\ m \ggeq liftStream \circ f$$

for every action m :: *m a and function f* :: *a* $\rightarrow$ *m b.*

7.5   Generalization Monad References to Monadic Structures

The above treatment of monadic streams seems to fit a fairly general notion of references to monadic structures. More precisely, we can define the type class:

    class (*MonadRefPlus m, Monad* (*t m*)) $\Rightarrow$ *MonadDataRef t m* **where**
    forkT :: *t m a* $\rightarrow$ *m* (*t Ref$_m$ a*)
    readT :: *t Ref$_m$ a* $\rightarrow$ *m* (*t m a*)

where, in any instance, primitives *forkT* and *readT* are required to satisfy the following laws:

$$(forkT\ s) \ggeq readT \equiv return\ s \tag{16}$$

$$forkT \circ readT \equiv return \tag{17}$$

$$forkT \ (s \ggg f) \equiv (forkT \ s) \ggg \lambda r \rightarrow forkT \ (readT \ r \ggg f) \tag{18}$$

for every monad structure $s :: t \ m \ a$ and function $f :: a \rightarrow t \ m \ b$.

Then, thanks to Lemmas 6 and 7 there is the following valid instance for monad stream references:

instance *MonadRefPlus* $m \Rightarrow$ *MonadDataRef Stream* m **where**
  forkT = *forkStream*
  readT = *readStream*

It is probably the case that such a construction can be generalized to arbitrary monadic versions of inductive types. However, such a study goes out of the scope of the present paper.

7.6   More Parallelism

So far, we can fork one monad action, or a stream of nested monad actions. One may wonder if such an asynchronous fork can be generalized to other structures such as lists, or, more generally, traversable structures. Actually, this can easily be done by defining:

forkAll :: (*Traversable t, MonadRef m*) $\Rightarrow$ $t \ (m \ a) \rightarrow m \ (t \ (Ref_m \ a))$
forkAll = *mapM fork*

The question then becomes, how to handle the resulting structure of monad references. One possibility is to uniformly define:

sortRefs :: (*Traversable t, MonadRefPlus m*) $\Rightarrow$ $t \ (Ref_m \ a) \rightarrow$ *Stream m a*
sortRefs = *foldMap* (*liftStream* $\circ$ *read*)

that turns a traversable structure of monad references into the monad stream of values returned by the referenced actions *ordered* by termination time. In other words, *sortRefs* generalizes *parRead* to arbitrary traversable structures. Moreover, using functions *forkAll* and *sortRefs*, much like using primitives *fork* and *read*, is safe for it yields no deadlock.

7.7   Asynchronous vs General Concurrency

The above generic definition of *sortRef* suffers from a rather severe drawback: its complexity in terms of call to *parRead*, therefore in number of *fork*, is likely to be quadratic in the size of the traversable structure.

With (fully) concurrent Haskell, this is not a necessity as shown by the following direct implementation of *sortRefs* in the IO monad:

$$sortRefs_{IO} :: Traversable\ t \Rightarrow t\ (Ref_{IO}\ a) \rightarrow IO\ (Stream\ IO\ a)$$
$$sortRefs_{IO}\ t = \mathbf{do}\ \{v \leftarrow newEmptyMVar;$$
$$mapM_{-}\ (\lambda r \rightarrow forkIO\ (read\ r \ggg putMVar\ v))\ t;$$
$$return\ \$\ mvarToStream\ v\ (length\ t)\}$$
where
$$mvarToStream\ \_\ 0 = mempty$$
$$mvarToStream\ v\ n = Stream\ \$\ \mathbf{do}$$
$$\{a \leftarrow takeMVar\ v; return\ \$\ Just\ (a, mvarToStream\ v\ (n-1))\}$$

with a linear number of forks.

In other words, despite the many and somewhat unexpected programming possibilities offered by asynchronous concurrency, illustrated among other things by monad stream references, asynchronous concurrency does not offer as many programming possibilities as a more general concurrent programming framework. This is no surprise. This is the price to pay for the increase of robustness and safety offered by asynchronous concurrency compared to general concurrency.

8   Related Works and Conclusion

The study proposed here started as an attempt to clarify the properties of an existing and somewhat ad hoc but succesfull experiment of realtime audio processing and control in Haskell [5]. As such, it was first designed as a stand alone approach that was a priori not much related with former theoretical investigations. A posteriori, our proposal offers an equational formalization of the semantics of (a kernel of) the existing *async* library. To the best of our knowledge, no such an axiomatization has yet been proposed.

We present a fairly generic notion of a monad extension. A first series of laws describes how to go back and forth between the underlying monad m and its extension $m \circ Ref_m$ via a retraction pair of natural transformations. The underlying general category theoretic schema seems rather orthogonal to more classical existing techniques for combining monads [2,10]. Such a notion of a monad extension is probably worth being studied more in the depth.

A second series of laws enforces concurrency as shown by ruling out pathological instances. However, there is no guarantee our proposal is complete. There could well be other pathological instances violating our intuition on what asynchronous concurrency should be. Moreover, all our examples are based on extending the strict IO monad. The underlying intuition is somewhat biased. What is the asynchronous concurrent extension of a non strict monad is yet not that clear. The successful extensions of the notion of monad references to more complex structures, such as monad streams or traversable structures of monad actions, only constitute partial answers to that question.

As already observed, the possibility of defining an equational theory for the additional primitives such as *tryRead* bumped into the lack of a denotional semantics that describes action durations. For instance, we cannot describe the property that between to monadic actions, one is finishing before the other unless they both block endlessly. A pure denotational approach might still be possible following the recent proposal of a timed extension of Scott domains [4]. However, investigating such a possibility goes out of the scope of the present paper.

Last, one could also examine the possibility of defining asynchronous concurrency as an algebraic effect [11]. The termination of a forked action indeed sounds like raising an effect that is eventually passed to all the readers of the monad reference bound to that action. The resulting API would be different than the current one. How the proposed axiomatization could be adapted to such a distinct modeling approach is an open problem.

References

1. Claessen, K., Hugues, J.: QuickCheck: a lightweight tool for random testing of Haskell programs. In: International Conference on Functional Programming (ICFP) (2000)
2. Dahlqvist, F., Parlant, L., Silva, A.: Layer by layer - combining monads. In: Theoretical Aspects of Computing (ICTAC), pp. 153–172 (2018)
3. Halstead, R.H.: Multilisp: a language for concurrent symbolic computation. ACM Trans. Program. Lang. Syst. **7**(4), 501–538 (1985)
4. Janin, D.: Spatio-temporal domains: an overview. In: Fischer, B., Uustalu, T. (eds.) ICTAC 2018. LNCS, vol. 11187, pp. 231–251. Springer, Cham (2018). https://doi.org/10.1007/978-3-030-02508-3_13
5. Janin, D.: Screaming in the IO monad. In: ACM Workshop on Functional Art, Music, Modeling and Design (FARM). ACM Press (2019)
6. Janin, D.: A timed IO monad. In: Komendantskaya, E., Liu, Y.A. (eds.) PADL 2020. LNCS, vol. 12007, pp. 131–147. Springer, Cham (2020). https://doi.org/10.1007/978-3-030-39197-3_9
7. Peyton Jones, S., Gordon, A., Finne, S.: Concurrent Haskell. In: Principles of Programing Languages (POPL). ACM, New York (1996)
8. Marlow, S.: Parallel and Concurrent Programming in Haskell. O'Reilly, Sebastopol (2013)
9. Minsky, Y., Hickey, J., Madhavapeddy, A.: Real World OCaml: Functional Programming for the Masses. O'Reilly, Sebastopol (2013)
10. Moggi, E.: A modular approach to denotational semantics. In: Pitt, D.H., Curien, P.-L., Abramsky, S., Pitts, A.M., Poigné, A., Rydeheard, D.E. (eds.) CTCS 1991. LNCS, vol. 530, pp. 138–139. Springer, Heidelberg (1991). https://doi.org/10.1007/BFb0013462
11. Pretnar, M.: An introduction to algebraic effects and handlers. In: The 31st Conference on the Mathematical Foundations of Programming Semantics (MFPS XXXI). Electronic Notes in Theoretical Computer Science, vol. 319, pp. 19–35 (2015)
12. Reppy, J.H.: Concurrent Programming in ML. Cambridge University Press, Cambridge (1999)
13. Wadler, P.: Comprehending monads. In: Conference on LISP and Functional Programming (LFP). ACM, New York (1990)

State Will do

Willem Seynaeve[⊠], Koen Pauwels, and Tom Schrijvers

Department of Computer Science, KU Leuven Belgium, Leuven, Belgium
willem.seynaeve@student.kuleuven.be

Abstract. The main strength of purely functional languages like Haskell is that they make reasoning about programs easy with a technique called equational reasoning. This ease of reasoning also extends to effectful programs provided the side-effects are modelled in a purely functional manner, for instance with monads.

This paper uses equational reasoning to reason about the modelling of the side-effects themselves. In particular, we consider non-determinism, which is a key side-effect in Prolog and other logic-programming systems. Non-determinism is typically modelled by the list monad, but efficient implementations of Prolog and other non-deterministic systems use a much more low-level approach based on mutable state. In this way we model those lower-level implementations with the state monad and use equational reasoning to show its correctness with respect to the high-level list-based model. We also show how this result can be further generalized to other models of non-determinism.

Keywords: Monads · Equational reasoning · Non-determinism · State

1 Introduction

One of the appeals of purely functional programs is that they possess the property that equals may always be substituted for equals [12], which makes reasoning about these programs more straightforward. This power comes at a disadvantage: our functions must be free of side effects, which makes some programs (for example, stateful or nondeterministic programs) harder to express. Wadler [14] shows how such effects can be encapsulated using the Monad interface. In Haskell the monad interface is captured in the following type class:

```
class Monad m where
    return :: a    -> m a
    (>>=)  :: m a -> (a -> m b) -> m b
```

This class is accompanied by three laws, which are rules we want any implementation of the monad interface to obey.

W. Seynaeve—Student.

K. Pauwels—Phd Student.

© Springer Nature Switzerland AG 2020
A. Byrski and J. Hughes (Eds.): TFP 2020, LNCS 12222, pp. 204–225, 2020.
https://doi.org/10.1007/978-3-030-57761-2_10

```
--Left identity:
return a >>= f  = f a
--Right identity:
m >>= return    = m
--Associativity:
(m >>= f) >>= g = m >>= (\x -> f x >>= g)
```

With monads to implement side effects, functions are still pure and so we can still use equational reasoning on our effectful programs.

One method of equational reasoning about effectful programs, shown by Hutton and Fulger [8], is to unfold the definitions of the effectful operations and to prove the properties directly in terms of the underlying code. Unfortunately, this breaches the abstraction boundaries and is a rather tedious task.

Gibbons and Hinze [4] address this problem. Instead of reasoning about a concrete implementation of an effect, they present an axiomatic approach: by exploiting algebraic properties of a monadic interface, they show that one can write equational proofs which preserve the monadic abstraction. In other words, the proof is entirely independent from the concrete implementation of an effect.

Of course, concrete implementations of effects have to make sure that they satisfy the expected algebraic properties. Pauwels et al. [9] investigate a layered approach, where a higher-level effect is implemented in terms of a lower-level effect. This way the axioms of the lower-level effect can be used to prove the algebraic properties of the higher-level one. Specifically, they investigate this for an implementation of non-determinism with backtrackable state in terms of non-determinism with non-backtrackable state. Unfortunately, because of the complex invariants involved in this implementation, the axiomatic reasoning approach of Pauwels et al. is rather involved.

In this paper, we investigate an alternative approach for establishing the correctness of a high-level effect's implementation in terms of a low-level effect. Instead of reasoning in terms of axiomatic specifications of the effects, we reason directly in terms of actual effect implementations. Seemingly this is a step back, but for our case study—the implementation of non-determinism in terms of state—it turns out that the proofs are very manageable. Moreover, because we are using initial implementations of the effects involved, we can generalize our result to other implementations.

Our main contribution is a technique for proving re-interpretations of a high-level effect in terms of a lower-level effect correct, which to the best of our knowledge is novel.

2   Overview

This section situates and motivates the problem we tackle, namely to simulate the *non-determinism* effect with a lower level implementation that uses *state*, and, more importantly, to prove the correctness of this approach.

2.1 Non-determinism

Non-determinism is a powerful high-level side-effect, often used in relational and logic programming, to enable concise and declarative programs.

As an example of non-determinism, consider the following Prolog program:

```
parent(lily,   harry).        parent(harry, albus).
parent(james,  harry).        parent(harry, lily2).
parent(arthur, ginny).        parent(ginny, james2).
parent(molly,  ginny).        parent(ginny, albus).
parent(harry,  james2).       parent(ginny, lily2).

grandChildren(X, Y) :- parent(X, Z), parent(Z, Y).
```

This program defines the **parent** relation extensionally, i.e., by enumerating all the parent–child pairs. In contrast, it defines the **grandChildren** relation intentionally, by means of a rule that refers twice to the **parent** relation.

When this program is loaded into a Prolog interpreter, we can ask it who the grandchild of **james** is with the query ?- **grandChildren(james,GC)**. Because the result is not uniquely determined, the Prolog interpreter will backtrack over multiple solutions.

```
?- grandChildren(james,GC).
GC = albus ;
GC = lily2 ;
GC = james2.
```

Here, the semicolon is a prompt asking the user whether they want to see the next answer.

We can model the above Prolog program and query in Haskell by using lists, and the list monad structure.

```
type Person = String

parent :: Person -> [Person]
parent "Lily"   = ["Harry"]
parent "James"  = ["Harry"]
parent "Arthur" = ["Ginny"]
parent "Molly"  = ["Ginny"]
parent "Harry"  = ["James II", "Albus", "Lily II"]
parent "Ginny"  = ["James II", "Albus", "Lily II"]
parent _        = []

grandChildren :: Person -> [Person]
grandChildren gp = do p   <-  parent gp
                        parent p
```

The Prolog query ?- **grandChildren(james,GC)**. can then be emulated as follows:

```
> grandChildren "James"
["James II", "Albus", "Lily II"]
```

Thanks to Haskell's laziness, computations in the list monad execute in very much the same order as Prolog's backtracking. However, actual Prolog implementations—such as those based on the Warren Abstarct Machine (WAM) [1,15]—do not implement non-determinism in terms of lists and the list monad (lazy or otherwise). Instead, they make use of a much more low-level side effect to simulate non-determinism, namely *mutable state*, as is typical for Prolog implementations in imperative, lower-level languages (like C and assembly) that are more careful about heap allocations.

2.2 Challenge and Approach

In this work we investigate the folklore technique, used by Prolog implementations among others, to simulate non-determinism by means of mutable state. We provide a functional model that abstracts from implementation details and focuses on the monadic renditions of both side-effects. Our main challenge, and the main novelty of this work, is to formally establish the correctness of this approach by means of equational reasoning.

The rest of this paper is structured as follows. First, Sect. 3 provides our functional model for the simulation of non-determinism in terms of state. Next, Sect. 4 formally proves the correctness of this simulation. Then Sect. 5 generalizes that result from the list monad to other non-determinism monads. Finally, Sect. 6 dicusses related work and Sect. 7 concludes.

3 Simulating Nondeterminism with State

This section shows how to simulate non-determinism with mutable state.

3.1 Non-deterministic Programs

As the starting point of our simultation we capture the syntactic structure of non-deterministic computations in a datatype:

```
data Nondet a = Ret a
              | Fail
              | Nondet a :| Nondet a
```

Here, `Ret x` denotes a computation that returns a single result x, `Fail` denotes a computation without results, and `p :| q` denotes a non-deterministic choice between the computations p and q.

This `Nondet` datatype is a free monad (also known as term monad):

```
instance Monad (Nondet a) where
  return x = Ret x
  Ret a  >>= f  =  Ret (f a)
  Fail   >>= f  =  Fail
  a :| b >>= f  =  (a >>= f) :| (b >>= f)
```

The monadic bind operator (>>=) implements the composition of syntax trees.

We can use the Nondet type to express the example of Sect. 2 as a syntax tree:

```
parent :: Person -> Nondet Person
parent "Lily"    = Ret "Harry"
parent "James"   = Ret "Harry"
parent "Arthur"  = Ret "Ginny"
parent "Molly"   = Ret "Ginny"
parent "Harry"   = Ret "James II" :| (Ret "Albus" :| Ret "Lily II")
parent "Ginny"   = Ret "James II" :| (Ret "Albus" :| Ret "Lily II")
parent _         = Fail

grandChildren :: Person -> Nondet Person
grandChildren gp = do  p   <-  parent gp
                       gc  <-  parent p
```

For a more compact example, consider the expression (Ret 1 :| Fail) :| (Ret 2 :| Ret 3) of type Nondet Int which can be depicted as a tree

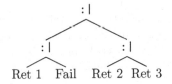

3.2   List Semantics

We can interpret Nondet programs in terms of lists.

```
runNondet :: Nondet a -> [a]
runNondet (Ret x)  = [x]
runNondet Fail     = []
runNondet (a :| b) = (runNondet a) ++ (runNondet b)
```

This implementation serves as an executable specification for the semantics of non-deterministic programs; this specification should also be respected by our future state-based implementation.

Here is a graphical illustration showing what runNondet does to the example program tree shown above:

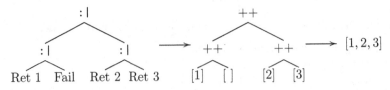

```
newtype State s a = State { runState :: s -> (s, a) }

instance Monad (State s) where
  return x  = State (\s -> (s, x))
  m >>= f  = State (\s -> let (s',x) = runState m s
                          in  runState (f x) s')

get :: State s s
get = State (\s -> (s,s))

put :: s -> State s ()
put s' = State (\s -> (s',()))
```

Fig. 1. Definition of the `State` monad

Also, with `runNondet` we can compute the grandchildren of James as follows:

```
> runNondet (grandChildren "James")
["James II", "Albus", "Lily II"]
```

3.3 State-Based Implementation

Now we turn to the state-based implementation of non-determinism. This implementation uses the well-known state monad `State s`, which is given in Fig. 1.

The main computation type for the simulation is `Prog a`, which is a `newtype` wrapper around the state monad:

```
newtype Prog a = Prog (State ([a],[Prog a]) ())

runProg :: Prog a -> (([a],[Prog a]) -> (([a],[Prog a]), ()))
runProg (Prog x) = runState x
```

The `Prog` type fixes the type of mutable state to a tuple with two components: 1) a list with the results obtained so far, and 2) a stack with the branches still to be explored. Those branches are themselves represented by `Prog a` computations. This makes the type recursive and explains the need for the `Prog` newtype.

We also provide a few helper functions to modify the state: `emit` adds a result to the end of the result list, `push` adds a branch to the the stack, and `pop` removes and executes the branch at the top of the stack—or does nothing if the stack is empty.

```
emit :: a -> Prog a -> Prog a
emit x (Prog k) = Prog $
  do { (xs,stack) <- get; put (xs++[x],stack); k }

push :: Prog a -> Prog a -> Prog a
```

```
push p (Prog k) = Prog $
  do { (xs,stack) <- get; put (xs,p:stack); k }

pop :: Prog a
pop = Prog $ do (xs,stack)  <- get
                case stack of
                    []              -> return ()
                    ((Prog p):ps) -> do { put (xs,ps); p }
```

With these auxiliary functions we define the core simulation of non-determinism:

```
simulate :: Nondet a -> Prog a
simulate Fail       = pop
simulate (Ret x)    = emit x pop
simulate (p :| q)   = push (simulate q) (simulate p)
```

The wrapper function `runNondet'` serves as a drop-in replacement for `runNondet`. It initializes the mutable state to an empty result list and an empty stack, and afterwards extracts the final result list.

`runNondet' nd = fst (fst (runProg (simulate nd) ([], [])))`

Figure 2 illustrates how the state-based simulation of non-determinism works on our running toy example. We push right subtrees of `(:|)` on the stack. When we reach a `Ret` leaf, we add its value to the list of results and pop the next branch from the stack. The latter also happens when we reach a `Fail` leaf. The execution stops when there is no more branch to pop.

4   Correctness Proof

This section provides a correctness proof of the state based simulation `runNondet'`. The proof combines induction with equational reasoning based on the definitions of the functions involved and the properties of list concatenation `(++)`.

Theorem 1. *For all p of type* Nondet *a it holds that:*

runNondet' p

=

runNondet p

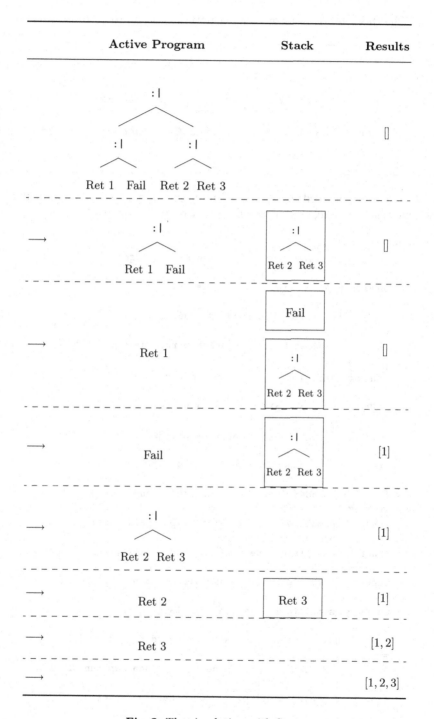

Fig. 2. The simulation with State

Proof. The theorem follows from setting both xs and qs to [] in Lemma 1.   □

Lemma 1.

> *runProg (simulate p) (xs, map simulate qs)*
>
> *=*
>
> *((xs ++ runNondet p ++ concatMap runNondet qs, []), ())*

Proof. The proof proceeds by structural induction on p and qs. We perform the case analysis on p here, and encapsulate that on qs in Lemma 2.

- **Case:** p = Fail

  ```
  runProg (simulate Fail) (xs, map simulate qs)
  = -- definition of simulate
  runProg pop (xs, map simulate qs)
  = -- Lemma 2
  (xs ++ [] ++ concatMap runNondet qs, [])
  = --definition of runNondet
  (xs ++ runNondet Fail ++ concatMap runNondet qs, [])
  ```

- **Case:** p = Ret x

  ```
  runProg (simulate (Ret x)) (xs, map simulate qs)
  = -- definition of simulate
  runProg (emit x pop) (xs, map simulate qs)
  = -- evaluation
  runProg pop (xs ++ [x], map simulate qs)
  = -- Lemma 2
  (xs ++ [x] ++ concatMap runNondet qs, [])
  = -- definition of runNondet
  (xs ++ runNondet (Ret x) ++ concatMap runNondet qs, [])
  ```

- **Case:** p = (r :| q)

  ```
  runProg (simulate (r :| q)) (xs, map simulate qs)
  = -- definition of simulate
  runProg (push (simulate q) (simulate r)) (xs, map simulate qs)
  = -- evaluation
  runProg (simulate r) (xs, simulate q : map simulate qs)
  = -- definition of map
  runProg (simulate r) (xs, map simulate (q:qs))
  = -- induction hypothesis
  (xs ++ runNondet r ++ concatMap runNondet (q:qs), [])
  = -- definition of concatMap
  (xs ++ runNondet r ++ runNondet q ++ concatMap runNondet qs, [])
  = -- definition of runNondet
  (xs ++ runNondet (r :| q) ++ concatMap runNondet qs, [])
  ```

□

Lemma 2.

```
runProg pop (xs, map simulate qs)
= --
((xs ++ concatMap runNondet qs, []),())
```

Proof.   The proof proceeds by case analysis on qs.

- **Case: qs = []:**
    ```
    runProg pop (xs, map simulate [])
    = -- evaluation
    ((xs, []), ())
    = -- neutral element of ++
    ((xs ++ [], []), ())
    = -- definition of concatMap
    ((xs ++ concatMap runNondet [], []),())
    ```
- **Case: qs = (r:rs):**
    ```
    runProg pop (xs, concatMap simulate (r:rs))
    = -- evaluation
    runProg (simulate r) (xs, concatMap simulate rs)
    = -- Lemma 1
    ((xs ++ runNondet r ++ concatMap runNondet rs, []), ())
    = -- definition of concatMap
    ((xs ++ concatMap runNondet (r:rs), []), ())
    ```

$\square$

5   Generalized Simulation of Non-determinism Monads

The state-based simulation we have created is specific for the list monad. However, we can generalize it to other non-determinism monads. **Note:** In this section we use some category-theoretical concepts such as initiality, which we define in Appendix A.

5.1   Non-determinism Monads

To express that generalization we create a type class for non-deterministic computations:[1]

---

[1] We avoid the standard `MonadPlus` type class because its intended purpose is overloaded and underspecified.

```
class Monad m => MonadNondet m where
  fail :: m a
  (||) :: m a -> m a -> m a
```

With this type class we can express non-deterministic computations in a way that is independent from the particular non-determinism monad. For instance,

```
p :: MonadNondet m => Int -> m Int
p n | n < 1     =  fail
    | otherwise =  return (n-1) || return (n+1)
```

Both the Nondet and list monad are possible instances of this type class:

```
class MonadNondet Nondet where
  fail = Fail
  (||) = (:|)

class MonadNondet [] where
  fail = []
  (||) = (++)
```

We can run the example program with a particular non-determinism monad by adding a corresponding type annotation. For instance, to use the list monad we may write:

```
> p 5 :: [Int]
[4,6]
```

For the sake of conciseness, we may use subscripts to denote the instantiating monad; e.g., we may write $p_{[]}$ 5.

Type classes are typically most useful when they come with some laws that restrict the possible behavior of the instances and thus enable reasoning. We assume that instances of MonadNondet satisfy the following five laws:

$$\text{fail} \ || \ m = m$$
$$m \ || \ \text{fail} = m$$
$$m1 \ || \ (m2 \ || \ m3) = (m1 \ || \ m2) \ || \ m3$$
$$\text{fail} >>= f = \text{fail}$$
$$(m1 \ || \ m2) >>= f = (m1 >>= f) \ || \ (m2 >>= f)$$

The first three laws express that $\langle m\ a, (||), \text{fail} \rangle$ forms a monoid, and the last two laws state that (>>=) is right-distributive over fail and (||).[2]

It is easy to see that the Nondet instance is lawless, while the [] instance is lawful. Both of these two instances play a special role among respectively all (lawful and lawless) and just the lawful instances: they are *initial* (see Appendix A).

---

[2] Some settings require additional laws, like commutativity of (||) or left-distributivity of (>>=), but we will use a more minimal set of laws.

```
newtype Prog m a = Prog (State (m a,[Prog m a]) ())

runProg :: Prog m a -> ((m a,[Prog a]) -> ((m a,[Prog a]), ()))
runProg (Prog x) = runState x

emit :: MonadNondet m => a -> Prog m a -> Prog m a
emit x (Prog k) = Prog $ Get $
  \(xs,stack) -> Put (xs || return x,stack) k

push :: MonadNondet m => Prog m a -> Prog m a -> Prog m a
push p (Prog k) = Prog $ Get $ \(xs,stack) -> Put (xs,p:stack) k

pop :: MonadNondet m => Prog m a
pop = Prog $ Get $ \(xs,stack) -> case stack of
   []              -> Return ()
  ((Prog p):ps) -> Put (xs,ps) p

simulate :: MonadNondet m => Nondet a -> Prog m a
simulate Fail       = pop
simulate (Ret x)    = emit x pop
simulate (p :| q)   = push (simulate q) (simulate p)

runNondet' :: MonadNondet m => Nondet a -> m a
runNondet' nd  = fst $ fst $ runProg (simulate nd) $ (fail, [])
```

Fig. 3. Simulation parametric in the non-determinism monad.

This means that there is a unique structure-preserving mapping from Nondet to any other instance, and from [] to any lawful instance. The former mapping is a generalization of the runNondet function form Sect. 3.2:

```
runNondet :: MonadNondet m => Nondet a -> m a
runNondet (Ret x)   =   return x
runNondet Fail      =   fail
runNondet (p :| q)  =   runNondet p || runNondet q
```

The latter mapping can be defined as follows:

```
choose :: MonadNondet m => [a] -> m a
choose []       =   fail
choose (x:xs)   =   return x || choose xs
```

5.2   Generalized Simulation

Based on naturality—which can be shown using free theorems [13], in particular for type constructor class [11]—it holds for any non-determinism monad N that

$$p_N = \text{runNondet} \, . \, p_{\text{Nondet}}$$

Simlarly, it holds for any lawful non-determinism monad M that

$$p_M = \texttt{choose} \cdot p_{[]}$$

We can combine the above two, with $N = []$, to get for lawful instances M:

$$p_M = \texttt{choose} \cdot \texttt{runNondet} \cdot p_{\texttt{Nondet}}$$

Now we can exchange `runNondet` for `runNondet'` to get a state-based, rather than a list-based interpretation.

$$p_M = \texttt{choose} \cdot \texttt{runNondet'} \cdot p_{\texttt{Nondet}}$$

This achieves the goal of simulating other lawful non-determinism monads with state. Yet, it is unsatisfactory in that the state-based simulation first builds an intermediate list and then converts that into the target monad. In the following, we *deforest* the above approach, i.e., we avoid the creation of this intermediate list.

Deforestation – Step 1: To enable deforestation of the intermediate list, Fig. 3 parameterizes the state-based simulation to generalize from a list-based result to an arbitrary non-determinism monad. The original implementation for lists is recovered as `runNondet'`$_{[]}$, yet we now also have a naturality property:

$$\texttt{choose} \cdot \texttt{runNondet'}_{[]} = \texttt{runNondet'}_M$$

We can use this to avoid the intermediate list in the above computation:

$$p_M = \texttt{runNondet'}_M \cdot p_{\texttt{Nondet}}$$

Deforestation – Step 2: Another intermediate datastructure we would like to eliminate is the `Nondet` structure built by $p_{\texttt{Nondet}}$. It might seem like we could appeal to naturality again and directly work with $p_{\texttt{Prog } M}$. However, upon closer inspection, that turns out to be invalid as `Prog m a` is not actually a monad in a. Indeed, in the underlying `State` monad the a parameter appears in the type of the state, but not in the result type, which is fixed to `()`.

To solve this problem we use the technique described by Schrijvers et al. [10] to turn a non-monadic interpretation (like `Prog m a`) of a free monad (like `Nondet`) into a monadic interpretation using the continuation monad.

Figure 4 shows the definition of a specialized monad `CProg m a` that wraps a continuation-layer around `Prog m a`. The continuation layer provides the monadic structure, while the non-determinism support is adopted

```
newtype CProg m a b
  = CProg { runCProg :: (b -> Prog m a) -> Prog m a) }

instance Monad (CProg m a) where
  return x  =  CProg (\k -> k x)
  m >>= f   =  CProg
    (\k -> runCProg m (\x -> runCProg (f x) k))

instance MonadNondet m => MonadNondet (CProg m a) where
  fail    = CProg (\k -> pop)
  p || q  = CProg
    (\k -> push (runCProg p k) (runCProg q k))

runNondetC :: MonadNondet m => CProg m a a -> m a
runNondetC p = fst $ fst $
  runProg (runCProg p (\x -> emit x pop)) (fail, [])
```

Fig. 4. Simulation into a continuation monad.

from `Prog m a`. Finally, the `runNondetC` function peels away the continuation layer and uses the underlying state-based representation to simulate a non-determinism monad.

As a consequence, we can write our final state-based simulation as follows, without unnecessary intermediate datastructures:

$$p_M = \texttt{runNondetC}_M \ \cdot \ p_{\texttt{CProg } M \texttt{ Int}}$$

This is also relevant if M is the list monad, because it avoids the intermediate `Nondet` structure.

6   Related Work

We were inspired by reading Hutton and Fulger's work on reasoning about effects [8]. We used their style of proofs to prove the correctness of the simulation of [] with the `State` effect. A different approach, proposed by Gibbons and Hinze [4] is to use axiomatic characterisations of effects to reason at a more general level. This work inspired us to give an axiomatic characterisation of the non-determinism effect and generalise our proof to hold for any effect that obeys these axioms.

Like Pauwels et al. [9] we simulate a high level effect with a more low level effect. For this they use Free Monads to separate between syntax and semantics. We used this technique in the state-based simulation.

We have directly modelled the folklore approach of simulating non-determinism with state and proven it correct with respect to a list-based semantics. An alternative route would be to tie together two different approaches in the literature:

- Firstly, Hinze [6] shows how to use Kan extensions and the Cayley representation to systematically derive a two-continuation representation from the list monad. This representation with two continuations (for success and failure) was already known much longer as a basis for implementating backtracking [3], and even derived before by Hinze [5] as a context-passing representation.
- Secondly, Biernacki and Danvy [2] show how to derive a so-called abstract machine for a continuation-passing interpreter of a propositional version of Prolog, which is related to our `Nondet` type.

  The obtained abstract machine comes with a program state that is related to ours. The derivation involves defunctionalization of the continuations which naturally gives rise to stacks. Their machine state does contain more information regarding execution control, namely the Prolog program to execute, which is external to our state. Also, it features three continuation stacks rather than one. The third continuation supports pruning (or cutting) branches. This cut continuation does not show up in our setting, and the success continuation is fixed and built-in (`push`). Hence, our state only keeps track of the failure continuation, i.e., the stack of unexplored branches. However, their machine does not compute any results; it only reports success or failure of the search. Hence, their state does not keep track of a result list.

7   Conclusion

This paper has shown how to model a folklore implementation of non-determinism in terms of mutable state in a purely functional fashion using the state monad. It has also demonstrated that this purely functional model makes it easy to establish its correctness with respect to a high-level model using the list monad. Indeed our proof uses basic equational reasoning and structural induction.

In a further step we have shown how to generalize these results from the list monad to other monadic models of non-determinism using reasoning techniques from the functional programming literature like free theorems and continuation monads.

7.1   Application and Future Work

We motivated our transformation with the example of modeling a Prolog program in Haskell. There we noted that the typical way of modeling the Prolog program, by making use of the list monad, is quite far removed from the approach followed by real Prolog implementations, such as those based on the WAM. Our mutable state modeling of non-determinism reflects the state-based WAM implementations more closely.

In short, we have shown that we can take an "obviously correct" implementation of a non-deterministic algorithm, and through a relatively simple sequence of reasoning steps, bring it closer to a real-world implementation. But just with the work of this paper, we aren't "there yet". In particular, non-determinism is not the only effect needed to model a WAM implementation. Prolog interpreters also need backtrackable state to keep track of unifications. They also implement more complex control flow constructs such as cuts, and they offer explicitly non-backtrackable state operations as well.

Practical implementations usually model all these effects on top of mutable state, which has the distinct advantage of offering a single framework in which the implementer can optimize their code. However, such an optimized interpreter is usually not *obviously* correct. As such, this work offers a first step in proving such a full system correct by starting from an obviously correct (but slow) implementation in terms of a complex, high-level effect set, and re-interpreting it in terms of a lower level effect set (in this case, just state), and subsequently applying optimizations through equational reasoning on the low level algorithm.

Furthermore, we believe our proof technique to be of more general interest than specifically the case of state and nondeterminism. Reasoning about programs with multiple effects is not new. But work around re-interpreting effect sets in terms of "lower-level" effect sets seems to be quite scarce, and we believe the established proof techniques have room for improvement. Compared to the work of Pauwels et al. [9], our proofs are considerably simpler and shorter.

A   Simulating Any Nondet Effect

In Sect. 5 we rely on the initiality of the []-implementation in the class of lawful instances of the MonadNondet class. In this section we formally define what the category theoretical concept of *initiality* means and provide proof that the []-implementation is initial.

A.1   Definition of Initiality

We consider the well-known category of Haskell types:

The category Type:

- The objects *ob*(Type) of this category are the Haskell types.
- The morphism from a type A to a type B, denoted Type(A, B), are the collection of all functions m : : a-> b.
- The composition of morphisms is Haskell's function composition (f . g)

We also define the category of monads over the base category Type:

The category Monad:

- The objects *ob*(Monad) of this category are the Haskell monads *M*.
- The morphisms from monads *M* to *N*, Monad(*M, N*), are the collection of all polymorphic functions m :: ∀ a: M a-> N a that satisfy two properties:
  - m (returnM a) = returnN a
  - m (x >>=M f) = (m x) >>=N (m . f)
- The composition of two monad morphisms is the composition of polymorphic functions.

We now define the concept of an *algebra*:

Definition: Given en endofunctor *F* over a category *A*, and an $a \in ob(A)$, an **algebra** is defined as a function: alg :: F a-> a

We are interested in a concrete algebra, the Nondet algebra. Lets begin by defining the endofunctor ND:

```
data ND a = Fail | Comb a a

fmap :: (a -> b) -> ND a -> ND b
fmap f Fail       = Fail
fmap f (Comb x y) = Comb (f x) (f y)
```

This is an endofunctor over the category of types and functions Type. We use this to define the category of ND-algebras over Monads:

Definition: NDA, the category of ND-algebras:

- *ob(NDA)* are all algebras algM :: ∀ a. ND (M a) -> M a, such that $M \in ob(\text{Monad})$ for which:
  - Fail is right and left zero:
    ```
    algM (Comb (algM Fail) x)
    = algM x
    = algM (Comb x (algM Fail))
    ```
  - Comb is associative:
    ```
    algM (Comb x (algM (Comb y z)))
    = algM (Comb (algM (Comb x y)) z)
    ```
  - left-distributivity:
    ```
    (algM (Comb x y)) >>= f = algM (Comb (x >>= f) (y >>= f))
    ```
  - left-zero:
    ```
    (algM Fail) >>= f = algM Fail
    ```
  W call these the Nondet-laws
- NDA(algM, algN) =
  $\{m \in \text{Monad}(M, N) \mid$ algM . m = (fmap m) . algN$\}$

The [] monad is an element of this category with:

```
alg[] :: ND [a] -> [a]
alg[] Fail    = []
alg[] Comb x y = x ++ y
```

Since [] is a monad, we know [] $\in ob(\texttt{Monad})$. Thus we know $\texttt{alg[]} \in ob(NDA)$. Now that we have defined the relevant categories and algebras, we can define and prove the initiality of $\texttt{alg[]}$ in the category NDA.

We say that an object is initial if there is exactly one unique morphism from it to any other object in the category. More formally:

Defnition Let C be a category and $init \in ob(C)$. $init$ is an intial object in the algebra iff: $\forall o \in ob(C) : |C(init, o)| = 1$

A.2   Proof of Initiality

In this section we prove $\texttt{alg[]}$ is the initial algebra. To prove this, we need to show two things:

1. There is an morphism from $\texttt{alg[]}$ to any other
2. There cannot be any more than 1

The first is proven by giving such a function, the second by showing that this function is unique.

Existence. Take any other element $\texttt{algM}$ in the category NDA, associated with the monad M. We define the function:

```
f :: [a] -> M a
f = foldr (\x xs -> (algM (Comb (returnM x) (f xs))))
          (algM Fail)
```

To show there is a morphism from $\texttt{alg[]}$ to $\texttt{algM}$, we show this is a Monad morphism and that it satisfies all the requirements to be a morpfism in the category NDA.

Theorem 2. $f \in Monad(\texttt{[]}, \texttt{M})$

Proof. Follows immediately from Lemma 3 and 4   □

Lemma 3. f $(return\texttt{[]}$ $x) = returnM$ x

Proof.

```
f (return[] x)
= --def of return[]
f [x]
= --def of f
foldr (\x xs -> (algM (Comb (returnM x) (f xs)))) (algM Fail)
= --def of fold
algM (Comb (returnM x) (algM Fail))
= --ND-law
returnM x
```

□

Lemma 4. f (x >>=[] g) = (f x) >>=M (f . g)

Proof. The proof proceeds by induction on x.

- **Case:** x = []

```
f ([] >>=[] g)
= --def of >>=[]
f []
= --def of f
algM Fail
= --ND-law
f (alg[] Fail) >>=M (f . g)
```

- **Case:** x = x:xs

```
f ((x:xs) >>=[] g)
= --def of >>=[]
f ((g x) ++ (xs >>=[] g))
= --def of alg[]
(f . alg[]) (Comb (g x) (xs >>=[] g)))
= --Monad law
(f . alg[]) (Comb (g >>=[] ([x])) (xs >>=[] g)))
= --property of algebra
algM . (fmap f) (Comb (g >>=[] ([x])) (xs >>=[] g)))
= --def of fmap
algM (Comb (f (g >>=[] ([x]))) (f (xs >>=[] g)))
= --Induction Hypothesis
algM (Comb ((f [x]) >>=M (f.g)) ((f xs) >>=M (f.g)))
= --ND-law
algM ((Comb (f [x]) (f xs)) >>=M (f.g))
= --definition of fmap
algM (fmap f (Comb [x] xs)) >>=M (f.g)
```

```
= --property of algebra
(f (alg[] (Comb [a] xs))) >>=M (f.g)
= --def of alg[]
(f (x:xs)) >>=M (f . g)
```

□

Now we can prove that the function f is an element of the category NDA.

Theorem 3. $f \in NDA([], M))$

Proof. From Theorem 2 all that is left to prove is (f . alg[]) x = (algM . (fmap f)) x. The prove proceeds by structural induction on x.

- **case: x = Fail**
  ```
  f (alg[] Fail)
  = --definition of alg[]
  f []
  = --definition of f
  algM Fail
  = --definition of f and fmap
  (algM . (fmap f)) Fail
  ```
- **case: x = Comb a b**
  This case is proven by structural induction on the list a.
  - **case: a = []**
    ```
    (f . alg[]) (Comb [] b)
    = --def of alg[]
    f b
    = --ND-Law
    algM (Comb Fail (f b))
    = --definition of (fmap f)
    (algM . (fmap f)) (Comb [] b)
    ```
  - **case: a = r:rs**
    ```
    f (alg[] (Comb r:rs b))
    = --definition of alg[]
    f (r:(rs++b))
    = --definition of f
    algM $ Comb (returnM r) ((f . alg[]) (Comb rs b))
    = --Induction Hypothesis
    algM $ Comb (returnM r) (algM (Comb (f rs) (f b)))
    = --ND law
    algM $ (Comb (algM $ Comb (f [r]) (f rs)) (f b))
    = --Induction Hypothesis
    algM $ Comb (f (r:rs)) (f b)
    = --definition of fmap
    (algM . (fmap f)) (Comb r:rs b)
    ```
    □

Uniqueness. To prove the uniqueness of this f we use a property called *universality of fold* [7].

Theorem 4. *Universality of fold:*
Say g : : [a] -> b then :
$$\begin{array}{l} g\ [] = v \\ g\ (x{:}xs) = f\ x\ (g\ xs) \end{array} \Leftrightarrow g = foldr\ f\ v$$

Using this property we will now prove that any morphism g : : [a] -> M a that has the same properties as f is equal to f

---

Theorem 5. *Say g : : [a] -> M a is a morphism in NDA, then*

$$g = foldr\ (\backslash x\ xs\ ->\ (algM\ (Comb\ (returnM\ x)\ (g\ xs))))$$
$$(algM\ Fail)$$

Proof. To prove this theorem we use Theorem 4. We need to prove two things:

1. g [] = algM Fail:
```
    g []
  = --definition of alg[]
    g (alg[] Fail)
  = --definition of algebra
    algM ((fmap g) Fail)
  = --defintion of fmap
    algM Fail
```
2. g (x:xs) = algM (Comb (returnM x) (g xs)):
```
    g (x:xs)
  = --definition of alg[]
    (g . alg[]) (Comb [x] xs)
  = --definition of algebra
    (algM . (fmap g)) (Comb [x] xs)
  = --definition of fmap
    algM (Comb (q [x]) (g xs))
  = --Monad law
    algM (Comb (returnM x) (g xs))
```

□

Since we have proven that f and g only differ in name, we conclude that f is unique.

References

1. Ait-Kaci, H.: Warren's Abstract Machine: A Tutorial Reconstruction. MIT Press, Cambridge (1991)
2. Biernacki, D., Danvy, O.: From Interpreter to Logic Engine by Defunctionalization. In: Bruynooghe, M. (ed.) LOPSTR 2003. LNCS, vol. 3018, pp. 143–159. Springer, Heidelberg (2004). https://doi.org/10.1007/978-3-540-25938-1_13
3. Carlsson, M.: On implementing prolog in functional programming. New Gener. Comput. **2**(4), 347–359 (1984). https://doi.org/10.1007/BF03037326
4. Gibbons, J., Hinze, R.: Just do it: simple monadic equational reasoning. SIGPLAN Not. **46**(9), 2–14 (2011)
5. Hinze, R.: Deriving backtracking monad transformers. In: Odersky, M., Wadler, P. (eds.) Proceedings of the Fifth International Conference on Functional Programming, pp. 186–197. ACM (2000)
6. Hinze, R.: Kan extensions for program optimisation *Or*: art and dan explain an old trick. In: Gibbons, J., Nogueira, P. (eds.) MPC 2012. LNCS, vol. 7342, pp. 324–362. Springer, Heidelberg (2012). https://doi.org/10.1007/978-3-642-31113-0_16
7. Hutton, G.: A tutorial on the universality and expressiveness of fold. J. Funct. Program. **9**, 355–372 (1999). https://doi.org/10.1017/S0956796899003500
8. Hutton, G., Fulger, D.: Reasoning about effects: seeing the wood through the trees. In: Trends in Functional Programming, Draft Proceedings (2008)
9. Pauwels, K., Schrijvers, T., Mu, S.-C.: Handling local state with global state. In: Hutton, G. (ed.) MPC 2019. LNCS, vol. 11825, pp. 18–44. Springer, Cham (2019). https://doi.org/10.1007/978-3-030-33636-3_2
10. Schrijvers, T., Piróg, M., Wu, N., Jaskelioff, M.: Monad transformers and modular algebraic effects: What binds them together. In: Proceedings of the 12th ACM SIGPLAN International Symposium on Haskell, Haskell 2019, pp. 98–113. Association for Computing Machinery, New York (2019). https://doi.org/10.1145/3331545.3342595
11. Voigtländer, J.: Free theorems involving type constructor classes: functional pearl. In: Proceedings of the 14th ACM SIGPLAN International Conference on Functional Programming, ICFP 2009, pp. 173–184. Association for Computing Machinery, New York (2009). https://doi.org/10.1145/1596550.1596577
12. Wadler, P.: A critique of abelson and sussman or why calculating is better than scheming. SIGPLAN Not. **22**(3), 83–94 (1987)
13. Wadler, P.: Theorems for free! In: Proceedings of the Fourth International Conference on Functional Programming Languages and Computer Architecture, FPCA 1989, pp. 347–359. Association for Computing Machinery, New York (1989). https://doi.org/10.1145/99370.99404
14. Wadler, P.: Monads for functional programming. In: Jeuring, J., Meijer, E. (eds.) AFP 1995. LNCS, vol. 925, pp. 24–52. Springer, Heidelberg (1995). https://doi.org/10.1007/3-540-59451-5_2
15. Warren, D.H.D.: An abstract prolog instruction set. Technical Report, 309, AI Center, SRI International, 333 Ravenswood Ave., Menlo Park, CA 94025 (1983)

Parallelism

Placement Strategies: Structured Skeleton Composition with Location-Aware Remote Data

Lukas Immanuel Schiller[✉][iD]

Fachbereich Mathematik und Informatik, Philipps-Universität Marburg, Marburg, Germany
schiller@mathematik.uni-marburg.de

Abstract. In this paper, we will extend algorithmic skeletons with the concept of *Placement Strategies*: a functional, structured mechanism to organize coordination of parallel computation placement. These Placement Strategies allow access to explicit and semi-explicit placement in a functional style. By doing so, we increase the flexibility and clarity of algorithmic skeletons. Example skeletons are implemented using an extension of Eden's Remote Data that allows for simple skeleton composition and drop-in parallelization of sequential programs. The scheme of Placement Strategies is transferable to other functional languages that allow for explicit placement. Preliminary experimental evaluations show the effectiveness of the extended skeletons and an mostly marginal overhead caused by the additional location information.

Keywords: Parallel · Functional · Language design · Process placement · Algorithmic skeleton composition

1 Introduction

The additional layer of complexity that parallelism adds to a computation can be reduced to the questions *"What* should be computed *where?"* and "How are the necessary communications organized?". When designing a programming language, we have to address these questions from different perspectives. The first perspective tackles the question:

"Where and by whom should be decided where a parallel computation is placed?" The question where a parallel computation should be placed is often subordinated to the question of what should be computed in parallel. However, at some point the decision where a certain computation is actually placed has to be made. The mechanisms to do so are as numerous as parallel systems are. The decision depends on the target hardware, concepts of the programming language used, as well as options of the operating system and of the program itself. It is made by the compiler (Futhark [12]), the OS (POSIX threads [13]), a VM (JVM threads [11]), the RTS (GpH [24]), a library (PFunc [15]), the programmer (MPI [10])

© Springer Nature Switzerland AG 2020
A. Byrski and J. Hughes (Eds.): TFP 2020, LNCS 12222, pp. 229–248, 2020.
https://doi.org/10.1007/978-3-030-57761-2_11

or various combinations of the above. From the programmer's point of view, the different approaches can be categorized into three groups: no influence on the placement is possible, the programmer needs to provide different hints to assist in the decision-making process, or the programmer needs to make explicit decisions on the placement of the computation. The question that sets apart the first two groups is:

Should the programmer be able to manipulate the placement of parallel processes? Some concepts try to hide as much as possible of the additional complexity parallelism adds to a program. This is, for example, often the case in exclusively data-parallel languages as it is most practicable for restricted classes of problems. There are situations in which the class of problems the programming language aims at is clear-cut. In this case, a highly optimized compiler yields more efficient code than a manual optimization of the program. Whenever the parallel task and the targeted hardware match well enough or the knowledge about a specific class of similar problems is sufficient, an adequate placement can often be chosen without any interference by the programmer. Good examples for this can be found in the advanced mechanisms used in various systems for data-parallel programming or GPGPU programming (e.g. Futhark [12], Accelerate [5]). However, with a wider range of targeted hardware or more complex problems, a prespecified analysis is often not sufficient and additional information about the specific problem needs to be passed to the decision-making mechanism (compare for example Repa's fine tuning [16], where, even in the quite specific domain of data-parallel programming, considerable improvements can be achieved by hints from the programmer). In general, the programmer's knowledge about the characteristics of a particular program is often a necessary ingredient for successful parallelization. This is especially the case if the programming language does not aim at a clearly restricted class of problems. Our goal is a programming language that offers a good balance between simplicity and the opportunity to address a wide range of programming problems. In the Chapel [6] community, a programming language aiming at different kinds of parallelism (data and task parallelism) and levels of parallel hardware (co-processors, multi-core processors, distributed computing, etc.) is sometimes called a "multifunctional" programming language. To avoid confusion with the term "functional" we will call such a programming language "multifaceted". In our opinion – with a good multifaceted programming language – the programmer should be able to manipulate the placement.

Should the programmer be able to determine a specific *parallel process placement?* The lack of possibilities to express an explicit placement may itself be considered a limitation. Not only in terms of fine-tuning: because for some algorithms placement is an essential component of the algorithm itself. On the other hand, the possibilities to express explicit placement are often kept basic or they struggle with functional paradigms.

A multifaceted parallel programming language should provide high-level constructs to express parallel problems regardless of the specific hardware while it should also allow for (hardware or problem specific) fine-tuning. This fine-tuning is – if the programming language is directed at a wide field of application – substantially made easier by the possibility to express an explicit placement, at best in a well-structured manner.

Where should the placement decision mechanism be placed and how can the programmer influence it? With the balance between simplicity and expressiveness in mind our goal should be a programming language where default implementation of parallel constructs exist but the possibility to influence the placement (up to explicit placement) is given. For this, it is crucial where to place the different parts of the placement mechanism and which possibilities of communication these parts have amongst each other. In existing languages, hints provided by the programmer can, for instance, express related tasks, either directly (e.g. architecture aware GpH [1], where boundaries for placements distances in a virtual architecture are hinted by the programmer) or through the data the tasks work on (e.g. HPF's alignment [22], where data fields in different arrays are linked with hints and then placed on the same processor element). But most of these approaches are motivated by a specific hardware setup or again by a specific class of problems. Therefore, their expressiveness is limited.

Algorithmic Skeletons. The complexity of dividing parallelizable programs into parallel parts and mapping these parts onto available processors requires a structured solution. Functional programming seems like an auspicious approach to control the complexity and numerous functional high-level approaches exist. Of all the different approaches to parallel programming the concept of algorithmic skeletons [7] is one of the most promising. Not least because skeletons are a known technique to achieve modularity. In this paper, we will use algorithmic skeletons for our structured approach of providing the precise computational control of explicit placement on a high level of abstraction. Algorithmic skeletons implement common computation or communication patterns of parallel algorithms and are both suitable for data and task parallelism. Many parallel algorithms can be expressed as an instance of an algorithmic skeleton. By doing so, the programmer can focus on the algorithm itself, leaving the details of the parallel implementation to the skeleton. The possibility to compose different skeletons enhances the capabilities of this high-level approach.

Separating the algorithm from its coordination of parallel communication has a long tradition in functional programming, evaluation strategies [20] being a prime example. Yet, the majority of functional parallel algorithmic skeleton concepts use a combination of semi-explicit parallelism and a scheduler for the placement of the parallel computations. But when it comes to parallel fine-tuning, this can be a limitation. In some cases, this can be solved by using different schedulers (e.g. the ParMonad) combining explicit placement with a scheduler [14]. But sometimes good hints for the scheduler result in essentially restricted schedulers [1]. Especially in the case of high communication costs between processor elements (e.g. if some of the processor elements are located on different computers connected by a relatively slow connection like Ethernet), a good placement is often obvious to the programmer but seldom to the scheduler.

We develop our approach in the context of the Eden programming language [17, 18], a parallel Haskell [19] dialect, which comes with an algorithmic skeleton library. These skeletons provide different options to improve performance. One distinguishes between procedural improvements of communication (for example controling the granularity of the parallelism by chunking) and the possibility to specify an explicit placement. Yet, the options to manipulate placement are limited. In this paper, we will explore various problems for which the possibility of intervention are either insufficient or clumsy.

Placement Strategies. Placement Strategies are functions that determine explicit placement in a flexible and elegant way and are passed to algorithmic skeletons as arguments. A specialized data type is used, that carries information about the current location of the contained data, called "Location-Aware Remote Data". It is fundamental, because it allows Placement Strategies to build a bridge between a user-friendly high-level approach and the possibility of expressive fine-tuning. It becomes possible to manipulate the placement systematically even when skeletons with different strategic profiles are combined. These simple ingredients break new grounds: by placing predefined structures of parallelism into a library or by allowing for more complex functions to be passed as arguments.

A Placement Strategy has more information to determine a placement than many other systems that merely use hinting. Our approach allows for structured composition, the nesting of algorithmic skeletons and the separation of the communication inside an algorithmic skeleton from the structure of the skeleton. Applying this approach, it is possible to combine work-pulling algorithmic skeletons (like a workpool) with work-pushing ones (like a map). Moreover it is possible to catch non-determinism in the placement of work-pulling skeletons and continue with the actual placement in a subsequent skeleton.

In the next section we will motivate the approach with an example. In Sect. 3 we will give a short introduction to the Eden programming language in which the realization of the concept is done. However, the conceptual idea itself is independent of any specific programming language. Section 4 introduces the Location-Aware Remote Data type and in Sect. 5 we will present different illustrative map and divide-and-conquer skeletons with Placement Strategies. The evaluation Sect. 6 shows the usefulness of this approach. In Sect. 7 related work is discussed and Sect. 8 concludes.

2   Running Example

In a first example we will adjust algorithmic skeletons in order to compose them in difficult situations. An implementation of a merger based on the bitonic sorting network [2, 23] will be parallelized. The structure of the network can be found in Fig. 1. Arrow boxes depict comparison elements and lines depict the data flow. It is obvious that this algorithm can be parallelized as every comparison element in the same column is working on independent data. In the given implementation a map function is applied several times. In every stage some permutations are

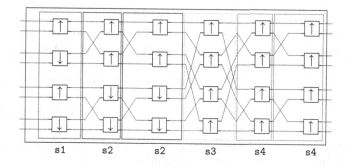

Fig. 1. Bitonic sorter of order 8

performed on the input list and then a comparator element is mapped over the permuted list. For this example, it is neither relevant which permutations are behind the different functions nor it is necessary to completely understand the structure of the sorting network. It is sufficient to know that the comparison element, a function with type `[[a]]` → `[[a]]` is mapped several times. The implementation is given as follows:

```
res = merger map cElem inp
[...]
merger mapSkel cElem = s4 o s4 o s3 o s2 o s2 o s1 where
     ac = mapSkel cElem
     s1 = perm1out o ac o perm1in
     s2 = perm2out o ac o perm2in
     s3 = perm3out o ac o perm3in
     s4 = perm4out o ac o perm4in
```

For a sequential version of the merger, Haskell's `map` function for lists can be used. Ideally, the parallelization is done by simply exchanging the `map` in the call of the `merger` function for a parallel map. But which requirements would this parallel map have to fulfill?

The map function is one of the most basic algorithmic skeletons. Consequently, parallel variants of map exist in almost all parallel Haskell variants. There are several ways to parallelize `map f [a1,..,an]`. Even in the most simple case if we want to create a process for each computation `f a1,..,f an` the strategies to place these processes are numerous. The best strategy to do so depends heavily on context:

- Where are the elements `a1,..,  an` located?
- Where do we need them and/or the computational results next?
- How expensive is the communication between (different) processor elements?

With this in mind, we can decide which strategy is the most suitable:

1. In some cases, we want to distribute the computations among all available processor elements (e.g. all elements are on the same processor element and we want the computation to be distributed equally).

2. In some cases, we know exactly where we want the computation to take place (e.g. if communication of the computational results is more expensive than the communication of the elements itself or a follow-up computation is supposed to be co-located on specific processor elements).
3. In some cases, we want the computations to be placed where the data is located (e.g. every element ai is already on a different processor element and we do not want to move them because of high communication costs).
4. In some cases, a more complex strategy is needed (e.g. "minimize the communication between processor elements but do not place more than three computations on the same processor element").

The first two methods of parallelizing the map function are already feasible in Eden. In this paper, we will present a safe (in terms of functional pureness) way to realize the latter two using Placement Strategies. Especially in the fourth case, when an arbitrary complex strategy is needed, a good interface to express and change the strategy is essential.

We will see that, in the merger example above, a naive parallel map does not co-locate processes and an explicit placement requires a complete understanding of the different permutations. This can result in an inflexible solution or the program might require deeper changes while a placement guided by data and strategy is possible, solving the parallelization problem with ease.

A row-wise placement would be possible. Although this seems like a good solution, it is not an optimal one. If the location of the results is not relevant (as is usual in distributed computing) and if we assume that communication between different processors is more expensive than communication on one single processor, a better placement is possible. The placement in Fig. 2 needs less communication between Processor Elements than a row-wise placement by keeping more data on consistent Processor Elements. For this, it is necessary to separate the placement from the given structure of the computation. This raises the question of how this placement can be communicated most suitably with the least intervention in the original definition of the algorithm and how this can be integrated into Eden's algorithmic skeleton approach.

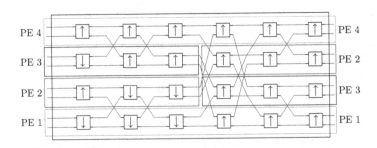

Fig. 2. Bitonic sorter with communication-minimized placement

3   Eden in a Nutshell

Eden[1] extends Haskell with explicit parallel function application via parallel
processes with implicit communication. A parallel process can be instantiated
with explicit or implicit placement. A parallel process abstraction can be created
and instantiated with explicit placement by the function `instantiateFAt` (read
"instantiate function at") where the first argument contains a processor element
(PE) on which the process is instantiated. Processor elements are also called
(logical) machines and they are numbered from 1 to the number of PEs. They
usually correspond to the number of CPUs in the system. The process output is
contained in the parallel action monad PA, thus it can be combined to a larger
parallel action.

```
instantiateFAt :: (Trans a, Trans b)
    ⇒ Place                 -- ^PE number
    → (a → b)               -- ^function for process
    → a                     -- ^process input
    → PA b                  -- ^process output
```

The class **Trans** is composed of *transmissible* values. **Place** is a type synonym
for **Int**. If the first argument of `instantiateFAt` is 0, the processes are placed
in a round robin fashion on all available processor elements.

`runPA $ instantiateFAt 0 f expr` with some function `f :: a → b` will create a (remote) child process. The expression `expr` will be evaluated (concurrently
by a new thread) in the parent process and the result `val` will be sent to the
child process. The child process will evaluate `f $ val` (cf. Fig. 3).

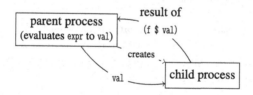

Fig. 3. The scheme of process instantiation [17].

With these basic constructs it is possible to build simple algorithmic skeletons and combine them into more complex ones. One form of a basic skeleton
is a parallel map. We structure the class of parallel map functions with our
ParFunctor class which is a parallel version of the **Functor** class. Instances of
ParFunctor should satisfy the same laws as the **fmap** function from **Functor**:

---

[1] Url: http://www.mathematik.uni-marburg.de/~eden.

```
class ParFunctor f where
    -- | parallel version of @'fmap'@.
    pmap :: (Trans a, Trans b) ⇒ (a → b) → f a → f b
```

Additionally, we define a `pmap` with explicit placement:

```
pmapAt :: (Traversable t, Trans a, Trans b)
    ⇒ t Place           -- ^places for instantiation
    → (a → b)           -- ^worker function
    → f a               -- ^tasks
    → f b               -- ^results
```

When composing skeletons an efficient connection between output and input is often essential for performance. The Eden programming language provides a sophisticated yet simple and effective concept for a division of computational and coordinational communication which is called Remote Data [9]. The Remote Data concept uses data handles to lighten the data volume of intermediate communication steps by enabling direct communication between both ends of a communication chain, thereby allowing for efficient skeleton composition. Between the skeletons, the smaller handle is transmitted instead of the computational data. The actual data is transmitted directly without the detour. The functions involved in converting local data into corresponding Remote Data and back again, are as follows:

```
release :: Trans a ⇒ a → RD a
fetch :: Trans a ⇒ RD a → a

-- list variants
releaseAll :: Trans a ⇒ [a] → [RD a]
fetchAll :: Trans a ⇒ [RD a] → [a]
```

Figure 4 demonstrates the communication scheme of a Remote Data connection. Two functions, f and g, are instantiated in succession by the same parent process. Without Remote Data the intermediate result is communicated through the PE on which the parent process is located.

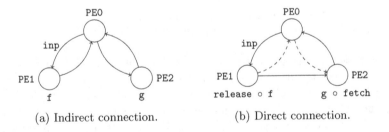

(a) Indirect connection.   (b) Direct connection.

Fig. 4. Remote Data scheme [17]. With RD, a handle is generated on PE1 and transferred via PE0 to PE2, the actual result is transferred directly.

The separation of computational and coordinational communication results in a largely intuitive coordination of communication while the algorithm remains unchanged. This adaptation is often particularly simple. For our running example we solely need to wrap the mapped function into `fetchAll` and `releaseAll` (cf. Fig. 5). If we use this modified version of a parallel map, all comparison elements on the same row are placed on the same PE.

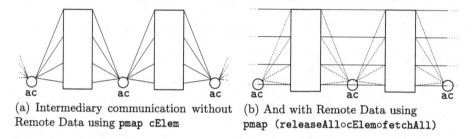

(a) Intermediary communication without Remote Data using **pmap cElem**

(b) And with Remote Data using **pmap (releaseAll∘cElem∘fetchAll)**

Fig. 5. Running example with and without Remote Data.

Using this, it is easy to get a row-wise placement as it is predefined by the computational structure. Even though Remote Data solves the accumulation problem when composing algorithmic skeletons, there is no easy way to manipulate the placement. In some cases the improved placement can be achieved with the explicit placement version of algorithmic skeletons, but, in some instances, at the cost of deep changes to the program. Hence, we want to emphasize the usefulness of the disengagement of the different layers of communication. While the Remote Data concept decouples computational communication and data communication, a third layer of (independent) placement communication is needed. This is the case whenever placement is not provided by the data structure.

In this paper, we will address this problem by placing the location of the data alongside the Remote Data handle and using specialized algorithmic skeletons which benefit from this additional information.

4   Location-Aware Remote Data

Dieterle [8] introduced the idea of tagging Remote Data with location. The previous definition

```
type RD a = ChanName (ChanName a)
```

is, therefore, replaced by a definition where an additional data field **place** is added. This data field contains the current position of the Remote Data:

```
data RD a = RD {place :: Place,
                rd :: ChanName (ChanName a) }
```

The location stored in the `place` data field is identical with the location where the Remote Data is created. We must ensure that the data selector `place` is not misused since it is not purely functional. A simple solution to achieve this is to use a hidden data field which is not exported and, therefore, to restrict its use to skeletons only. The new field can be used for co-located function application in a natural way.

As an example, we will define an instance of `ParFunctor` for `Remote Data`:

```
instance ParFunctor RD where
    pmap f rd = runPA $
          instantiateFAt (place rd) (liftRD f) rd
    pmapAt places f rd = runPA $
          instantiateFAt (head (toList places)) (liftRD f) rd
```

`liftRD :: (Trans b, Trans a) ⇒ (a → b) → RD a → RD b` lifts a function to work on Remote Data.

Let `rdd = release d` for some data d. Then `pmap f rdd` computes f $ d on the PE where the Remote Data handle was created. Based on this, we can define a parallel map for functors containing Remote Data with a co-locational placement.

```
rdmap :: (Trans a, Trans b, Functor t, ParFunctor t)
      ⇒ (a → b)               -- ^map function
      → t (RD a)              -- ^inputs
      → t (RD b)              -- ^outputs
rdmap f = fmap (pmap f)
```

The mapped function is placed where the inputs are located. Therefore the inputs need to have been distributed already. A possible solution to this is the following function:

```
releaseAt :: (Trans a, Traversable f, ParFunctor t)
          ⇒ f Place              -- ^target locations
          → t a                  -- ^input data
          → t (RD a)             -- ^Remote Data handle output
releaseAt places inp = pmapAt places release inp
```

With this function the data can be distributed first and the computation can follow the data. As an example `rdmap (+5) ∘ releaseAt [2,7] [3,6]` will compute `((+5) 3)` on PE 2 and `((+5) 6)` on PE 7.

Even though this function is extremely useful, it is not sufficient for the problem introduced by the running example. In that example, the input for the map function is a list of lists containing two elements each. So, the optimal placement depends on a nested data structure and it is more complex than the simple mapping used by `rdmap`.

5   Example Skeletons and Placement Strategies

In this section we will explore the possibilities of skeletons equipped with Placement Strategies. The Placement Strategy passed to the skeleton is a function with three arguments:

```
(ParFunctor f, Traversable t, Trans a)
  ⇒ ((RD a1 → Place)        -- place selector
      → t Place             -- valid target places
      → f a                 -- data input
      → t Place)            -- placement output
```

The third argument is the data structure containing the Location-Aware Remote Data. The location of the data can be extracted by the Placement Strategy with the help of RD's data selector `place`. The `place` function itself is a hidden field. Thus, it needs to be passed to the Placement Strategy (as the first argument) by the skeleton. It is visible to the skeleton but not to the programmer. Note that the data has type 'a' which can also be a nested data structure (containing elements of type `RD a1` inside a deeper level). The second argument is a `Traversable` containing the places ("valid target places") from which the Placement Strategy selects a subset and returns it to the skeleton as the placement. This is necessary for nested parallelism. Based on this, we can define skeletons with a semi-explicit placement that can be used as drop-in replacements in sequential programs. Many useful strategies are possible and they can become arbitrarily complex.

5.1   Parallel (Nested) Map Skeletons

A parallel map with Placement Strategy support is given by the definition:

```
rdmapPStrat :: (ParFunctor f, Traversable t, Trans a, Trans b)
  ⇒ ((RD a1 → Place)
      → t Place
      → f a
      → t Place)             -- placement strategy
  → t Place                  -- valid target places
  → (a → b)                  -- map function
  → f a → f b                -- input / output
rdmapPStrat pstrat targets f xs = pmapAt places f xs where
    places = pstrat place targets xs
```

With `rdmap` we introduced a map in which the computation is co-located with the data. If we have a list $l = [a1, .., a4] :: [RD\ a]$ and $a1, .., a4$ are, for example, located on PEs 1, 3, 5 and 7, then `rdmap f l` results in four processes being located on PEs 1, 3, 5 and 7. But if we have a list $l2 = [b1, .., b4]$, which is located on PEs 1, 1, 2 and 2 again, we may consider locating the four processes of the parallel map on four different PEs. Each one can be achieved using explicit relocation with the function:

```
moveTo :: (Trans a, Traversable f, ParFunctor t)     ∤
   ⇒ f Place                      -- ^target locations
   → t (RD a) → t (RD a)     -- ^input / relocated RD
moveTo places inp = pmapAt places (release o fetch) inp
```

The same can be achieved in a more elegant and universal fashion using a Placement Strategy. At the same time, this will motivate the programmer to define the placement in a declarative style, usually resulting in a solution that can be more easily adapted to changes. A function that returns a balanced list of places (e.g. placing the processes on the PEs 1, 3, 2 and 4 if the data is located on 1, 1, 2 and 2) is easily defined. Indeed, a linear time solution to this task can be found in [3]. While the cited source is not connected to parallel process placement, the problem to be solved is sufficiently universal for a reusable solution to exist. This is a regular phenomenon.

A strategic solution to the problem posed in the running example is now easy to find. A suitable strategy takes the smallest non-colliding index for every sublist. If, e.g., the Remote Data is located at [[1,2], [3,4], [1,2], [3,4]], then the chosen placement is [1, 3, 2, 4]. For sorting networks, this strategy results in exact placement. This means that in each stage of the algorithm not more than one process is placed on the same PE (if the number of PEs is at least the width of the sorting network) and communication is minimized. Necessary changes to the sequential program are limited to replacing the map in the function call with an instance of rdmapPStrat. With the original pmap only a row-wise placement is possible and with pmapAt an efficient placement would only be possible with a complete restructuring of the original algorithm. The Placement Strategy can be defined separately and the original algorithm can stay untouched.

5.2   Divide-and-Conquer Skeletons

The idea of Placement Strategies is transferable to other skeletons. All skeletons from Eden's skeleton library can be updated. The necessary adjustments can be easily done and usually previous skeletons are an instance of derived skeletons.

As an example, a distributed divide-and-conquer skeleton with placement strategies has the following type signature:

```
rdPStratDC :: (Traversable f, Traversable t, Trans a, Trans b)
   ⇒ ((RD a1 → Place)
         → f Place
         → t a
         → t Place)                -- placement strategy
   → f Place                       -- tickets
   → (a → Bool)                    -- trivial?
   → (a → b)                       -- solve
   → (f Place → a → t a)           -- split
   → (f Place → a → t b → b)       -- combine
   → a → b                         -- input / output
```

6   Examples and Preliminary Experimental Evaluation

With Placement Strategies the algorithmic skeletons become more modular. They allow for a communication structure that is independent of the one pre-determined by the structure of the algorithmic skeleton. If skeletons are composed or nested, a better coordination of communication is possible. They extend Eden's algorithmic skeletons with an interface that can also manage a non-deterministic distributed input.

In this section we will see examples, taken from different categories of problems, in which Placement Strategies prove beneficial.

6.1   Nesting Skeletons and Algorithms with Diverging Communication

The bitonic merger in the running example can also be expressed through divide-and-conquer skeletons, describing it as a nested divide-and-conquer algorithm [23]. The algorithm consists of two parts: a bitonic merger and a bitonic sorter, both of which are divide-and-conquer schemes intertwined with one another. Describing the algorithm with this scheme yields the advantage of simplified proof of correctness and scalability. Conveniently, the same Placement Strategy suitable for the parallel map implementation can be used for both divide-and-conquer instances. The algorithm is an example of nesting skeletons with dependent placement and a communication scheme that is not guided by the computation. This results in nonideal performance, when the original algorithmic skeletons from Eden's skeleton library are used.

We will compare the new Placement Strategy skeleton with a manually tuned version of the bitonic merger and an implementation which builds upon the original skeleton from Eden's skeleton library. In the manually tuned version – called placed – all optimizations regarding communication used in the skeletons are included. Furthermore, the placement is ideal. Compared to the algorithmic skeleton using a Placement Strategy, this version does not need to store the location of Remote Data and the explicit placement is precalculated. These two factors is what we will call the additional overhead of Placement Strategies. On the basis of said optimizations, we expect it to be the fastest implementation and therefore an upper bound for the speedup of these skeleton implementations. Of course, this solution comes with disadvantages: compared to algorithmic skeletons, this monolithic solution not only requires the programmer to know all the complexity hidden in the skeleton, it requires more code to be written, which is less modular and less flexible.

We tested the algorithms on our multi-core computer hex, equipped with an AMD Opteron CPU 6378 (64 cores) and 64 GB memory. In our test, a list containing $5 \cdot 10^7$ elements of pseudo-random Int numbers has to be sorted. For each test, a list is generated with the same initial seed to ensure comparability.

As Fig. 6 demonstrates, the manually tuned version has approximately the same parallel speedup as the new algorithmic skeleton equipped with the fitting Placement Strategy (called RDDC). The difference of speedup is within the usual dispersion – indicating that the additional overhead of the Placement Strategy is marginal. On the other hand, the distributed divide-and-conquer skeleton from the Eden skeleton library (called disDC) does choose a different placement, which is hard-coded into the skeleton and cannot be changed without defining a new skeleton. This placement is, in general, a good placement for many different divide-and-conquer algorithms. But for our example, the fine-tuning of the Placement Strategy has proven clearly superior.

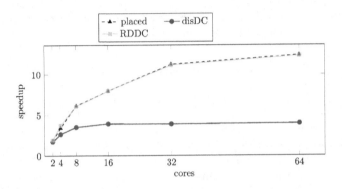

Fig. 6. Speedup of the different implementations of the bitonic merger

6.2 Combination of Non-deterministic with Deterministic Placement

In the second example we will see another major advantage of Placement Strategies. Some of the algorithmic skeletons in Eden's skeleton library, for example workpool skeletons, have a non-deterministic placement of parallel processes. The decisive advantage of these algorithmic skeletons lies in deciding on the placement in a dynamic fashion. Since process placement does not affect the computational result, a non-deterministic placement is compatible with functional programming concepts. But this means that subsequent algorithmic skeletons get non-deterministic distributed input, which they have to handle adequately. The switch from an algorithmic skeleton with non-deterministic placement back to (semi-)explicit placement can be coordinated using a Placement Strategy.

In the following example, a mandelbrot set is computed, including second stage coloring and other post-processing. We will compare three different implementations: in the first one both stages use a parallel map, in the second one the first step is handled by a workpool and the second step uses a parallel map. In the third implementation, the first step is handled by a workpool skeleton and the second step is based on a parallel map using a Placement Strategy.

As we will see, that the workpool skeleton represents a significant improvement. But ignoring the actual location of the data from the output of the workpool skeleton results in speed reduction.

We tested the algorithms on a multi-core computer, equipped with an Intel Core i7-3770 CPU (8 cores) and 8 GB memory. In the test a picture of the mandelbrot set with approximately 10^6 pixels is computed. The implementation using a Placement Strategy organizes the communication between two skeletons employing a heuristic that chooses the placement with the help of a cost function based on a discrete metric. With this, we achieve a decent trade-off between coordination cost and optimized placement (Table 1).

Table 1. Runtimes of different skeleton instances, averaged over 10 runs.

Skeleton	Avg. runtime
pmap ∘ pmap	45.1 s
pmap ∘ workpool	40.9 s
rdmapPStrat ∘ workpool	30.4 s

The example demonstrates that Placement Strategies are a suitable solution to connect algorithmic skeletons with distributed input and output in general, and with non-deterministic distributed input and output in particular. In addition, specifying the placement functionally dependent upon the actual location of the input has the advantage that placement specifications are easily adaptable to program changes as redundancies are avoided. The connection between different placement specifications can be made re-usable and transparent.

6.3   Architecture Awareness

It is possible to define a Placement Strategy based upon a metric. This has the advantage that the metric can reflect the underlying structure such as the hardware used. A change of hardware can be accounted for by the used metric without needing to redefine the whole Placement Strategy. While in most cases a discrete metric might represent the communication costs adequately, more complex situations can be represented by it just as well. For example, on heterogeneous hardware like clusters, the communication costs between different processor elements may vary significantly due to different types of connection (e.g. communication between PEs on the same computer and different computers in the same cluster).

In the following example, we will use a scattering placement on the previously used multi-core computer hex, in order to make additional use of AMD's Turbo Core feature. In contrast to common situations where a high locality is most suitable, in this setup, a dispersed placement is beneficial if not all cores are being used. The 64 cores of the CPU are grouped into 8 groups with 8 cores each. Distributing parallel computing among groups is sometimes beneficial as cores are clocked dynamically, depending on power consumption.

A list with 10^7 elements is sorted with a distributed merge sort on eight processor elements, first of all using a default round robin placement (resulting in a placement on the first 8 cores) and then moving on to a sparse placement. Changing the placement yields an implementation which is 6.5% faster (Table 2).

Table 2. Runtime of different skeleton instances, averaged over 10 runs.

Skeleton	Avg. runtime
pmap	73.7 s
rdmapPStrat sparse	68.9 s

Yet, the most important feature of Placement Strategies is the option to define complex placement methods that are far more adjustable than common static placement methods like blockwise or cyclic placement. With Placement Strategies it is possible to consider additional information (e.g. estimated communication costs depending on the actual location of the distributed data) when making a placement decision. Depending on our requirements, explicit, semi-explicit or dynamic placements are possible and can be combined.

7   Related Work

This section discusses different forms of placement organization and their relation to Placement Strategies as well as other concepts structurally connected to the idea of Placement Strategies. Apart from the different functional placement concepts, some non-functional concepts use sophisticated forms of placement organization.

Not only is the explicitness of expressing placement treated differently, even the location of the decision-making mechanism is very different in various parallel systems. The type as well as the amount of information accessible to the decision-making mechanism also differ.

7.1   Implicit Placement

Implicit placement is superior whenever the benefits of the compiler's knowledge about specific hardware outweighs the programmer's knowledge about the program. In that case, explicit placement becomes uneconomic. This has led to a well-justified coexistence of both concepts. While explicit placement is especially popular in distributed computing (with heterogeneous hardware), implicit placement is, for example, very popular in functional data-parallel languages. It is not unusual for modern parallel systems to use a mixture of distributed computing and hardware acceleration. While explicit and implicit placement are fundamentally opposed concepts, some data-parallel languages organize their parallel expressiveness in specialized functions that are close to the conceptual idea of algorithmic skeletons (e.g. Futhark's Second-Order Array Combinators [12]). Thus, a good connection between concepts using a closely related syntax is possible wherever parallelism (and parallel placement) is coordinated by separate, higher-order functions.

7.2 Annotation-Based Semi-explicit Placement

Within the realm of annotation-based parallelism attempts to affect placement exist as well. Approaches, closely related to Placement Strategies, are characterized by a structured influence on the placement as a goal of annotation. A common way to influence placement is through the expression of co-location. For example, in High Performance Fortran [22], the keyword "align" can be used to align the data distribution of a data structure to another already distributed data structure. Similar effects can be achieved by using Location-Aware Remote Data and Placement Strategies. It is possible to adapt a placement to the distribution of one or more distributed data structures. Often the alignment is the immediate result of the Remote Data concept and no additional efforts must be made to achieve co-location.

Another interesting idea is to express (relative) locality, which is very useful if the hardware used is inhomogeneous. In an architecture aware variant of GpH [1] the (maximal) relative distance between two computations can be expressed. The explicit equivalent would be a Placement Strategy with a representation of hardware structure as a function argument. Thereby, all kinds of cost-functions and metrics can be used.

7.3 Explicit Placement

Functional Explicit Placement. There is a variety of functional languages supporting explicit placement. Common constructs are the option to specify a place for a specific computation (Clean's "@", Eden's "instantiateFAt", Erlang's "spawn/4") and a function that returns the current location (Clean's "self", Eden's "selfPE", Erlang's "self/1"). The use of algorithmic skeletons to organize more complex parallel patterns is popular [4,18]. Yet, the placement is usually decided exclusively by the skeleton and the only way to manipulate the placement is to choose a different skeleton or reorganize the data input.

Non-functional Explicit High-Level Placement. Explicit placement is very common in non-functional languages. Apart from a direct placement similar to the explicit placement discussed in the previous paragraph, some concepts for structured placement exist.

MPI [10] provides a rich set of options for process selection and therefore placement determination. However, it is focused on communication models and differs fundamentally from the function-based communication model used in Eden and other functional languages.

Designed for high performance computing, Chapel [6] provides a so-called "multifunctional" programming approach. While we agree with almost all of the conceptual ideas presented as the basis of the Chapel programming language, chosen implementations differ. Domain Maps are used to express data distribution in a wide-ranging and compositional fashion.

7.4   Evaluation Strategies

Different functional approaches that intervene in the parallel evaluation exists. Evaluation strategies [20, 24] are a well-known technique to control parallel behaviour by controlling the evaluation degree of an expression. The placement is handed over to the runtime system. Halide [21] uses separated schedules which define the partitioning and evaluation of a parallel algorithm. The goal of both is therefore to answer the question of *"how?"* and not *"where?"*. Conceptually, these both are related to Placement Strategies in the way their goals are pursued. All of them are written in the same language as the algorithm and therefore extensible by the user. Amongst all these concepts, the goal is to separate the algorithm from the organization of parallel behaviour.

8   Conclusion and Future Work

The vast majority of parallel functional concepts use either a scheduler (in the runtime system) or parallel data structures. This paper has tried to offer a middle ground to change the parallel strategy depending on the skeleton used. In combination with improved connection opportunities, the composing and nesting of algorithmic skeletons is enhanced. A precise parallelism control is made possible through the expressiveness of explicit placement, offering improved elegance. Whenever a strategy requiring a data location is appropriate, this approach is well suited. The solution fulfills many different goals at once:

1. Functional programming style: In our opinion Placement Strategies fit perfectly into a functional programming style. They encourage the programmer to express a placement as a function. The use of auxiliary constructs like the selfPe function becomes unnecessary.
2. High level of abstraction: The combination of algorithmic skeletons and Placement Strategies divide an algorithm into a computational and an organizational part.
3. High level of manipulation possible: Placement Strategies combined with Location-Aware Remote Data can determine a parallel placement relative to the actual position, thus facilitating co-locating tasks and even more sophisticated placement.
4. Nesting algorithmic skeletons: It is possible to nest algorithmic skeletons in any way.
5. Skeleton composition with (non-deterministic) distributed input: By locating the organisation of the parallelism into algorithmic skeletons it is possible to combine work-pulling skeletons with work-pushing skeletons. A Placement Strategy can cope with non-deterministic placement by applying a (semi-)explicit placement.

The advantages of algorithmic skeletons can only be harnessed if the algorithm that is parallelized can be expressed adequately. We have shown that Placement Strategies can be an improvement to algorithmic skeletons in several different situations. They generalize the definition of algorithmic skeletons while the additional overhead of coordination remains manageable.

Future work should focus on a library of Placement Strategies that complements Eden's algorithm skeleton library. Moreover a more detailed (experimental) evaluation is necessary.

Acknowledgments. The author thanks Rita Loogen and the anonymous reviewers for their helpful comments on a previous version of this paper.

References

1. Aswad, M.K., Trinder, P., Loidl, H.: Architecture aware parallel programming in Glasgow parallel Haskell (GPH). Procedia Comput. Sci. **9**, 1807–1816 (2012). https://doi.org/10.1016/j.procs.2012.04.199. Proceedings of the International Conference on Computational Science, ICCS 2012
2. Batcher, K.E.: Sorting networks and their applications. In: Proceedings of the 30 April–2 May 1968, Spring Joint Computer Conference, AFIPS 1968, pp. 307–314. ACM, New York (1968). https://doi.org/10.1145/1468075.1468121
3. Bird, R.: Pearls of Functional Algorithm Design, 1st edn. Cambridge University Press, New York (2010). https://doi.org/10.1017/CBO9780511763199
4. Brown, C., Danelutto, M., Hammond, K., Kilpatrick, P., Elliott, A.: Cost-directed refactoring for parallel Erlang programs. Int. J. Parallel Prog. **42**(4), 564–582 (2013). https://doi.org/10.1007/s10766-013-0266-5
5. Chakravarty, M.M., Keller, G., Lee, S., McDonell, T.L., Grover, V.: Accelerating Haskell array codes with multicore GPUs. In: Proceedings of the Sixth Workshop on Declarative Aspects of Multicore Programming, DAMP 2011, pp. 3–14. ACM, New York (2011). https://doi.org/10.1145/1926354.1926358
6. Chamberlain, B., Callahan, D., Zima, H.: Parallel programmability and the Chapel language. Int. J. High Perform. Comput. Appl. **21**(3), 291–312 (2007). https://doi.org/10.1177/1094342007078442
7. Cole, M.: Algorithmic Skeletons: Structured Management of Parallel Computation. MIT Press, Cambridge (1991). https://homepages.inf.ed.ac.uk/mic/Pubs/skeletonbook.pdf
8. Dieterle, M.: Structured parallelism by composition. Ph.D. thesis, Philipps-Universität Marburg (2016). https://doi.org/10.17192/z2016.0107
9. Dieterle, M., Horstmeyer, T., Loogen, R.: Skeleton composition using remote data. In: Carro, M., Peña, R. (eds.) PADL 2010. LNCS, vol. 5937, pp. 73–87. Springer, Heidelberg (2010). https://doi.org/10.1007/978-3-642-11503-5_8
10. Forum, T.M.: MPI: a message-passing interface standard. Technical report, Knoxville, TN, USA (2012). https://www.mpi-forum.org/docs/mpi-3.0/mpi30-report.pdf
11. Gosling, J., Joy, B., Steele, G.L., Bracha, G., Buckley, A.: The Java Language Specification, Java SE 8 Edition. Addison-Wesley Professional, 1st edn. (2014). https://dl.acm.org/doi/book/10.5555/2636997
12. Henriksen, T., Serup, N.G.W., Elsman, M., Henglein, F., Oancea, C.E.: Futhark: purely functional gpu-programming with nested parallelism and in-place array updates. SIGPLAN Not. **52**(6), 556–571 (2017). https://doi.org/10.1145/3140587.3062354

13. IEEE: IEEE Std 1003.1-2001 Standard for Information Technology – Portable Operating System Interface (POSIX) Rationale (Informative) (2001). Revision of IEEE Std 1003.1-1996 and IEEE Std 1003.2-1992) Open Group Technical Standard Base Specifications, Issue 6
14. Jones, Jr., D., Marlow, S., Singh, S.: Parallel performance tuning for Haskell. In: Proceedings of the 2nd ACM SIGPLAN Symposium on Haskell, Haskell 2009, pp. 81–92. ACM, New York (2009). https://doi.org/10.1145/1596638.1596649
15. Kambadur, P., Gupta, A., Ghoting, A., Avron, H., Lumsdaine, A.: PFunc: modern task parallelism for modern high performance computing. In: Proceedings of the Conference on High Performance Computing Networking, Storage and Analysis, SC 2009, pp. 43:1–43:11. ACM, New York (2009). https://doi.org/10.1145/1654059.1654103
16. Lippmeier, B., Chakravarty, M., Keller, G., Peyton Jones, S.: Guiding parallel array fusion with indexed types. SIGPLAN Not. 47(12), 25–36 (2012). https://doi.org/10.1145/2430532.2364511
17. Loogen, R.: Eden – parallel functional programming with Haskell. In: Zsók, V., Horváth, Z., Plasmeijer, R. (eds.) CEFP 2011. LNCS, vol. 7241, pp. 142–206. Springer, Heidelberg (2012). https://doi.org/10.1007/978-3-642-32096-5_4
18. Loogen, R., Ortega-Mallén, Y., Peña-Marí, R.: Parallel functional programming in Eden. J. Funct. Program. 15(3), 431–475 (2005). https://doi.org/10.1017/S0956796805005526
19. Marlow, S.: Haskell 2010 language report (2010). http://citeseerx.ist.psu.edu/viewdoc/summary?doi=10.1.1.179.2870
20. Marlow, S., Maier, P., Loidl, H.W., Aswad, M.K., Trinder, P.: Seq no more: better strategies for parallel Haskell. In: Proceedings of the Third ACM Haskell Symposium on Haskell, Haskell 2010, pp. 91–102. ACM, New York (2010). https://doi.org/10.1145/1863523.1863535
21. Ragan-Kelley, J., Adams, A., Paris, S., Levoy, M., Amarasinghe, S., Durand, F.: Decoupling algorithms from schedules for easy optimization of image processing pipelines. ACM Trans. Graph. 31(4) (2012). https://doi.org/10.1145/2185520.2185528
22. Rice University, C.: High performance fortran language specification. SIGPLAN Fortran Forum 12(4), 1–86 (1993). https://doi.org/10.1145/174223.158909
23. Schiller, L.I.: An agglomeration law for sorting networks and its application in functional programming. In: Schwarz, S., Voigtländer, J. (eds.) Proceedings 29th and 30th Workshops on (Constraint) Logic Programming and 24th International Workshop on Functional and (Constraint) Logic Programming, Dresden and Leipzig, Germany, 22 September 2015 and 12–14 September 2016. Electronic Proceedings in Theoretical Computer Science, vol. 234, pp. 165–179. Open Publishing Association (2017). https://doi.org/10.4204/EPTCS.234.12
24. Trinder, P.W., Hammond, K., Loidl, H.W., Jones, S.P.: Algorithm + strategy = parallelism. J. Funct. Program. 8(1), 23–60 (1998). https://doi.org/10.1017/S0956796897002967

Author Index

Printed in the United States
By Bookmasters